D0989876

THE WHIG PARTY AND
THE FRENCH REVOLUTION

THE WHIG PARTY
AND THE
FRENCH REVOLUTION

F. O'GORMAN

ASSISTANT LECTURER IN HISTORY
AT THE UNIVERSITY OF MANCHESTER

MACMILLAN
LONDON . MELBOURNE . TORONTO
ST. MARTIN'S PRESS
NEW YORK
1967

Published by
MACMILLAN & CO LTD
Little Essex Street London W C 2
and also at Bombay Calcutta and Madras
Macmillan South Africa (Publishers) Pty Ltd Johannesburg
The Macmillan Company of Australia Pty Ltd Melbourne
The Macmillan Company of Canada Ltd Toronto
St Martin's Press Inc New York

Library of Congress catalog card no. 67–18077

Printed in Great Britain by
ROBERT MACLEHOSE AND CO LTD
The University Press, Glasgow

TO ELSE

Contents

Preface

This work first appeared in 1965 in the form of a doctoral dissertation in the University of Cambridge. Since then, I have enlarged, revised, and almost entirely rewritten it. In doing so I have profited from the criticisms and suggestions of Professor J. H. Plumb and Professor I. R. Christie, who examined the dissertation in its original form.

To all the librarians and owners of manuscripts who most kindly allowed me to examine papers in their care or possession I am deeply grateful. I wish to express my particular thanks to Earl Fitzwilliam and the Trustees of the Wentworth Woodhouse Estates, and to Captain Adam of Blair-Adam, Kinross. I was able to draw upon the expert knowledge and the kindly assistance of the staff at the following libraries: the City Library, Sheffield, the County Record Office at Northampton, the Scottish Record Office and the General Register House at Edinburgh, the university libraries at Durham and Nottingham and, of course, the Public Record Office and the British Museum.

Many historians have been kind enough to answer my enquiries and to further the writing of this book in other ways. I should like to mention here Professor A. Aspinall of the University of Reading, and Professor G. R. Potter of the University of Sheffield. Mr. J. Brooke allowed me to make extensive use of his advice and his wide knowledge of this period of English history. Professor T. W. Copeland, the general editor of the Burke correspondence, generously placed at my disposal copies of otherwise inaccessible Burke material. To him and to all members of the 'Burke Factory' at Sheffield I would like to acknowledge my gratitude.

Dr. John Woods of the University of Leeds first suggested this subject to me several years ago and he has always provided invaluable assistance by acting as a constant source of information, advice and encouragement. To Professor Herbert Butterfield, Master of Peterhouse, I can do no other than express my most sincere and grateful thanks for his patience, kindness and counsel while he supervised the writing of this work in its dissertation form, and for the interest and encouragement he has bestowed upon me ever since.

F. O'GORMAN

Manchester
September 1966

ABBREVIATIONS

Ad. MS.	British Museum Additional Manuscript.
Copeland Transcript	Letter to or from a member of the Burke family which has not been examined in the original but in transcript, through the courtesy of Professor T. W. Copeland, general editor of the most recent edition of the correspondence of Edmund Burke.
C.U.L.	Cambridge University Library, where are deposited copies of Pitt letters from various sources.
E.H.R.	*English Historical Review*
H.M.C.	Historical Manuscripts Commission
N.R.O.	Northamptonshire County Record Office

Introduction

The gradual break-up of the Whig party is usually regarded as the inevitable sequel to a long period of weakness and internal decay. It is not clear when this process is supposed to have begun. Perhaps the general election of 1847, which wrought such havoc upon the party, was a blow from which the Whigs never really recovered. Perhaps the animosities which came to the surface during the Regency Crisis never really healed. Perhaps the destruction of the party was the work of Burke, who had been increasingly indifferent to the party even before the French Revolution produced fresh points of disagreement between himself and Fox. Perhaps the Whig party was never a real party at all, and perhaps its disintegration was merely a further manifestation of the essentially unstable and unreliable nature of eighteenth-century factions.

Yet the disruption of a political party is never a simple event with neatly labelled causes which obligingly assemble themselves into neat categories and compartments. The seeds of the decay of a party can be found in the elements of unity, for unity itself is conditional upon the fulfilment of certain provisions. Thus, disruption may threaten when those concerned are unaware of the danger. There could have been few members of the Whig party in 1791 — when the opposition attained an impressive drive and unity in its lively and convincing attacks upon the incompetent bungling of Pitt's foreign policy — who would have dreamed that within a year the party would be fighting for its very existence. The sudden event, the unexpected crisis and the startling realization that events have run out of control were the dramatic means by which politicians were brought abruptly to understand the urgency of the situation in which they found themselves and of which they themselves were a part.

If there were elements of disunity in the Whig party before 1789 — and who would doubt it? — then there were, too, sources of strength and coherence. (To read the history of the party in the 1780s in the light of what happened in the 1790s merely distorts both stories.) Chapter 1 attempts to give both sides of the picture. The weaknesses of the party are described, the failings of its leaders are assessed and its unfortunate connection with the Prince of Wales related. Yet beneath the surface of the personal jealousies and the factional politics which characterized the proceedings of the Whig party in the years after 1784, developments had been set in train which are only now being recognized by historians, and which may lead them to adjust their ideas about the status of party in the later eighteenth century. The activities of William Adam, the growth of organizational and financial institutions within the party, the development of electoral and procedural techniques show that the party was beginning to assume something of a more modern character and to divest itself of the exclusively proprietary and family characteristics which had for so long dominated it.

After the Regency Crisis the Whigs were in a sorry condition. Their leaders seemed more interested in involving themselves in the unsavoury domestic disputes which were endemic in the Hanoverian household than in attempting to look to, and plan for, a future which appeared bleak and unpromising. Burke was drifting further and further away from the centre of the party, and the indifference of his friends to the impeachment of Warren Hastings angered and distressed him. The French Revolution thus found the party at odds with itself, with its leaders divided and its purposes unclear. Yet the disputes between Fox and Burke on the French Revolution were, until 1792 at least, of lesser importance than posterity might assume. The revival of the opposition in the session of 1791, the delirious feeling that office and power were at hand characterized the mood of the Whigs as they merrily set about trouncing Pitt for his handling of the Oczacov crisis. Pitt weathered the storm and was able to emerge from it with undiminished authority. However, from the façade of unity which the Oczacov crisis had lent to the opposition appeared the fateful Association of the Friends of the People, which aroused within the conservative section of the opposition the fear that the reform agitation in the country, of which it already strongly disapproved, was about to be sponsored and led from within the ranks of the Whig party itself.

There followed perhaps the nine most important and confusing months in the history of the Whig party between 1784 and 1806. Pitt was aided in his attempts to weaken the party by those members of it who were either anxious for office or sincerely apprehensive about the dangerous state of the country and the consequent need to reinforce Pitt's weak administration. The struggle for the party ended in the early months of 1793 as a stalemate. Fox had succeeded in restraining Portland from breaking the party; Burke and Windham had succeeded in forming a 'Third Party', largely carved out of the Whig party, which dedicated itself to opposing Fox and to supporting the ministry. And Pitt had succeeded, wittingly or not, in splintering the opposition and in beginning the process of enticing individuals away from it. The next eighteen months tell the story of how Portland finally brought himself to break with Fox and thus to reassert his authority over the 'Third Party', of how Pitt was able after much effort to dispel some of the mists of suspicion and distrust with which the conservative Whigs regarded him, and, most of all, of how the conservative Whigs gradually managed to swallow their pride, and what they believed to be their principles, by coming to accept the need for coalition with the ministry. This latter process was perhaps the most significant — certainly it is the most interesting — element in the story of the Whig party in these years, for it is the story of how the leading party men wrestled with their consciences and their ideals and how they managed ultimately to satisfy their ambitions without compromising either.

1. *The Whig Party in the Age of the French Revolution*

1784–90

I. THE POLITICS OF THE WHIG PARTY, 1784–9

After the political upheavals and the excitement of the short-lived ministries which characterized the two years following the fall of Lord North's ministry, political stability returned to Great Britain in 1784. Pitt's appointment to the Treasury, the failure of Charles James Fox and his party to oust him from office and Pitt's overwhelming victory at the general election of 1784 condemned Fox to what seemed a futile and hopeless opposition. The King could rest well satisfied with the outcome of the struggles of 1782–4 which had threatened, and even annihilated for a time, his dearest prerogatives. Now he had a minister in whom he could repose his confidence and who was supported by large majorities in both Houses of Parliament. George III felt himself well rid of the obnoxious men whom he considered to be responsible for the dissipation of his son and heir, George, Prince of Wales;[1] and he was unable to forget, or forgive, the humiliations to which he had been subjected during the Coalition ministry in 1783. The monarch's continuing antipathy to the Whigs was thus double-edged. He had nothing but contempt for the opposition, whose hopes he had dashed and whose political future he had seemingly destroyed. Because the King thought that he was at last safe from his enemies he could well afford to dismiss them as an unprincipled, factious clique.

[1] In Aug. 1782 the Prince established a residence at Carlton House which rapidly became a meeting-place for members of the Foxite party. But the connection between the heir apparent and the Whigs seems to have arisen during the Rockingham–Shelburne administration. As early as 10 May 1782 the Prince had written to Prince Frederick that 'the new Administration seems to wish me better than the former one'. *The Correspondence of George, Prince of Wales*, ed. A. Aspinall (Cambridge University Press, 1964), i. 88.

George III was not quite so secure as he thought. If Lord Chatham were to die, then his brother, Pitt, would go to the Lords and his well-known disdain for party connections might prove as damaging to him as it had been to his father less than twenty years earlier. In the House of Lords, Pitt could command an overwhelming majority, but his ministry was weak in debating talent.[1] In the Commons, Pitt appealed to 'the approbation of impartial and independent men',[2] but it was the Court and Administration group which gave him his majority.[3] For Pitt stood aloof from the ordinary member. He did not mix with him and he did not know his opinions. Even by eighteenth-century standards, Pitt's nepotism was lavish, while his indulgence of Dundas was popular neither with the King nor with the independents.[4] Occasional defeats in parliament could be sustained but there were, perhaps, limits to the severity of the reverse which might be inflicted. When Pitt brought forward proposals to reform parliament in 1785, the Lord President of the Council, Camden, could write that the ministry was 'in some danger of being shaken, if his motion is defeated by a considerable majority'.[5] But it was Pitt's weaknesses which ultimately rendered him impregnable. Members might grumble at his inattention 'but they will think twenty times before they go into Opposition'.[6] Whenever his position was threatened, his indispensability was recognized. In the cabinet, Pitt had to contend with frequent disagreements on policy, ministerial incompetence and the sulky hostility of Lord Chancellor Thurlow. Yet his supremacy was never

[1] About one-half of the government peers were amenable to the King rather than to Pitt. See D. Large, 'The Decline of the Party of the Crown and the Rise of Parties in the House of Lords, 1783–1837', *E.H.R.* (Oct. 1963), lxxviii. 675.

[2] Pitt to Sir A. Edmonstone 2 Jan. 1784, H.M.C. *Various Collections*, v. 180.

[3] According to the *Third Party Circular* of 1788, Pitt commanded a parliamentary following of 52 members, only 20 of whom would remain faithful to him out of office.

[4] W. S. Sichel, *Sheridan* (2 vols., 1909), i. 159; *Bland-Burges: Letters and Life*, ed. J. Hutton (1885), 88; D. Pulteney to the Duke of Rutland 13 Aug. 1784, H.M.C. *Rutland*, 131.

[5] Camden to Grafton 19 Mar. 1785, Grafton MSS. IIIa, f. 99.

[6] Lord Bulkeley to Lord Buckinghamshire 27 Apr. 1789, *Memoirs of the Court and Cabinets of George III*, ed. Duke of Buckingham and Chandos (4 vols., 1853–5), ii. 154.

in doubt. The Oczacov crisis in 1791 actually reinforced his position in the cabinet in spite of the resignation of the Foreign Secretary, the Duke of Leeds.[1] A year later, Thurlow's opposition in the Lords to a ministerial finance measure put Pitt in a position to threaten resignation unless the King agreed to part with his Lord Chancellor, and Pitt's ultimatum was effective. Although there were no formed groups in the cabinet consistently opposing him,[2] ministers who were usually well-disposed towards Pitt would at times address him in language which his father would never have permitted.[3]

Although Pitt had his weaknesses, he was careful to present the fewest possible fronts upon which the opposition might concentrate its attack. When they found a chink in his armour they would seize the opportunity of mounting an assault on the ministry. It was the opposition speakers who looked for openings and led the attack, who introduced legislation and tried to amend or repeal government measures. Sometimes ministers were worsted in debate and sensed that the feeling of the House was running against them. In fact, in the changed political circumstances of the years following the election of 1784, the struggles of earlier years seemed to lose their relevance. The exciting session of 1785 found Pitt testing the sympathy of his supporters to a dangerous extent, while his mistaken handling of the Westminster election scrutiny, a particularly clumsy and distasteful political manœuvre designed to unseat Fox, acted as a rallying-point for the opposition. Other subjects such as the Irish Trade proposals tended to inflame partisan feeling in the House and roused the opposition. Now that the constitutional conflicts of earlier years had been settled, politics had been cast into a fresh mould and the Whig party was forced to accommodate itself to its new situation. Yet it is misleading to depict the opposition as a declining and demoralized group and to interpret the history of these years as a prelude to the divisions which racked the party in the 1790s. By 1786 Wraxall was talking about a revival of the opposition.[4] Even in a routine and fairly quiet session,

---

[1] *Bland-Burges*, 174–5.   [2] A. G. Olson, *The Radical Duke* (Oxford, 1961), 77.

[3] For example, see Lord Hawkesbury to Pitt 20 Aug. 1789, P.R.O. Pitt Papers, 152; Lord Grenville to Lord Buckinghamshire 16 Apr. 1789, *Court and Cabinets*, ii. 142.

[4] Sir N. Wraxall, *Posthumous Memoirs* (3 vols., 1836), ii. 55.

such as that of 1788, Pitt was several times on the defensive. The opposition cheerfully trounced him in debate when he produced the India Declaratory Bill and it accused him of accepting the principles of its own ill-fated India Bill of 1783. On a minor issue concerning the promotion of certain naval officers, the opposition ran the government uncomfortably close. Its motion for a committee was lost by only sixteen votes.[1] There are other instances in which, by the active criticism of Pitt's measures, the opposition made itself felt in parliament; but on these occasions the effect was all too frequently lost. Because it was so concerned with embarrassing Pitt and belittling his achievements, the opposition tended to present a factious appearance to the world. In spite of their much-vaunted fidelity to the notion of party connection, members of the opposition found it expedient to deny party motives in an attempt to draw the independent vote on controversial issues, such as the Fortifications proposals of 1786. When the Whigs had a good case to argue, they were hampered by the fact that their motives were discredited in advance. On other occasions, the best oratory in the world might be wasted in arguing a bad one. Although these were not propitious years for an opposition, for many of their weaknesses the Whigs themselves were responsible.[2]

In an age when opposition to the government implied personal opposition to the court, the activities of the Whig party assumed a social as well as a political aspect. The Whigs enjoyed the allegiance of many of the most talented and charming men and women of the time, but the intercourse of aristocratic families, of brilliant writers and artists, sometimes seems to have outshone the political exploits of the party of Charles Fox. The debates at Westminster may appear incidental to the extravagant and dazzling lives of the fashionable *élite* of London society. While it is misleading to view the opposition

---

[1] 'In truth, it is a frightful question. They talk of repeating it, but I hope they will not.' T. Steele to Wilberforce 30 Apr. 1788, *The Correspondence of William Wilberforce*, ed. by his sons (2 vols., 1840), i. 54–55.

[2] 'When you were with Fox, tho' I wished the Opposition most cordially to be popular, I never could find, that it was generally so; and it was the only Opposition I ever remember, (I mean from 1784) that was not so.' E. Malone to Windham 29 Nov. 1795, Ad. MS. 37854, ff. 137–40, Windham Papers, printed in *The Windham Papers*, ed. Lord Rosebery (2 vols., 1913), i. 317–22.

exclusively through the eyes of the popular diarists and writers of the period, it is hard to deny that all too frequently the leaders of the party consoled themselves for their political misfortunes by allowing their personal whims and jealousies to be indulged in the delightful — if brittle and hollow — world of the Duchess of Devonshire and Mrs. Crewe. Only by constant and assiduous application to the political problems in hand could the Whigs have restored their reputation and convinced the world — and the King — that they were, after all, fit to govern the country. Years of wearying and remorseless routine had to be endured before they could purge themselves of the sins of the past. While they continued to suffer the bitter fruits of the defeat which the King and Pitt had inflicted upon them in the winter of 1783-4, and until there seemed some prospect of their party achieving office, it is not altogether surprising that members of the opposition languished in the years following. They were buffeted from one political storm to the next, lacking a general purpose and a general direction. They lived upon the expectation that Pitt might provide them with an occasional opportunity of humiliating him and consequently the life of opposition was unsatisfying and even factious. In truth, the Whigs were waiting for the King to die.[1] Until he was gone there seemed to be no purpose in exerting themselves in a hopeless cause and in a fortuitous search for public sympathy. Proscribed from positions of power and influence in the state for an indefinite period, they were perforce driven to make a principle out of their proscription, for proscription was to them a proof of their own fundamental honesty and incorruptibility.[2]

The leaders of the party were not the men to solve the political difficulties in which the opposition had enmeshed itself; still less were they capable of guiding the party into more constructive activities.

[1] On 2 Aug. 1786 the King was nearly murdered by a lunatic, Margaret Nicholson. Yet the Whigs did not join in the celebrations held to mark the King's fortunate escape and derided the danger to the royal person as imaginary and his escape as a misfortune. N. Wraxall, op. cit. ii. 157.

[2] '... ours is not the Party of Riches and Honours — our principles lead not to them — in short we have principles, which never will be acceptable to the Fountain of Rewards'. Fitzwilliam to Edmund Burke 29 May 1791, Wentworth Woodhouse MSS., Burke Letters 1.

Fox's determination — and perhaps, too, his confidence — had been shaken by the events of 1782–4. He had underestimated the skill and the resourcefulness of the King, and for this mistake he and his friends were paying dearly. He did not yet fully appreciate the role of party in the political arena; even if he had understood it, he lacked the conviction that might have translated theory into action. He was uninterested in the refinements of speculative doctrine. Even worse, he lacked the capacity for grasping the simple realities of the present when by so doing he might have transformed the future. His none-too-frequent assessments of the political scene are, almost invariably, astonishingly unrealistic. However indispensable his talents may have been to the opposition, he was not a good party leader. He lacked the authority which might have imposed restraint upon his followers. His mercurial temperament plunged him into periods of lethargy and pessimism. Then there would follow a burst of energy which would soon exhaust itself and weaken his enthusiasm for politics, while he dreamed of the peace and serenity of St. Anne's. He did not possess the qualities of patience and serious application to business which were necessary to perform the drudgeries of party organization. Although he was sometimes more assiduous during sessions than is often realized, he behaved during the recess as though the party did not exist. Yet Fox was, of course, indispensable to the party. The charm of his private companionship and the generosity of his public conduct gave him unrivalled leadership and attracted many younger politicians into the opposition party. Whatever his failings, his public stature and, at times, his notoriety, served to polarize politics between himself and Pitt. Whatever the weaknesses of the opposition, Fox was its undisputed leader and its clearest focus of unity.

The nominal head of the party was the Duke of Portland. He was hardly the nonentity so often described by historians. He was much more attentive to business than Fox or, indeed, most of the other leading men of the party. He is frequently to be found writing to party members, concerning himself with attendance in both Houses, striving to provide guidance on electoral matters and involving himself in many aspects of party organization. His crucial weakness was lack of assurance in his own judgement. He was compared unfavourably with Rockingham, who had possessed a greater firmness of character and

who was thus less likely to be influenced by others.[1] He looked to Fox
for that energy and confidence which he himself did not possess.
Although devoid of profound political sagacity, he enjoyed all those
aristocratic virtues which endeared him to the Whigs and which they
demanded and expected in a party leader. Not the least of these were
his scrupulous honesty and his undoubted integrity. His London
residence, Burlington House, was a more important meeting-place for
the party than Carlton House, largely because the Duke was on
intimate terms with all the important men in the party and because he
kept open house for all members of the party during sessions.[2] The
Duke of Portland was a respected and popular leader but, because he
was always looking for advice, he was usually unable to give any. His
dilatoriness and his inability to make up his mind drove party agents
and members to despair. Most fatal of all, he was unable to guide —
or restrain — Charles Fox.

The failings of its leaders had serious consequences for the party.
During the summer and autumn months political contacts between
party leaders were rare and haphazard and thus members returned to
town unprepared for the new session, lacking both a plan and a policy.
Tactics had thus to be concerted hurriedly at the meeting at Burlington
House on the eve of the debate on the Address. Fox rarely divided the
House on the Address[3] not, as he declared, because he did not wish to
introduce divisions between members — these existed already — but
because pains had not been taken to bring members to town. After the
session was under way, opportunities were lost and embarrassments
were caused by lack of preparation and planning.[4] Even when policy
had been worked out, the decisions which had been taken were rarely
communicated to the party at large. It is hardly surprising that many

[1] W. Combe, *Letter from a Country Gentleman to a Member of Parliament* (1789),
20–21.

[2] *Portrait of a Whig Peer*, ed. B. Connell (1957), 183; Wraxall comments that
Portland 'could not shut his doors, even had he been so inclined, against his
followers'. Op. cit. i. 11–12.

[3] Fox divided the House in the first session of the new parliament in 1784 and
was in a minority, 282–124. He did not divide again on the Address for the rest
of this parliament, that is, not until 1790.

[4] This was the party's greatest weakness, according to the Duchess of Devonshire. Sichel, *Sheridan*, ii. 400.

members of the opposition, remote from the party leadership, unaware
of party policy and ignorant of the order of business, were not to be
found in their seats when they were needed. On the rare occasions
when a debate on a major issue brought the ordinary member to town,
he was given little attention and rarely allowed the opportunity of
speaking.[1]

Effective organization of the party required the co-operation of its
leading members. Through personal rivalries and suspicion, lethargy
and indifference, this was not to be found. Crippling animosities
gnawed at the fragile unity of the opposition. Sheridan was distrusted
by Fox and disliked by Grey. His elevation in the counsels of the Prince
was deeply resented by many in the party, not least by Burke and
Windham.[2] Charles Grey, who entered parliament in 1786, was a
restless and disruptive force. He quickly endeared himself to the
Duchess of Devonshire and thus incurred the antagonism of Fox and
others.[3] On the other hand, several talented members of the Whig
party such as Elliot and Windham, and, of course, Burke, were unable
to find an adequate outlet for their political energies in the dreary party
routine, and their enthusiasm for the party conflict correspondingly
declined. Divided by trivial personal animosities, the party was thus
further weakened in its parliamentary proceedings. Nor were these
personal differences without a greater political significance, for they
were to bear bitter fruit for the party in the years to come.

Even more serious were the problems which the opposition brought
upon itself through its connection with the heir-apparent. During the
Coalition ministry in 1783 there are signs that Fox attempted to
manipulate the Prince for direct political purposes,[4] while the Prince
used the Whigs to assist him in his financial difficulties. Neither party
benefited much from its association with the other. The Prince did
not receive the money which the Coalition had promised to obtain
for him and it took all the persuasive arts of the Duchess of Devonshire

---

[1] The bulk of the speeches were made by six or seven members of the opposition.
About one-half of the party did not speak in the parliament of 1784–90.

[2] Burke to Windham 24 Jan. 1789, Wentworth Woodhouse MSS. Burke Letters 1.

[3] Sichel, op. cit., ii. 112.

[4] Fox to the Prince of Wales 4 Mar. 1783, Aspinall, *Correspondence of George,
Prince of Wales*, i. 103–4.

to reconcile the Prince to this outcome.[1] The King's anger with the Whigs was heightened and he was henceforward even more bitterly hostile towards them than he had previously been. Moreover, the affair was unpopular in the party, whose continued connection with the Prince lost it much public credit.[2] After the election of 1784 the Prince began to tire of his politically useless friends and the connection between them tended to weaken. There is some evidence, in fact, that both Fox and Portland were none too happy about the continued relationship between themselves and the Prince[3] but it was by this time too late to undo the damage which the connection had caused and worse was yet to come. When the Prince's financial difficulties became so acute that he was forced to consider living abroad, the King unjustly blamed Fox for encouraging the plan although Fox had been urging economy and retrenchment upon the heir to the throne for some time.[4] The matter came to something of a climax when the Prince desired the Whigs to bring the question of his debts before parliament in 1787. Fox and Portland were reluctant to involve themselves more deeply in the Prince's affairs and well knew that opinion in the party was divided. But, having antagonized the King, they could ill afford to alienate the heir to the throne and thus they acquiesced. Elliot saw the consequences as 'a sort of separation and schism in the party, that may perhaps lead to discussion on other occasions'.[5] If the issue of the Prince's debts was futile and unpopular, then his morganatic marriage was so dangerous as to strike at the very legitimacy of opposition itself. Fox was unable to prevent the Prince from contracting the marriage and during the debates in 1787 on the Prince's debts widespread rumours concerning the secret marriage gave rise to a first-rate public scandal. If the

---

[1] Ibid. 99.

[2] Ibid. 100. The Prince was present in the Commons during some of the debates in early 1784. Sir N. Wraxall, *Historical Memoirs of My Own Time*, ed. R. Askham (1904), 655. The Prince was never popular. He was despised not so much for his dissipation as for his shiftiness, extravagance and bullying.

[3] The Prince of Wales to Mrs. Fitzherbert 3 Nov. 1785, Aspinall, op. cit., i. 92; Combe, *Letter from a Country Gentleman*, 18–19.

[4] Fox to the Prince of Wales 16 July 1786, ibid. 247–9.

[5] Elliot to his wife 5 May 1787, *Life and Letters of Sir Gilbert Elliot*, ed. Countess of Minto (3 vols., 1874), i. 159–62 (hereafter referred to as Minto).

marriage were to be made public the consequences would be disastrous. An almost unprecedented constitutional crisis would have been created because the marriage infringed both the Royal Marriages Act and the Act of Succession. Because of his wife's religion, the Prince might be deprived of the succession, and then the Whigs might not come into office as they expected. If the public were to hear about the marriage then the party's reputation would suffer a catastrophic blow. Fox's denial that the marriage had taken place did nothing to quell rumours. Even worse, the conflicting statements made by Fox and Sheridan only served to strengthen the intensity of public speculation. Although the excitement soon died away, the affair remained to embarrass the Whigs during the Regency Crisis of 1788–9 when it produced further friction within the party. Not least, Sheridan's influence with the Prince was confirmed and enhanced and was correspondingly envied and disliked. Further personal animosities followed from these events. Portland, influenced by his wife, refused to receive Mrs. Fitzherbert, and it was to be two years before he resumed his former relations with the Prince.[1] The Devonshire House circle, on the other hand, was rather more sympathetic to the Prince and therefore somewhat estranged from Portland for a time. The Prince was offended by Fox's statement to the Commons and their relations never really recovered the warmth of previous years. Although these quarrels and disputes were serious enough, it would be unwise to exaggerate their significance. It is doubtful if they were a really serious cause of party disunity. Most members of the opposition remained unmoved by it all and took little interest in the squabbles of the more fashionable elements in London society.

But there was one who thoroughly disapproved of the whole proceeding and who distrusted the Prince. Edmund Burke, drifting away from that position of influence and prestige which he had enjoyed in the party when Rockingham was alive, suspected that when the Prince came to the throne he might not form a Whig ministry but rather one chosen from 'a few of his own doubtful people'.[2] Burke's party enthusiasm was rapidly declining. He was, by this time, confining his

[1] W. H. Wilkins, *Mrs. Fitzherbert and George IV* (2 vols., 1905), i. 142.

[2] C. M'Cormick, *Memoirs of Edmund Burke* (1798), 291. For a discussion of this point, see A. S. Foord, *His Majesty's Opposition* 1714–1830 (Oxford, 1964), 410–11.

political attention to the impeachment of Warren Hastings and took little interest in purely party matters. In 1784 he had confessed his unwillingness to continue the struggle against the influence of the crown because the people had so decisively rejected the Whig party at the general election.[1] He felt himself spurned by the party which he had done so much to establish, and he began to voice criticism of Fox's tactics in 1783–4. After 1784 he disapproved of the party's proceedings because the opposition 'proceeded upon the separate measures as they separately arose, without any vindictive retrospect to Mr. Pitt's conduct in 1784'.[2] Disillusioned with the Prince and weary of the hopeless party struggle, Burke was occupied almost exclusively with the affairs of India. Yet he did not regard this as a party question, he was angry when Fox tried to treat it as such and he even attempted to persuade the ministers to commit themselves more whole-heartedly to its support.[3] Yet he was no more successful in this than he was in his efforts to maintain the enthusiasm of those of his colleagues who were managing the impeachment.[4] Nevertheless, too much was at stake for Burke to allow himself to be deflected from his purposes by the indifference of men like Grey and Sheridan. Not only did he wish to impeach Hastings. He wished also to 'acquit and justify myself to those few persons, and to those distant times, which may take a concern in these affairs'.[5] Burke's concern for his own reputation doubtless arose from the odium with which his ill-fated India Bill of 1783 had been greeted and his subsequent wish to salvage his character. But there was more than this to Burke's gruelling persecution of Hastings. There is no doubt that it daunted him, that he was rarely optimistic as to its outcome, that, once begun, he could not turn back without acknowledging Hastings's innocence. But the amazing pertinacity and the laborious industry which Burke expended upon the impeachment

---

[1] Burke to Baker 22 June 1784, Baker MSS. Acc. 452, no. 77.

[2] *Observations on the Conduct of the Minority*, in *The Works of Edmund Burke* (2 vols., 1834), i. 627.

[3] Burke to Francis 10, 23 Dec. 1785, Wentworth Woodhouse MSS., Burke Letters 1; Burke to Dundas 1 Jan. 1787, Melville MSS. Copeland Transcript.

[4] Sichel, *Sheridan*, ii. 404; *Bland-Burges*, 101–2; Burke to O'Beirne 29 Sept. 1786, Wentworth Woodhouse MSS., Burke Letters 1.

[5] Burke to Francis 10 Dec. 1785, *The Correspondence of Edmund Burke*, ed. Lord Fitzwilliam and Sir R. Bourke (4 vols., 1844), iii. 42.

cannot be explained away by references to his disordered imagination. Belief in an insidious East India group, a 'Bengal Squad', was confined neither to Burke nor to members of the opposition. His thinking on India is part of the essential Burke. He feared that self-interested motives would destroy a hierarchical society which was blessed by prescription and sanctified with religion. All the more heart-breaking then was his bitterness towards the indifference of those who called themselves his friends. Burke's future looked bleak in the years after 1784. His life was distorted by loneliness and despair, by the knowledge of frustrated ambition, by the debts and the ill health which sharpened his temper and soured his spirit. The ties of loyalty which continued to bind him to the party were slowly loosening. The party had failed to achieve the aims which he had set before it many years ago and of this failure had been the first and most pitiful casualty.[1]

II. The Consolidation of Party, 1784–90

The rise of party has long been recognized as one of the most important constitutional developments of the late eighteenth and early nineteenth centuries. Yet it is not at all clear what the rise of party was, when or how it occurred, or how it affected politics. Although it is difficult to define party attachments with any great precision in this period, there can be little doubt that the Whig party of Fox and Portland was larger and more stable in its membership than many of the family and patronage groups of the eighteenth century. The party survived the crisis years 1782–4 without substantial loss of numbers. Indeed, the Fox–North Coalition added further numbers and, despite the heavy losses suffered by the Coalition at the polls in 1784, Fox could still command the support of over 130 members in the new parliament. By 1790 this number had crept up to over 140 because Fox was rather more successful than Pitt in attracting new talent from among the intake of members

[1] Burke's keen awareness of his own failings and his own unpopularity was perhaps the most potent factor contributing towards the testiness of his public behaviour. 'If a man is disabled from rendering any essential service to his principles or to his party, he ought at least to contrive to make his conversation as little disagreeable as he can to the society which his friends may still be indulgent enough to hold with him.' Burke to Francis 23 Nov. 1785, *Memoirs of Sir Philip Francis,* ed. J. Parkes and H. Merrivale (2 vols., 1867), ii. 246.

from by-elections.[1] This large and stable opposition did not depend entirely upon patronage or upon family connection for its survival. Indeed, voluntary association and attachment on principle played significant roles in providing for the strength and coherence of the party. Nevertheless, 'The durability of Parties depends less on the ideas they represent than on the strength and coherence of party organizations.'[2] If this is to be our principal criterion for judging of party development then we can observe interesting and significant events taking place within the Whig party after 1784 and which present a totally different picture from the traditional caricature which concentrates upon Fox's failings, the Prince of Wales's flirtations and Burke's impatience with the opposition.

One aspect of the Whig organization which has already attracted the attention of historians has been the establishment of clubs and societies within the party during the years after 1784. These could be temporary, informal attempts to secure co-operation during sessions,[3] but the Whig Club was a more important vehicle for establishing party activities on a more permanent institutional basis.[4] It grew out of the Westminster Election Club of 1780, but it rapidly became a general party association. The Whig Club was active in disseminating propaganda and in maintaining contacts 'with a variety of other clubs in the provincial towns of the kingdom, [which] may be considered the offspring of this prolific parent'.[5] Black remarks that although the club was financed by Portland and Fitzwilliam[6] it was used by Fox 'as a vehicle through which to secure ascendancy over the remains of the Rockinghamite party'.[7] But by the end of the decade it was beginning

---

[1] For an attempt to estimate the size of the Whig party from 1780 to 1792 see Appendix 1.

[2] Sir L. Namier and J. Brooke, *The House of Commons, 1754–1790* (3 vols., H.M.S.O., 1964), i. 186.

[3] See p. 81 n. 1, for a good example of this type of association.

[4] The Whig Club is discussed by Foord, *His Majesty's Opposition*, 406–7, and by E. C. Black, *The Association* (Harvard University Press, 1963), 217.

[5] C. Pigott, *The Whig Club* (1794), 5–6.

[6] Rockingham left no issue and thus the greater part of his estate and borough interests descended to his nephew, Fitzwilliam, in 1782.

[7] Black, op. cit., 217. *The World*, a ministerial paper, ran a series of articles in June and July 1790 entitled 'Whigs and Whig Club'. One of the many unsavoury

to show itself unwilling to accept tamely the leadership of Fox, still less that of Portland, a fact which was to be of the first importance in the history of the Whig party after 1789. In that year a Whig Club was established in Ireland, at Dublin. The Irish Whigs justified their readiness to organize their activities on a party basis by rehearsing the virtues of party in Burkeian terms. They proclaimed proudly that they were closely connected with the English Whigs not merely through family ties but also because the Whigs of both countries should unite to secure the much-needed reformation in government in both England and Ireland.[1]

This recognition of the need for party institutions and a greater measure of party organization characterized the history of the Whig opposition after 1784. But the establishment of political societies is only a very small part of the opposition's efforts to organize the party on a more efficient and rational basis. Far-reaching political changes sometimes arise naturally as a response to urgent financial needs, and the party developments of this period are no exception. Since the early 1780s a general fund had been in existence 'for payments to newspapers and to individuals constantly in the service of the party and for various debts incurred by the party'. This fund was subscribed by the leaders of the party, and by the early 1790s was realizing over £1,000 per annum.[2] But it was the heavy cost of elections which set in train more extensive and systematic attempts to place party finances upon a more secure footing. In 1788 Lord Hood, one of the members for Westminster, was appointed a Lord of the Admiralty and had thus to seek re-election. Against the wishes of their leaders, the Whigs decided on a contest and chose Lord John Townshend as their candidate.[3] After the

charges which the paper made was that the Club acted as a source of recruitment for likely party members.

[1] *A Fair Exposition of the Principles of the Whig Club* (Dublin, 1790); *Thoughts on a Letter addressed to Thomas Connoley, by a Whig* (1790).

[2] In much of what follows I have relied heavily upon the important article by Donald E. Ginter, 'The Financing of the Whig Party Organization, 1783–1793', *American Historical Review* (Jan. 1966), lxxi, (2), 421–40.

[3] Lord Sheffield to William Eden 2 Aug. 1788, *Journals and Correspondence of William, Lord Auckland*, ed. Bishop of Bath and Wells (4 vols., 1861–2), ii. 222–3. *The Morning Post* of 25 Aug 1788 stated that the Whig Club was responsible for Lord John's candidature.

Whigs had spent a sum estimated as high as £50,000 the party's campaign was successful and Lord John was returned. His victory owed much to party organization. Whig members of parliament left their homes to travel, in some cases, hundreds of miles, to canvass for him.[1] More important, however, was the readiness of the Whigs to subscribe to a second party fund to finance the staggering expenses of the election. Such subscriptions were not, in fact, uncommon. It was simply good sense for the party leaders to pool their resources in a common fund for party purposes. If Wraxall is to be trusted, the expenses of the Westminster scrutiny of 1784–5 were borne by the Whig party grandees.[2] Such funds were usually temporary, directed to an immediate objective and closed soon after the business in hand had been completed.[3] But the enormous expense attending the Westminster election of 1788 led to a more permanent arrangement. An informal subscription launched in September 1788 quite failed to raise the enormous sums needed and in 1789 the fund was placed in the care of William Adam, who by that date was playing a remarkable and hitherto totally unrecognized role in party management.[4]

Adam had formerly been a Northite and had held government office between 1779 and 1782. Yet he possessed an overwhelming admiration for Fox which ripened into friendship and mutual respect, rather curiously, after the two men had fought a duel in 1779. He was thus one of the most prominent advocates of the Fox–North Coalition and he was active in the party's services during the 1784 election. He rapidly became one of Fox's closest political associates and most trusted advisers. Not least, he was a great success in Whig society. A lawyer by training, endowed with great patience and perseverance, Adam was a natural choice as one of the managers of the impeachment of Hastings. His friendship with Tom Pelham led to his appointment to the post of Solicitor-General in the household of the Prince of Wales. His attempts to retrieve the Prince's dismal financial situation endeared him to Carlton House. During the Westminster election of

[1] Lists of such members may be found, *inter alia*, in *The Morning Chronicle* for 19 July and 5 Aug. 1788. [2] Wraxall, *Posthumous Memoirs*, i. 238.

[3] Although the fund would be closed, claims might still be made upon it, e.g. debts incurred by Fox at Westminster between 1780 and 1783 were still outstanding in 1793. J. Almon to W. Adam 20 May and 2 July 1793, Blair-Adam MSS.

[4] For the Westminster subscription see Ginter, op. cit., 424–7.

1788 Adam was in London, canvassing for Lord John and in close touch with the leaders of the party. His own financial straits, however, did not allow him to make a contribution to the fund.[1] During the Regency Crisis of 1788–9 William Adam acted as party whip and established himself as an indispensable party manager. He was rewarded by a firm promise of the Secretaryship to the Treasury. His jubilation was double-edged. This lucrative appointment would rescue his family from the debts into which it had fallen of late. But what fascinated Adam was the opportunity of exercising the power which went with his promised situation. For he took an almost Harringtonian view of politics. He saw that in recent decades the funded, trading and commercial interests represented in the Commons were challenging the entrenched landed interest which was largely represented in the House of Lords, where it would be more directly amenable to the influence of the crown. Adam wanted to be the man to control the rising interests and the new powers in the land, and to harness them to the Whig party.[2] The recovery of George III in 1789 dashed Adam's high hopes, but he swallowed his disappointment and lent his talents ever more rigorously to the service of the opposition party.

He had learned one important lesson from the Westminster election of 1788: that an adequate supply of money was an irresistible advantage in electioneering. In July 1789 Portland and Adam established yet a third party fund, the proceeds from which were to be applied to general election expenses.[3] Although the party grandees sympathized with these aims, the money was slow in coming and it was only by a last-minute effort on the part of Adam, Lord Fitzwilliam and Lord Spencer in the summer and autumn of 1790 that it was collected at all.[4] But it is not only the existence of these funds which indicates a fairly

---

[1] Adam to John Adam 9 Jan. 1789, Blair-Adam MSS.   [2] Ibid.

[3] The target which they set themselves to raise was over £20,000. Adam to G. Elphinstone (n.d. 1789), Blair-Adam MSS.; Lord Spencer to Adam 5 Sept. 1790, Blair-Adam MSS.; Lord Spencer to Fitzwilliam Aug. 1790, Wentworth Woodhouse MSS., F. 115e.

[4] The Duke of Devonshire to Fitzwilliam 11 June 1790; Lord Spencer to Fitzwilliam Aug. 1790, Blair-Adam MSS. and Ginter, op. cit., 427–8. George, 2nd Earl Spencer held office in 1782 but is reputed to have declined an offer of the Irish Vice-Royalty in the Coalition ministry of 1783.

sophisticated party organization. Nor is the readiness of certain individuals to subscribe sums which occasionally can be counted in thousands rather than hundreds the factor upon which the historian fastens his attention. How the money was spent is probably more indicative of the state of party development than the manner in which it was collected.

Even before the Regency Crisis Adam had been preparing the party for the forthcoming general election. He acted as the manager of the opposition's campaign in Scotland, 'our party being in total want of anyone to unite our friends in one common mode of exertion'.[1] Details of electoral interests in the Scottish counties were meticulously prepared and annotated, while the loyalties of every voting freeholder in the burghs were ascertained and tabulated.[2] The recovery of the King did not halt these preparations because rumours of an impending dissolution continued to tantalize the political world until the summer of 1789.[3] Adam's activities during the election of 1790 are only now being investigated,[4] but already it is possible to indicate the nature and the significance of his work. It is now a commonplace to be told that an interest in a constituency did not depend on a party but on landed property, services to constituents and the goodwill of the electors.[5] Nevertheless, it would benefit candidates in many constituencies to obtain the assistance of men of local standing to further their nomination, and this was, in fact, one way in which a man like Adam was able to place at the disposal of party candidates such machinery, influence and resources as the party commanded. We are also told that 'Despite the growth of party during this period, there was little change in the

[1] F. MacKenzie to Adam 8 Oct. 1788, Blair-Adam MSS.

[2] L. Hill, *View of the Political State of Scotland* (1788); unidentified writer to Adam Jan. 1789; W. Robertson to Adam 7 Nov. 1788; L. Hill to Adam 4 Jan. 1789; Adam to L. Hill 29 May 1789, Blair-Adam MSS.

[3] Adam was one of the few members of the opposition to have rejoiced in the fact that they did not come to power by virtue of the King's madness in 1789, for he felt that the party would soon have been dismissed had it done so. He was content for the Whigs to remain out of office and build up their numbers from a more solid, enduring and reputable motive than that of the mere expectation of office. W. Adam to John Adam 12 Feb. 1789, Blair-Adam MSS.

[4] Mr. Ginter is publishing a volume of documents and comment on the subject of Adam's electoral activities in 1790 which will greatly illuminate this neglected field of Whig history.

[5] Namier and Brooke, *House of Commons*, i. 46.

C

essential nature of the patronage system'.[1] But this does not exclude the possibility that the patronage system might have been used for party purposes. Members of parliament might not owe their seat directly to a party but a party might be used to assist a candidate either to find a seat or to fight a contest. Party could thus begin to operate at the constituency level and, with the beginning of a systematic party organization directed by William Adam, this began to be the case. He was, indeed, well placed to perform these services. Close to the Duke of Portland and the other party grandees, he was recognized and accepted as party secretary and 'principal agent' to the Duke. He seems to have received a stream of information about prospects in many constituencies and he was thus able to warn a friendly candidate about an impending contest or perhaps to send details of constituency interests which the candidate might attempt to gain.[2] The election fund allowed financial assistance to be distributed to party candidates and even allowed the opposition to contest seats they had not recently fought. In this latter context Mr. Ginter has observed a most significant development, namely that the party sent out its own agents from party headquarters to help candidates fight these difficult contests.[3] Adam also helped members to find seats, either through the patronage system, informing prospective candidates of patrons who wanted reliable members, or by informing them of seats on the open market.[4] The extent of Adam's work is difficult to assess. It would be true, for example, that the need for his interference would be lessened wherever there was already in existence a strong local party machine under the direct control of one of the more considerable patrons of the party but, even in these cases, money and propaganda may well have been provided by Adam. If it is difficult to know exactly how many constituencies felt the effects of this nascent party organization, the best possible commentary upon it is that it survived. Such assistance as it

[1] Ibid. 56.

[2] See, *inter alia*, Sir W. Cunnynghame to Adam 27 Apr. 1789; A. Dalzal to Adam 3 May 1789; Sir D. Carnegie to Adam 30 Oct. 1789; Portland to Adam 25 Jan. 1790, Blair-Adam MSS.

[3] Ginter, op. cit., 428–30.

[4] G. A. North to Adam 3 Apr. 1789; Adam to G. A. North 10 Apr. 1789; J. Anstruther to Adam 27 Aug. 1789; Portland to Adam 25 Jan. 1790, Blair-Adam MSS.

provided was taken for granted and even expected at the general election of 1796, and Adam continued to manage elections for the Foxite Whigs for many years afterwards.[1]

An essential and integral part of electioneering in the eighteenth century, as in any other period, was the publication and distribution of party propaganda. The Whigs showed a timely awareness of publicity throughout the 1780s,[2] but it was the Regency Crisis which supplied the impetus towards the development of propaganda techniques and organization which had hitherto been lacking. A subcommittee met frequently 'at a well-known tavern, in Covent Garden, to shape paragraphs, frame hand-bills and propagate falsehoods'.[3] Early in 1789 a 'central office' was in existence with a full-time, paid staff which received annual allocations from the general fund.[4] From this source flowed a stream of loyal addresses, circular letters, party notices and subscription demands to all parts of the kingdom.[5] Nor was the party blind to the potential importance of the newspaper press, and during the Regency Crisis both *The Morning Post* and *The Morning Chronicle* became party organs, largely through the exertions of Sheridan.[6] Afterwards Adam seems to have been charged with the control of party propaganda. Not only did he subsidize pamphleteers.[7] Unlike the government, he had the wit to see that the country papers might be of use to the party in the forthcoming elections and there are some few traces of his financial dealings with them.[8] Through Adam's energy and foresight, therefore, the indispensable business of

---

[1] M. A. Taylor to Adam 9 Oct. 1794; Lord Guilford to Adam 22 Oct. 1794; Dr. S. Parr to Adam 2 May 1795; Adam to Parr 5 May 1795, Blair-Adam MSS.; Ginter, op. cit., 439.

[2] Ginter, op. cit., 433, 436.

[3] Combe, *Letter from a Country Gentleman*, 48.

[4] Ginter, op. cit., 430–3; Fitzwilliam to Adam 8 Sept. 1791; Portland to Adam 3 Sept. 1792, Blair-Adam MSS.

[5] Sandwich to Adam 27 Jan. 1789; North to Adam 12 Dec. 1789, Blair-Adam MSS.

[6] Foord, *His Majesty's Opposition*, 407–8; Sichel, *Sheridan*, ii. 420; A. Aspinall, *Politics and the Press* (1949), 274–81, 396–7.

[7] S. Haywood to Adam 23 Dec. 1789, Blair-Adam MSS.; Adam to Fitzwilliam 19, 20 Sept. 1793, N.R.O. Box 45; Ginter, op. cit., 434–5.

[8] R. Frazer to Adam 6 May 1790; Lord Spencer to Adam 5 Sept. 1790, Blair-Adam MSS.

party publicity had been placed upon a systematic financial basis, and party propaganda was regularly disseminated throughout the kingdom.

The question of the novelty of Adam's achievements naturally arises. It can be argued with some justification that part or all of his work had been anticipated by politicans earlier in the eighteenth century and the services which Burke rendered to the Rockingham Whigs spring immediately to mind. Yet, as we have observed, the party developments of the 1780s rested upon a secure financial footing and a solid institutional framework which did not exist during the life of Lord Rockingham. In the age of Fox and Adam the leaders of the party were willing to contribute to the maintenance of central party institutions administered by an energetic and industrious secretary. This represents, in some small degree at least, nothing less than a purposive attempt to overcome the predominantly local nature of politics and electoral contests which so frequently dissipated the exertions and the energies of eighteenth-century parties. Nor is it difficult to explain why Adam was able to undertake this task with some success. His role at the centre of party organization was unprecedented. Although he was handling a party which was larger than that of Burke and Rockingham in the 1770s and which had correspondingly larger and more complex requirements, the party organization manipulated by Adam did not rest upon the authority which he himself derived from a single patron or friend. It depended partly upon Adam's industry but, more important, it depended upon his own unique position within the party. He was close to all the party leaders. He was the agent and adviser to the Duke of Portland[1] and he was on ever increasingly intimate terms with Fox.[2] He maintained his old affection for the rapidly declining Lord North and brought himself to the notice of the Duke of Bedford and was put in charge of his affairs.[3] His promotion in the household of the Prince of Wales has already been mentioned and it was not long before he was enmeshed in the murky

[1] Interviews with Portland were sometimes arranged through Adam, and matters for the Duke's notice occasionally passed through his hands.

[2] Adam was one of Fox's closest confidants during the Regency Crisis, but it was not until 1791 that their friendship seems to have reached its maturity. See Fox to Adam 2 Feb. 1789, and 16 Nov., 30 Dec. 1791, Blair-Adam MSS.

[3] Adam to John Adam 29 Nov. 1791, Blair-Adam MSS.

business of the Prince's debts and, later, those of the Duke of York.[1] He was even liked by Burke, and was one of the few managers of the impeachment who did not drive him to desperation by unkindness and indifference.[2] Although he lacked the personal qualities and the public ability (he was never a good parliamentary speaker) which might have allowed him to cut a figure in politics, Adam was at the very heart of the Whig party and in a position of immense potential influence. He understood well the web of political interests and personal connections which helped to combine the disparate elements of the party into something resembling a political organization. The institutions which were at his finger-tips soon acquired a life and a force of their own. Their authority and their power became detached from the control of the aristocratic patrons who had enabled them to be born. In the struggle for the Whig party after 1789, the mechanisms of the party were to play a significant if not a vital role.

All this does not exhaust the sum of William Adam's services to the Whig party of Portland and Fox. During parliamentary seessions he acted as party whip.[3] His advice was sought by party members on attendance and he was sometimes personally responsible for sending out cards.[4] He was informed by members of the opposition of their absences, and it was he who received instructions from opposition peers concerning the use of their proxies.[5] Although pairing remained a private and not a party matter, and although Adam did not arrange pairs for his members, he was often informed of such arrangements.[6]

[1] Adam was frequently approached for his interposition with the Prince in the matter of the heir's influence and patronage. In 1791 Adam played a prominent part in the unsavoury attempts to contract a loan for the Prince from Antwerp. By the end of the same year he had been placed in charge of efforts to reduce the debts of the Duke of York. Adam to John Adam 29 Nov. 1791, loc. cit.

[2] Burke to Sir Philip Francis 17 Dec. 1789, Parkes and Merrivale, *Memoirs of Sir Philip Francis*, ii. 263–5; Adam to Burke 2 Jan. 1791, Fitzwilliam MSS. N.R.O., Burke Letters A. iv. 57.

[3] For the party whip in earlier years, see Foord, op. cit., 405–6.

[4] See, *inter alia*, Fox to Adam, 15 Mar. 1789; J. Lee to Adam (n.d. 1788–9); Portland to Adam 10 Jan. 1792, Blair-Adam MSS.

[5] E.g. Lord Mountstuart to Adam 12 Jan. 1790; G. N. Edwards to Adam 9 Dec. 1790; Elliot to Adam 3 Feb. 1792; Blair-Adam MSS.

[6] E.g. Lord Charles Spencer to Adam 3 May 1789; J. MacPherson to Adam 24 May 1791, Blair-Adam MSS. MacPherson had paired off with a ministerialist

As party secretary and whip he sometimes received information from government whips or from Pitt himself concerning the order of business. This was not entirely novel but it became more common and more systematic than the 'gentlemanly co-operation' of which Professor Foord writes in connection with the relations between Lord North and the Rockingham Whigs in the 1770s.[1] During the Regency Crisis, Steele seems to have been in fairly close contact with Adam and was particularly concerned to warn him of changes in the order of business so that Adam might have an opportunity to bring his members to the House.[2] In the following years such contacts between government and opposition appear to have become the regular method of arranging controversial business. In 1791 the Clerk of the House of Commons suggested to Adam a convenient arrangement by which to accommodate a matter raised by the opposition.[3] In May 1793 Sheridan negotiated with Pitt for the date of the debate on the East India Company Charter Bill and, through his friendship with Canning, a convenient date for the debate on the Aliens Bill.[4] Such developments illustrate that acceptance of organized party and formed opposition which characterized the later eighteenth century. The routine of politics and the practices of parliament were beginning to accommodate party. This was reflected not only in political organization but also in the customs and habits of members. As is well known, members of the opposition began to seat themselves to the Speaker's left about 1740. Yet many years were to pass before that side of the House became reserved exclusively for the opposition. Opposition parties were too small in numbers to fill up one side of the House and, even in the 1770s, other groups would sit with or among the Rockingham Whigs. Nevertheless, at this time the phrases 'treasury benches', 'opposition benches' and 'under the gangway' become common coin, indicating

---

who had promised to inform one of the government whips, Long, of the arrangement, and 'I agreed to do the same to you'. For the earlier history of 'pairing', see Foord, op. cit., 200 n.3; E. and A. Porritt, *The Unreformed House of Commons* (2 vols., Cambridge, 1909), i. 506–7.

[1] Foord, op. cit., 358.

[2] T. Steele to Adam 24 Dec. 1788 and 26 Jan. 1789, Blair-Adam MSS.

[3] J. Hatsell to Adam 10 Nov. 1791, Blair-Adam MSS.

[4] D. Marshall, *The Rise of Canning* (1938), 66, 68.

the location of a supporter of the government, of the opposition, and members independent of both.[1] After 1784 there was a large and distinctive opposition party whose members habitually sat together, but on non-party issues seating arrangements might be confused, especially when there was a scramble for seats before an important debate. Bland-Burges, for example, heard Pitt's Benares speech from 'a snug corner of one of the Opposition benches, just facing the Treasury bench'.[2] Yet, in general, the location of a member's seat was regarded as a manifestation of his political loyalties. Dundas, gloating over Eden's defection from the opposition, exhibited him as a government supporter by seating him on the Treasury bench and several years later, when Edmund Burke quitted the Whig party, he wandered uneasily among the benches for a time, before crossing over to the ministerial side of the House.[3]

There were other, more bizarre, ways of demonstrating party attachments. The Rockingham Whigs had adopted the colours of the uniform of Washington's regiment, the buff and blue, and they wore these colours in the House of Commons.[4] They became the colours of the Whig party and after 1784 they were much in evidence at election times.[5] Even in Whig society the colours were worn at important functions and acquired minute elaboration.[6] The straight political fight between Pitt and Fox, and the centenary of the Glorious Revolution encouraged members to wear party uniform. Some ministerialists wore orange cloaks in the Commons — the colours of the Revolution. When Sir Joseph Mawbey wished to castigate the Whigs in 1789 he caused the House much amusement by his sarcastic references to the buff and blue.[7] And during all the social bickering which followed the Regency Crisis, London was split into two hostile camps, resplendent

[1] These phrases are common in writers like Wraxall. See *Posthumous Memoirs*, i. 28–29.

[2] *Bland-Burges*, 84.   [3] Wraxall, *Posthumous Memoirs*, ii. 18, iii. 344.

[4] *Miscellanies*, ed. Lord Stanhope (2 vols., 1861, 1864), i. 100–7; Sir G. C. Lewis, *Administrations of Great Britain* (1864), 70 n.2.

[5] Stanhope's *Miscellanies*, i. 100–7; *The Diary of William Windham*, ed. Mrs. Frances Baring (1866), 109.

[6] W. C. Sydney, *England and the English in the Eighteenth Century* (2 vols., 1891), ii. 157.

[7] *The Parliamentary Register*, xxvi, 299, 447.

in their respective liveries.[1] It is impossible to say how many Whigs wore the buff and blue, but it was not confined to Fox and his friends. Burke wore the party colours as late as 1788.[2] Nor was the wearing of party uniform devoid of political significance, for Fox made the buff and blue the colours of his party after the split with Portland. At this, the Prince of Wales adopted a different uniform for himself and his friends.[3] The buff and blue, in fact, was worn long into the nineteenth century and it became part of Foxite mythology and Whig tradition. Such idiosyncrasies are, perhaps, typical of political parties, and to ignore them is to miss something of the flavour and the continuity of politics.

When parliament thus began to accommodate party, the role of the Speaker was inevitably significant. Earlier in the century, George Onslow had disliked party as 'a combination for factious or illegitimate or tyrannical purposes' and he consequently disliked divisions because they introduced partisan feeling into the House. He used his great prestige and authority to assist the government, in which he held office, in striving to maintain harmony within the Commons and 'in shaming an opposition into decency'.[4] After Onslow left the Chair, his notion of 'a basic agreement between all men of patriotic good-will super-imposed upon faction and self-seeking' became increasingly irrelevant to an assembly torn by the new issues of Wilkes and America. The patriotic line of conduct was now by no means obvious and it could not easily be found. The absence of strong party organizations, through which some kind of procedural arrangements might have been negoti-ated, dissolved the sittings of the House into chaos. Thus the activities of Adam and the emergence of a more highly organized opposition party stabilized the working of parliament. Although the Speaker continued to have close links with the government,[5] the ideal of the impartiality of the Chair had made an unmistakable appearance.

[1] Wilkins, *Mrs. Fitzherbert and George IV*, i. 257.

[2] Burke to Wilkes 18 Aug. 1788, Wentworth Woodhouse MSS., Burke Letters, 1.

[3] Wraxall, *Historical Memoirs*, xvii.

[4] On this subject I have relied upon J. Steven Watson, 'Arthur Onslow and Party Politics' in *Essays in British History presented to Sir Keith Feiling*, ed. Hugh Trevor-Roper (1963), and the same author's 'Parliamentary Procedure as a Key to an Understanding of Eighteenth Century Party Politics' in *The Burke Newsletter* (1962).

[5] This is particularly true of Grenville and Addington, both of whom were close friends of Pitt.

Although the 'Patriotic Line' reappeared after 1793 during the war against revolutionary France, the procedural and organizational developments of earlier years were not reversed. Inside the House of Commons, party had come to stay.

The consolidation of party in the routine of politics had come far since the accession of George III, and this is reflected in the size and stability and organizational activities of the opposition after 1784. But, like many oppositions of the unreformed parliament, it was based upon a coalition, and one, moreover, between men with different political beliefs and principles. It is hard to believe that the Northites really shared the conviction of the Portland and Foxite Whigs that the influence of the crown ought to be diminished. Surely this violates Burke's dictum — that a party should be agreed on fundamental principle. By recalling the foundations upon which the Coalition had been constructed in 1783 it might be possible to approach this question. Historians now realize that 'the grand principle of distinction and separation between parties', the American war, was no longer an issue in politics.[1] Some form of coalition was necessary in 1782–3 if there was to have been a government at all. Should Fox have waited for Shelburne to have allied with North? Could Fox have formed a coalition with Shelburne after what he imagined to be Shelburne's treachery during the Rockingham–Shelburne administration of 1782? There had never been personal animosity between North and the Whig leaders, and Fox made it clear to North that a coalition ministry would not practise the form of government which had prevailed during the ministry of 1770–82.[2] Fox did promise to drop parliamentary reform but this had never been an agreed party measure. In the Coalition cabinet, the Whigs obtained all but two of the 'efficient offices'. North, moreover, was ill-suited for leading a party. Nor were his followers accustomed to acting in party, and Adam was worried that they might defect.[3] After 1784 North aged rapidly and rarely attended parliament.

[1] Elliot to Sir J. Harris (n.d. Mar. 1782), Minto, i. 75.

[2] Foord, *His Majesty's Opposition*, 391. See also I. R. Christie, 'George III and the Debt on Lord North's Election Account', *E.H.R.* (Oct. 1963), lxxviii, for a discussion of the financial necessities which led North to ally with Fox.

[3] Adam to North 15 Jan. 1784, *The Later Correspondence of George III*, ed. A. Aspinall (Cambridge University Press, 1962), i, pp. xxxii–iii.

His eyesight was failing and he became hesitant and indecisive in his conduct.[1] This was not the sort of man to lead a party within a party and, to all intents and purposes, he surrendered the leadership of his following to Fox. Thus the Northites joined with Fox in his ill-fated assault on Pitt's ministry in 1783–4. And there is remarkably little to suggest that Fox was ever restrained in his conduct by feelings of delicacy for the Northites after 1784. Slightly over fifty members of the old party of North survived the election of 1784, but the absorption of his followers within the opposition as a whole proceeded apace. By 1788, although there were still over forty Northites in the House, less than twenty of them could be distinguished as a separate entity within the opposition.[2] Even if the Northites had been a larger or more distinctive group it is doubtful if their influence within the party would have been great. Most of the Northite leaders and patrons had been discredited during the American war and they lacked real ability. This was recognized during the Regency Crisis when the list of projected offices in the new Whig administration was scarcely generous to them and included very few of their number in anything like responsible situations.[3]

Fox enjoyed undisputed leadership of the opposition. The only rivals he may have had came, not from the Northites, but from among his own followers. As new members entered the party they received their political education at his hands and they adopted his principles. What characterizes the opposition to Pitt after 1784, then, is the whittling away of incongruous elements within it — although these existed. There is a sense, for example, in which the almost 'monolithic' appearance of the opposition can be misleading, for individual patrons still counted for much. Great lords, like Bedford and Norfolk were prepared to accept the leadership of Fox and Portland. Although it was customary for all sections of the opposition to co-operate in parliament, it was the older Rockingham and newer Foxite–Portland groups which contributed to the party fight an altogether disproportionate amount of talent and ability. The great lords of the old Rockingham connection

---

[1] Fitzpatrick to Ossory 22 Feb. 1783, *Memorials and Correspondence of Charles James Fox*, ed. Lord John Russell (4 vols., 1853–7), ii. 19.

[2] See Appendix 1.

[3] Fox to Portland 21 Jan. 1789, *Fox's Memorials*, iv. 282–5.

enjoyed respect, prestige and patronage which were equalled by none of the Northite peers. It was the Foxites who stood close to the Prince of Wales and who formed the fashionable *élite* of London society. Inside the Whig section of the party it is possible to discern a shift of power, a shift towards Fox and away from the Lords of the party such as Lord John Cavendish, a shift which left Burke alone and neglected. Fox's influence with Portland, his intimacy with Adam and his friendship with the Prince of Wales, together with his own personal qualities, kept that power securely in his own hands.

In 1780 there had been in opposition to North's ministry a number of small political groups which had acted independently of the Rocking-ham Whigs.[1] The confusing years of 1782–4 had eliminated most of these groups as autonomous political forces. In 1788 the *Third Party Circular* aptly described the opposition as '*The Party attached to Mr. Fox*' together with '*Remnants of Ld. North's Party*'. There is no mention of other opposition parties. A large and unitary opposition had emerged. 'Third Parties' still arose from time to time but they were only of slight importance. An 'Armed Neutrality' appeared during the Regency Crisis but most of its members returned later to their former independence, although a handful adhered to Fox.[2] Such parties usually declined after the circumstances which had given them birth passed away.

What cohesive forces kept this opposition together? Patronage and family connection, while forming the necessary structural backbone of the Whig party, fail to take account of many members. In any case these factors rarely provide adequate explanations of political conduct. Christie has shown that voluntary attachment could play a role in party connection at the beginning of the 1780s[3] and the same is prob-ably true of oppositions throughout the century. But more general factors need to be adduced before we can reach a satisfactory explana-tion of party coherence. The leadership of Fox is undoubtedly such a factor. The rivalry between himself and Pitt and the enduring pro-scription which the Whigs suffered after 1783 also played their part in lending to contemporary politics a superficial 'two-party' appearance.

[1] I. R. Christie, *The End of North's Ministry, 1780–82* (1958), 220–6.
[2] Combe, *Letter from a Country Gentleman*, 32.   [3] Christie, op. cit., 220.

The operation of new party institutions and political organization had stamped some measure of uniformity upon the large opposition grouping. On another dimension, common experience of shared conflicts and mutual loyalties rendered desertion of the party unthinkable.[1] When patronage and friendship are viewed in this manner they assume a more realistic complexion. A patron who had remained loyal to the Rockinghams throughout the 1770s, who had participated in the constitutional struggles of 1782–4, and who continued in opposition after 1784 would naturally return members who would support the party. Lying behind patronage itself as a materialistic process exist the motives of the patron himself and the reasons for his continued loyalty to the party.

As early as 1780 the Rockingham Whig party had 'survived the principles and circumstances which had first given it life'.[2] By 1790 the situation had changed once more. The American war and Economic Reform were no longer urgent political issues. The opposition was proscribed for the rest of the reign and thus its members had to be content with retiterating their principles and with emphasizing their usefulness as an opposition. Tirades against the influence of the crown tended to give way to attacks on a domineering minister and assaults upon the doctrine of confidence by which Pitt claimed the trust of the Commons as a reason for refusing to disclose papers and information. Fox admitted that 'when he spoke of kings, he desired always to be understood as speaking of courts and cabinets . . . for the actions of princes their ministers were responsible'.[3] The opposition had to hand something like an alternative programme of measures: on Ireland, India and Economic Reform. They continued to proclaim their party proclivities and the doctrine of party, with its claims to appoint the First Minister, the cabinet and the minor office-holders. Moreover, the Whigs realized that their opposition must have defined purposes. Naturally, their first task was to exercise vigilance over the conduct of the executive but they should restrain their own potential wilfulness by refusing to bring forward measures which they would not execute

[1] For the few cases of defection from opposition, see Appendix 1.

[2] Christie, op. cit., 220–1.

[3] *The Parliamentary History*, xxx. 1479; see also Foord, op. cit., 345, 411–414.

in office.[1] Further, they should always be ready to justify their own former activities whether in office or in opposition. It is difficult to grasp the mentality of party politicians of the later eighteenth century unless one realizes how deeply they were gripped with the conviction that constitutional rectitude consisted in constant displays of personal consistency. As Portland said in 1793, political principles 'call for a consistency of conduct as a security, as a title for confidence'.[2] A principle was that which underlay 'measures which will infallibly recur'[3] and thus the search for consistency was the constant pre-occupation of honest party men.

The significant party changes of the period after 1784 are to be found less in the realm of ideas than in the machinery of opposition politics. Nor did the break-up of the Old Whig party in the 1790s stifle these developments. Little, if any, of the progress towards the consolidation of party was lost as a result. The ideas, the functions and the organization of the party were taken over by the Foxite Whigs and carried by them into the nineteenth century. Yet the deprecation of party remained a powerful psychological factor retarding its growth.[4] Nevertheless, other factors need to be recognized if party developments are to be viewed in a true perspective. While great prestige attached to independent men, the traditional hostility of the eighteenth century towards formed opposition and party was fading and was being replaced by some measure of recognition and acceptance of the constitutional functions which they could perform.[5] Men might prate against

[1] See, *inter alia*, Portland to Lawrence 14 Sept. 1789, Portland MSS.; Fox to Fitzwilliam 13 Nov. 1789, Wentworth Woodhouse MSS., F.115a.

[2] Portland to Burke 10 Oct. 1793, Portland MSS.

[3] R. Burke jnr. to Fitzwilliam 16 Aug. 1793, Fitzwilliam MSS. N.R.O. Burke Letters, A. iv. 19.

[4] Even in the minds of a few party men themselves. See Namier and Brooke, *House of Commons*, i. 203.

[5] Foord, op. cit., 411–12; O. Browning, *The Flight to Varennes and other Historical Essays* (1892), 177; W. Miles, *Authentic Correspondence with LeBrun* (1796), 48 n.8 See also W. Combe, *Considerations on the approaching Dissolution of Parliament* (1790), 9–12. Combe deplores the spread of party 'from the Houses of Parliament to the corporations of borough towns', yet he recognizes that the trend was irreversible and even remarks that it was 'useless and ridiculous' to be of no party. Thus he reviles 'this amiable, but fallacious theory of independence' and asserts

systematic opposition but it was practised throughout the eighteenth century. And cries against organized party did absolutely nothing to prevent William Adam establishing a rudimentary party organization. Even the reappearance of the 'Patriotic Line' of conduct in the 1790s did little to abate his activities.

Yet in 1790 the role of party in the constitution was still very limited. A ministry did not and could not yet rest solely upon a majority of the House of Commons. To the survival of the ministry the support of the Court and Administration group was still necessary, and for this the confidence of the King was essential. Before 1832 party politicians were always too small in number to be able to form a government and thus they were forced to bid for the independent vote.[1] Moreover, there persisted the eighteenth-century notion that a small party of talented men might find it possible to obtain high office through their own abilities, and then proceed to build up a party when safely installed in the government. But there could be no mistaking the fact that party was becoming necessary for the conduct of business. The Younger Pitt disclaimed party and was able to govern for seventeen years, in spite of occasional defeats in the House of Commons. But the Court and Administration group was declining and the King's influence in politics was diminishing as George III grew older and more frail. When the King himself could no longer be the first of party leaders it was natural for that responsibility to be assumed by the ministers, and by 1806 the 'Friends of Mr. Pitt' had divested themselves of their Chathamite principles and had become a party.[2] Meanwhile, the opposition, in spite of the fragmentation of politics during the first decade of the nineteenth century, reasserted itself during the ministry of Liverpool and maintained a very respectable numerical stability.[3] As Dr. Fraser comments: 'The strength of either side remained fairly

that a man could act in party 'perfectly consistent with the spirit and honour of an independent character'.

[1] For a discussion and documentation of this situation, see P. Fraser's unpublished doctoral dissertation, 'The Conduct of Public Business in the House of Commons 1812–1827' (London, 1957), 23.

[2] A. S. Foord, 'The Waning of the Influence of the Crown', *E.H.R.* (Oct. 1947), lxxii.; Foord, *His Majesty's Opposition*, 420–39.

[3] Fraser, op cit., 25–26. Estimates given here vary from 140 to 173, and the criterion of party membership is the receiving of attendance notes.

constant', and he demonstrates this thesis by referring to the fact that three-quarters of the members of the Commons voted consistently for government or opposition.[1] Thus, even if one takes a structurally atomistic view of politics, it is possible to see in the early decades of the nineteenth century something resembling a two-party system in operation, or, at the very least, a dualistic tendency which encouraged small parties and individuals to align themselves with either government or opposition. The origins of these developments lie in the eighteenth century. During the reign of George II the government had begun to organize its electoral activities on a sound, systematic basis and, by the judicious distribution of patronage, had attempted to unite its adherents. But as Mr. Ginter aptly comments: 'The modern political party was not clearly part of the political atmosphere nor yet an integral part of the constitutional process of modern Britain until it had formed the basis of British political life in opposition as well as in office.'[2] By 1790 this had happened and neither the split in the Whig party in the 1790s nor the factional politics of the early years of the nineteenth century destroy the essential continuity of the Whig party organization fashioned and developed by William Adam.[3]

[1] Ibid. 24–25.   [2] Ginter, op. cit., 439.

[3] For the years after 1794, Mr. Ginter comments: 'while organizational activity was more sporadic and in some of its aspects less intensive among the new Foxite opposition, nevertheless it did persist and continue to develop significantly'. Ibid.

2. The Whig Party and the French Revolution

March 1789–*May* 1791

In the early months of 1789 the Whigs obstinately clung to the conviction that the King was mad and thus they stubbornly anticipated that they would be called to office when the Prince of Wales became the Regent. It seemed that fate had at last rescued them from their demoralizing proscription, that long years in office stretched before them, that personal ambitions were about to be fulfilled. The recovery of the King in March dashed their hopes and blighted their prospects. Soon afterwards, the French Revolution brought English politicians to face new movements and philosophies which often appeared to them unintelligible, and therefore frightening. Torn between bewilderment and fear, men of all parties sought to interpret these problems. Yet the innumerable instances in contemporary diaries and letters of passionate hatred and contempt for the French indicate not only an inability to carry this interpretation beyond a comparison with the traditions of English political life but also, perhaps, an absence of that much-vaunted faith in the superiority of English institutions with which the men of the eighteenth century are supposed to have been imbued. Such anxieties and fears were shared by the Whigs. Unhappily there was never any real agreement in the party about the nature of the problems which the French Revolution raised in English politics, still less was there the statesmanship and the resolution which might have sought to resolve these tensions and to produce some solution to the delicate problems in hand.

The months which followed the Regency Crisis thus witnessed a new threat to the unity of the party. But even in 1789 unity seemed fragile and precarious. That consolidation of the party which characterized the years after 1784 was not accompanied by a greater measure of harmony or restraint among the Whig leaders, especially at times when such qualities were most needed. The malevolence, the asperity and the rivalry which sapped the unity of the party during the Regency Crisis have recently been catalogued minutely by historians.[1] Murmurs of discontent and dissatisfaction with the political tactics adopted so carelessly by Fox were not confined to Burke. They were to be heard among the 'Armed Neutrality',[2] the shrunken following of North and, not least, among the old corps of the Rockingham Whigs. The respectable division figures which Fox enjoyed throughout the crisis of the winter of 1788–9 were merely the consequence of the opposition's hunger for office and the result of the efficient operation of party institutions. Yet the political disputes and the personal feuds of the Regency Crisis do not correspond significantly with the later lines of schism in the party and it is therefore misleading to exaggerate the effects of the Regency Crisis on the unity of the Whig party. It was in a different climate of political opinion — when the crisis had been almost forgotten and when politicians were confronted with new issues — that the split in the party occurred. The unity of the party may have been weakened by the Regency Crisis but it was not destroyed. Nor was a party split in any sense inevitable thereafter.

Nevertheless, the disputes which raged within the opposition during the winter of 1788–9 demonstrated that the party lacked real coherence and effective leadership. Even good and loyal Whigs like Lord George Cavendish could murmur against 'some misfortune and perhaps some mismanagement on our side'.[3] In truth, the party leaders were, in the last analysis, unable to impose discipline upon their adherents. The unconcealed ambitions of Charles Grey, for example, could not be restrained. In his determination to cut a figure in politics and assert his claims to office he fell into bitter and reckless disputes with Sheridan.[4] In this he was not alone. Sheridan's ascendancy with the Prince of

[1] J. W. Derry, *The Regency Crisis and the Whigs, 1788–9* (Cambridge University Press, 1963); C. C. Trench, *The Royal Malady* (1964).

[2] The 'Armed Neutrality' was a temporary union of independents which, while wishing Pitt to continue in office, disapproved of his policy of limiting the Prince's rights. Thus it voted several times with the opposition.

[3] Lord George Cavendish to Lady Louisa Ponsonby 25 Dec. 1788, Grey MSS.

[4] Sichel, *Sheridan*, ii. 410–14.

D

Wales was resented by the lords of the party, who distrusted him and who watched suspiciously the progress of the negotiations which he opened with Lord Chancellor Thurlow.[1] In spite of the renewal of Portland's friendship with the Prince and Fox's reconciliation with Mrs. Fitzherbert, the Prince of Wales was a further source of dissension. Although there was no truth in the rumours that he was tiring of Fox and preparing to conciliate Pitt, such speculations heightened the atmosphere of paralysing distrust within the party. The Prince was indifferent to the interests of the opposition and acted 'more from his own counsels than those of the D. of Portland, Fox, Loughboro' etc.'.[2] They had to stifle their dissatisfaction with the negotiation with Thurlow and his rash distribution of offices, for they could not risk offending the vehicle of their hopes and ambitions.[3] Such dependence upon the Prince reacted unfavourably upon the party, for it shared in his unpopularity and his ruthless, almost inhuman, indifference towards the welfare of the monarch. Worst of all, the ominous spectre of the Fitzherbert marriage was raised once more in parliament during January 1789, thus reviving, at one stroke, the dangers and the embarrassments of earlier years.[4]

Such a sorry picture provides a most significant commentary upon the effectiveness of Fox's leadership. He was in Italy when the illness of the King was publicly announced and by the time he returned to London Sheridan and Loughborough had taken charge of affairs. Overcome with exhaustion after his gruelling journey across the continent, and uninterested in the complex and baffling problems which surrounded the Prince's claim to the Regency, Fox never succeeded in establishing effective leadership in the party during the Regency Crisis. His sudden declaration of 'the doctrine of right', for which his friends were totally unprepared, and of which they thoroughly disapproved, was a rash mistake from which the opposition never recovered. Charles Fox's failure to provide his party with a sound and convincing case

[1] Lord Bulkeley to Lord Buckinghamshire 25 Nov. 1788, *Courts and Cabinet*, ii. 15; Wilkins, *Mrs. Fitzherbert and George IV*, i. 236; Derry, op. cit., 65–66.

[2] William Eden to Lord Beauchamp 17 May 1789, Egerton MS. 3260, f. 72, Hertford MSS.

[3] Elliot to his wife 27 Dec. 1788, Minto, i. 250.

[4] Sichel, op. cit., ii. 419; Derry, op. cit., 101, 131–2, 146–8.

reduced his stature in the Whig party and rendered him incapable of mitigating the rivalries which beset his followers.[1] Throughout the Crisis, he remained airily confident of the outcome of the struggle and until a remarkably late date persisted in his optimistic view of the political scene. Against a mounting body of evidence he clung to the conviction that the King would not recover.[2] The political future of the party — and of Fox — hung on the state of George III's mind. It was thus with gloom, despondency and disbelief that Thurlow's announcement of the King's convalescence, on 19 February 1789, was greeted by many members of the opposition.

Faced with a renewed proscription from positions of power and influence in the state, which was all the more galling because success had seemed to be at hand, the Whigs refused to accept the bitter reality of the King's recovery, finding it more comforting to themselves to dismiss reports of his improved health as ministerial fiction. They seized upon every shred of evidence of George III's weakness as a proof of his persisting insanity. The King made few public appearances during the spring and therefore the opposition press spoke of his confinement as evidence of his inability to fulfil his royal functions.[3] The fact that Dr. Willis, the physician who had done so much to restore the King's health, stayed on in attendance for a while was even more compelling proof of the royal incapacity.[4] Fox and his friends assumed that the Queen was the evil genius behind these machinations. She wished to exercise the powers and the patronage of the monarchy herself. In this insidious design she was assisted by Pitt, whose sole concern was to remain in office.[5] The Queen was reluctant to allow the Prince of Wales and the Duke of York to see their father, pre-

---

[1] For Sheridan's almost contemptuous treatment of Fox, see Derry, op. cit., 88, 108. There were some who believed Fox's illness to be feigned and 'that the party . . . is very angry with Mr. Fox'. George Selwyn to Lady Carlyle 4 Dec. 1788, *Letters and Life of George Selwyn*, ed. E. S. Roscoe and H. Clergue (1899), 245.

[2] Fox to Portland 16 Feb. 1789, Ad. MS. 47561, f. 109; Fox to Adam 22 Feb. 1789, Ad. MS. 47568, f. 257 (copy), Fox Papers.

[3] *The Morning Post*, 10, 17 and 22 Mar. 1789.

[4] Ibid. 11 Mar., and on 23 Mar.: 'Dr. Willis for shame go home again.'

[5] Elliot to his wife 25 Apr. 1789, Minto, i. 304; Windham to J. Hutchinson 2 Apr. 1789, H.M.C. *Donoughmore Mss.*, 323: Tom Pelham to his wife 17 Feb. 1789, Ad. MS. 33093, ff. 84–85, Pelham Papers.

sumably because she wished to conceal the true state of his health from them. Revealing a compassion for the King which had not hitherto been in evidence, the Princes reacted violently against their mother. Only with difficulty were Portland and Fox able to restrain them from severing relations with her entirely. They were able to convince the Princes of the necessity for keeping open some communication between themselves and their father because only thus could he learn the true facts of the situation.[1] For her part the Queen could not forgive the Princes their recent conduct: their public jubilation at the madness of the King and their avowed association with the enemies of the throne. She had in fact permitted them an interview with their father as early as 23 February, when 'care was taken that the conversation should be cordial but without running into particulars'.[2] This did nothing to diminish the hostility between mother and sons. The Queen could be vindictive when she chose and insinuated that the Princes were not welcome at Windsor. They continued to accuse her of selfish ambition and ruthlessness. By the beginning of April the country was provided with the absorbing — yet dreary and unedifying — spectacle of a bitter family quarrel which permeated throughout London society, dividing it into two delighted factions.[3] When the Queen had given undeniable proof of her malevolence and hostility to her sons (through her reported indifference to the safety of the Duke of York when he involved himself in a duel), there followed evidence that she had succeeded in her efforts to turn the mind of the King against the Princes. During May, the Duke of Clarence submitted to his father an application for an increased allowance which had been drawn up by Burke, Sheridan and Elliot. The King's reply left the Princes in no doubt of his attitude towards them.[4] By the end of May they had thus realized that their

---

[1] Elliot to his wife 22 Mar. 1789, Minto, i. 287; *The Morning Post*, 23 Mar. 1789.

[2] The King to Thurlow 23 Feb. 1789, Aspinall, *Later Correspondence of George III*, i. 398.

[3] The Queen snubbed Fox at a Drawing-Room on 26 Mar. (*The Morning Post*, 27 Mar. 1789). Lady Duncannon's Diary, 18 Mar.–20 Apr., gives a detailed account of the quarrel (*Lady Bessborough and her Family Circle*, ed. Earl of Bessborough and A. Aspinall (1940), 43–53) as does Elliot in his letters to his wife 14 Mar.–25 Apr. (Minto, i. 283–303).

[4] Aspinall, *Later Correspondence of George III*, i. 417–8; Elliot to his wife 2 June 1789, Minto, i. 319–21.

father thoroughly disapproved of their activities during the Regency Crisis. It was therefore necessary to act quickly to attempt to challenge the influence which their mother wielded over his sick mind. They could do so only by informing and convincing him of the true motives which had inspired their conduct during the winter.

The task of composing a suitable Memorial (as it came to be called) for the King's edification was entrusted to Elliot on 31 May. It was hoped that the Memorial would impress the King with the good intentions of the Princes by rehearsing their former conduct in the most favourable light. During the next few weeks, the leaders of the opposition spent their time and energies in secret discussions as they strove to perform the difficult, if not impossible, task of trying to improve Elliot's drafts and to inject into them the conviction which, in their hearts, the Whigs knew they lacked.[1] Yet, when the invidious task of composing the Memorial had been completed, they were not sure what they were to do with the papers thus assiduously prepared. At a meeting at Carlton House on 25 June, they timidly decided that the Prince of Wales should contact his father and request permission to submit the Memorial.[2] At this point, the Duke of York fell ill and the Prince of Wales had to assume the filial posture of faithfully reporting to his father the state of the Duke's health.[3] The impetus which had brought the scheme thus far was lost and it was not until 14 August that the preliminary note was at last written to the King.[4] By this time both Fox and the Prince had tired of the scheme. Three weeks passed before the King replied and his letter summarily dis-

---

[1] For the composition of the Memorial, see the letters of Sir Gilbert Elliot to his wife between 2 and 24 June 1789, Minto, i. 319–33. The Memorial is printed in *Fox's Memorials*, ii. 308–38.

[2] The meeting is described in Elliot's letter to his wife 26 June 1789, Minto, i. 333–4.

[3] This 'affectionate correspondence', as Elliot termed it, is described in Elliot to his wife 9 July 1789, Minto, i. 337, and is given in Aspinall, *Later Correspondence of George III*, i. 429–31, and in the same editor's *Correspondence of George, Prince of Wales*, ii. 20–22.

[4] Elliot to his wife 23 July 1789, Minto, i. 338; Fox to Portland 2 Aug. 1789, Ad. MS. 47561, ff. 113–14, Fox Papers. The introductory letter from the Prince of Wales to the King is given in *Later Correspondence of George III*, i. 439–40, and the King's reply of 5 Sept. 1789 to the Duke of York, ibid. i. 442.

posed of the whole hypocritical proceeding. George III wrote that he was 'willing to suppose the P. of Wales's conduct has proceeded from errors of judgement, the moment his public as well as private conduct towards the Queen and myself shall mark that respect and affection, which parents have a right to claim'. Here the matter ended. Indeed, it is hard to see how it could have been otherwise. Mistaken in their interpretation of the role of the Queen, underestimating the perspicacity of the King and possessing a naïvely confident view of their own righteousness, the friends of the Prince could hardly have done themselves — or him — more harm than by indulging in specious explanations of conduct which had depended for its success upon the continued madness of George III.

Fox's role in this misguided proceeding was a curious one. He had throughout attempted to moderate the tone of the Memorial and had consistently striven to restrain the Prince and his friends from extreme courses of action which might have severed completely the ties which still bound them to the royal family. He wrote to the Prince on 18 July, ostensibly to advise him against presenting the Memorial to the King. But he also begged the Prince to

take some favourable occasion of laying me at the King's feet and of assuring his Majesty that, if ever it should suit the convenience of his Majesty's affairs to make use of so humble an instrument as I am, and to repose any confidence in me, I shall be as ready as any other of his subjects to do all that is in my power to evince my attachment to his Majesty, and to serve him in the way he may most approve.[1]

There was little time to be lost for the promotions of Chatham and Grenville had weakened the position in the cabinet of Thurlow, 'the person most fully possessed of the King's confidence'. Through the Prince, Fox tried to arrange an interview with the King but there is no indication that the Prince acted upon any of Fox's requests. It is hard to see what Fox could have hoped to gain. By this time he was aware of the King's attitude to the conduct of both the Prince and the opposition during the Regency Crisis, and it could only have been a desperate and futile wish which led him to imagine that he might yet convince the King of his own loyalty. Still less could he have expected

---

[1] Aspinall, *Correspondence of George, Prince of Wales*, ii. 20–22.

office in Pitt's administration. Perhaps the humiliating realization of his own disastrous mistakes distorted Fox's judgement and led him to grasp at any expedient which could have saved him from a bleak political future. His authority in the party was declining, his reputation had recently suffered one of the worst political scandals of his career. Perhaps he realized that he was increasingly little better than a liability to his friends. Yet, far from attempting to compose the discordant rivalries which weakened the opposition, he was prepared to abandon the party and to leave it to the hopeless fate which he himself had done so much to bring upon it.

The activities of the opposition during the session of 1789 reflect the weariness and hopelessness, and perhaps, too, the incompetence of the Whig party. The months of tension and excitement during the Regency Crisis had drained the zeal of so many members that attendances were lower than usual, and this at a time when there were no great party issues before the House.[1] Discredited by their conduct of the winter, demoralized by the failure of their expectations and dismayed by the ministerial reaction which followed the King's recovery, the opposition looked more factious than usual. All too frequently one or other of the leaders of the party harangued a thin and disapproving House from sparsely occupied opposition benches, striving to demonstrate the hypocrisy of Pitt or the unconstitutional nature of his proceedings. With their motives so easily called in question, it was difficult for the Whigs to take the initiative. Their only real success of the session was the repeal of the Shop Tax and this passed only with Pitt's agreement.[2] There was a respectable minority vote against Addington's election to the chair but there are all too few instances of effective, well-informed or even constructive opposition during this session.[3]

If the Regency Crisis and its aftermath mark one of the saddest periods in the history of the Whig party and the career of Charles

---

[1] *The Diary* on 18 and 20 July commented upon the slack attendance of the opposition, especially during the vital, early stages of bills.

[2] Fox disclaimed party motives when he moved the repeal on 2 Apr. 1789. *The Parliamentary History*, xxvii. 1341.

[3] Elliot was nominated by the opposition and he was defeated by the surprisingly narrow margin of 215–174.

James Fox, the year 1789 is the very nadir of the political fortunes of
Edmund Burke. As one of the few members of the Whig party to take
seriously the indecisive and confusing constitutional issues raised by the
Regency Crisis, Burke had sought to influence the tactics of the opposition from his position of isolation and neglect.[1] Despite Portland's
attempts to treat him generously and to humour him, his advice was
brushed aside and his conduct reprobated. Once more, he was offered
merely the office of Paymaster and excluded from the projected Whig
cabinet. Burke's simmering resentment was translated into trenchant
criticisms of the party's ineffective political tactics and of Fox's handling
of the opposition's case against Pitt. The great constitutional issues
which impressed themselves on his imagination were seemingly
neglected by his colleagues who were indifferent to the great question
of the succession.[2] Although the Regency Crisis marks a further stage
in the deterioration of Burke's relations with the Whig party, it would
be unwise to ignore what had gone before and what came after. It is
true that Burke did look back with some bitterness at the treatment he
had suffered at the hands of the party and at the party's mistaken
handling of the Crisis but, compared with the French Revolution and
everything which followed in its wake, the Regency affair was merely
another of those 'mere toys and Triffles' of politics.[3] As he told the
House of Commons on 9 February 1790, 'the differences of opinion
on that occasion were small, when viewed and compared with the
tumult of the present times'.[4]

In the session of 1789 Burke's major concern was, once more, the
impeachment of Warren Hastings, but ill health prevented him from
expending upon it the devotion and industry he would have wished.
Further, Major Scott, Hastings's agent, preferred charges in the
House of Commons which accused Burke of having introduced
damaging, irrelevant material into the speech with which he had opened

[1] Burke to Fox Nov. 1788, Wentworth Woodhouse MSS., Burke Letters 1,
printed in *Correspondence of Edmund Burke*, iii. 81–85.

[2] Burke to Windham 24 Jan. 1789, ibid. iii. 88–102.

[3] Burke to Fitzwilliam 5 June 1791, Wentworth Woodhouse MSS., Burke
Letters 1; Burke to Weddell 31 Jan. 1792, *Correspondence of Edmund Burke*, iii. 402.

[4] *The Parliamentary Register*, xxvii. 64–65; see also Burke's fairly moderate
remarks in his letter to Charlemont of 10 July 1789, Royal Irish Academy MSS.
Copeland Transcript.

the impeachment in 1788. The dreary debates on this question were remarkable only for Burke's embarrassingly inept performances and Fox's tepid speeches. The latter's tactless remarks during the debate on 4 May, in fact, evoked a more strongly worded censure upon Burke than had been in contemplation.[1] It is little wonder that Burke declared that the difficulties attending the impeachment 'have been much encreased by the conduct of those, whom every principle of honour, of duty, and of public and private faith had engaged to make them as little embarrassing to me as possible'.[2] After public reprobation had been thus added to private neglect and indifference, Burke convinced himself that his problems were insuperable, that the Queen was sheltering Hastings and that Fox, upon whose assistance Burke probably felt that the success of the impeachment hung, was rapidly cooling towards him.[3] Worry made him tetchy and resentful. Yet his more generous instincts were not dead. He supported the abolition of the slave-trade and the revision of the criminal law during the session of 1789. Although it is possible to exaggerate the extent of his isolation within the party — he was, for example, on intimate terms with Elliot and Windham — he was painfully aware that he was shunned by the more important leaders of the party. Consequently, he was unhappy and unsure of himself, for he needed the encouragement and the companionship of his friends.[4] The hopelessness of the future prospects of the impeachment and the nagging consciousness of his own unpopularity 'rendered it very unfit for me to exert myself in the common routine of opposition'. He realized that he was nothing more than a liability to Fox. He realized, too, that continued failure 'may be in part . . . the Cause of the inactivity of others of our friends'.[5] Although Burke professed his continued attachment to the idea of party, he had become

[1] On 27 Apr. Fox told the Commons that he would continue with the impeachment 'as long as there was any prospect of doing good with it, or rendering the prosecution effectual'. *The Parliamentary History*, xxvii. 1368–9; see also Elliot to his wife 5 May 1789, Minto, i. 307.

[2] Burke to Bright 8/9 May 1789, Wentworth Woodhouse MSS., Burke Letters 1.

[3] Burke to Fox 11 May 1789, *Fox's Memorials*, ii. 355–8. 'It is unlucky that things are so circumstanced that we can seldom meet.'

[4] 'My strength was always in those admirable Men . . . with whom I have been connected. Stripped of them, I am nothing.' Burke to Bright 8/9 May 1789, loc. cit.

[5] Burke to Charlemont 10 July 1789, loc. cit.

thoroughly disillusioned with the conduct of his political friends.

Party is absolutely necessary at this time. I thought it always so in this Country ever since I have had anything to do in publick Business; and I rather fear, that there is not virtue enough in this period to support party, than that party should become necessary on account of the want of Virtue to support itself by individual exertions.[1]

In the following months, none the less, Burke's isolation continued and his distress mounted. In November 1789 he made some attempts to encourage Fox and Sheridan to take a more active part in the impeachment, 'our strange derelict business'.[2] Their indifference was now such that they remained unmoved by Burke's pitiful pleading. His anger, so long suppressed, now knew no bounds:

What is the conduct of our pretended friends. Put an end to the trial; you have spun it out too long; the people are tired of it. . . . I have done with that sort of friends. It rests only with me in what manner I am to conduct myself in this defeat produced by their desertion.[3]

Burke had never used such strong language before, although he had suffered comparable disappointments. There can be no doubt that his lack of intimacy with the other managers of the impeachment was beginning to endanger the progress of the trial. But worse was still to come. It was not long before Burke learned that Fox had no confidence in the outcome of the impeachment. All he wanted was to secure an honourable retreat.[4] Despite attempts on the part of Francis and Loughborough to mollify him, Burke remained acutely aware of Fox's indifference to the progress of the trial amidst the dangers which further delay threatened.[5]

Burke felt that the impeachment was to be, in a sense, the measure by which posterity would judge of him. He was thus much more

[1] Burke to Charlemont 9 Aug. 1789, Royal Irish Academy MSS. Copeland Transcript.

[2] Burke to Francis (n.d. Nov. 1789), Parkes and Merrivale, *Memoirs of Sir Philip Francis*, ii. 262–3.

[3] Burke to Francis (n.d. Dec. 1789), ibid. ii. 264.

[4] Burke to Francis 2 Jan. 1790, Wentworth Woodhouse MSS., Burke Letters 1.

[5] Burke to Elliot 3 Jan., *post* 6 Jan. 1790, Osborn Collection, Copeland Transcript. According to *The Public Advertiser* of 3 Feb. 1790, Burke was 'greatly disturbed in his mind' about the possibility that the impeachment might be delayed.

preoccupied with matters arising from the trial than with the Revolution in France. At first he seems to have shared with many Englishmen a sensation of 'astonishment at the wonderful Spectacle', but he was uneasy and saw 'something in it paradoxical and Mysterious'.[1] The disapproval of the Revolution which he voiced in the summer of 1789 was based mainly on lurid newspaper accounts and letters, and thus Burke's suspicions were founded on a rather superficial fear of mob rule and the overthrow of property.[2] It was not until the end of the year that this rather sententious and melodramatic view of proceedings in France ('where the Elements that compose Human Society seem all to be dissolved, and a world of Monsters . . . produced in place of it').[3] gave way to a more informed and profound judgement. By November 1789 the essence of the theories which he was later to expound so eloquently in the *Reflections* had been articulated. The emphasis on order and restraint as preconditions of liberty, the distaste for abstract theorizing which was unrelated to the circumstances or the men in question, the conviction that the monarchy and its chief supports, the church and the aristocracy, were doomed to extinction and the gloomy prognostications of what might follow — all these occur in Burke's letters before the end of the year.[4] Theoretical condemnation was in itself innocuous. But it was not long before Burke began to connect up in his own mind the renewal of reform agitation in England[5] with the French Revolution.

I see some people here are willing that we should become their scholars too, and reform our state on the French model. They have begun; and it is high time for those who wish to preserve the *morem majorem*, to look about them.[6]

1 Burke to the Earl of Charlemont 9 Aug. 1789, MS. in the Royal Irish Academy. Copeland Transcript.

2 Burke to Windham 27 Sept. 1789, Ad. MS. 37843, ff. 15–16, Windham Papers.

3 Burke to Richard Burke *c.* 10 Oct. 1789, N.R.O. A. xiv. 7c. Burke Letters.

4 See Burke's letter to De Pont, *post* 4 Nov. 1789, wrongly dated Oct. 1789 in *Correspondence of Edmund Burke*, iii. 102–21. Wentworth Woodhouse MSS., Burke Letters 1.

5 G. S. Veitch, *The Genesis of Parliamentary Reform* (1913), 103–7, 121–5; P. A. Brown, *The French Revolution in English History* (1918), 27–31.

6 Burke to De Pont, C. McCormick, *Memoirs of Edmund Burke* (1798), 326–30. The letter is undated but is probably early 1790 as it appears to be a reply to a letter from De Pont of 29 Dec. 1789 printed in *English* (1950–1), viii.

When he came to realize that 'The Revolution in France is certainly a Fore runner to other Revolutions in Europe'[1] this only served to confirm his growing suspicion that England might yet witness havoc and anarchy comparable to that in France unless the people were warned in time. When Charles James Fox delivered a lukewarm eulogy upon the French Revolution to the House of Commons on 5 February 1790, Burke was led to fear that it was the Whig party itself which stood most in need of those warnings.[2]

Fox, indeed, had shown little interest in the two matters which absorbed Burke, the impeachment and the French Revolution. Such activity as there was in the party during the recess had been directed along different lines. While preparations for the long-awaited dissolution and election were going forward,[3] Fox was anxious to court the Dissenters by arranging to move for the repeal of the Test Act in the coming session. Although Portland strongly disapproved of the whole affair, Fox characteristically ignored the wishes of the leader of the party.[4] There were other sources of friction and disunion. The Prince of Wales's journey to the north of England may have helped to revive the party's cause in the constituencies but it caused some antagonism between Fitzwilliam and the Northite peer, Carlisle.[5] *The Morning Post* of 3 November 1789 felt it necessary to deny rumours that the opposition was so divided that it could make no exertions in the coming session, while the ministerial press made much of the supposed divisions between Sheridan and the Prince on the one hand, and Fox and Port-

---

[1] This ominous warning is contained in a letter of none other than Tom Paine to Burke 17 Jan. 1790. There is a copy of the letter at N.R.O. A. iv. 73a, and it is printed in *The Durham University Journal* (1951), xliii. 50–54. Burke probably received this letter when he returned to town for the new session in late Jan., about which time he read Price's sermon at the Old Jewry of 4 Nov. 1789.

[2] 'The new form which the government of France was likely to assume . . . would render her a better neighbour, and less disposed to hostility, than when she was subject to the cabals and intrigues of ambitious and interested statemen.' *The Parliamentary History*, xxvii. 330–2.

[3] Even a ministerial paper, *The Diary*, of 21 July 1789, admitted that the opposition, 'if not successful, will at least be vigorous' during the coming elections.

[4] Portland to F. Laurence 14 Sept. 1789, Portland MSS. P.W.F. 6238; Fox to Fitzwilliam 13 Nov. 1789, Wentworth Woodhouse MSS., F. 115i.

[5] Aspinall, *Correspondence of George, Prince of Wales*, ii. 4, 31 n.2; G. Selwyn to Lady Carlisle 3 Sept. 1789, H.M.C. Carlisle, 667–9.

land on the other.[1] In short, after the humiliating reverse which they
had suffered at the hands of Pitt during the previous winter, the Whigs
had apparently done little, if anything, to compose their rivalries and
prove to the world that they were anything like responsible politicians.
Inevitably, they made a poor showing in the early days of the session.
There was hardly any debate on the Address and the opposition did not
attempt to divide the House.[2]

It was against this background that the celebrated debate on the
Army Estimates occurred on 9 February 1790. By this time, Burke's
dissatisfaction with the party and his anger towards those managers of
the impeachment who were neglecting their duties were at their height.
In particular, he had seen little of Fox since the discussions of the
previous June concerning the Memorial and it is doubtful if Fox was
really conversant with Burke's opinions on the French Revolution.
Indeed, it is difficult to be sure how far Fox's own approval of the
Revolution went. In his famous panegyric of 30 July 1789, he declared:
'How much the greatest event it is that ever happened in the world!
and how much the best'. Yet he went on to say 'that all my pre-
possessions against French connections for this country will be at an
end, and indeed most part of my European system of politics will be
altered, *if this Revolution has the consequences that I expect*'.[3] For
most of the recess he had ignored politics and confessed that he had
spent only a few days in town.[4] His spontaneous approval of the
Revolution was rather a reflection of Fox's own instinctive compassion
for freedom and his hatred of despotism. His opinions were not based
on the lengthy perusal of letters and official documents, as were Burke's.
For long afterwards, Fox was prepared to shade over into obscurity his
views on the French Revolution and to use them as a political means of
composing dissensions within his own party. The careless ambiguity,
the lack of logic and, sometimes, the ruthlessness which characterized
his opinions on the French Revolution are all an indication of the fact

---

[1] *The Public Advertiser*, 2 Feb. 1790.

[2] 21 Jan. 1790. *The Parliamentary History*, xxviii. 303–7.

[3] Fox to Fitzpatrick, *Fox's Memorials*, ii. 361. (My italics). He had already told
the House of Commons on 10 July 1789 that the Revolution 'might produce the
freedom of France'. *The Parliamentary History*, xxviii. 286.

[4] Fox to Fitzwilliam 13 Nov. 1789, Wentworth Woodhouse MSS., F. 115a.

that Fox possessed no systematic or profound interpretation of it to which he might stubbornly have clung. And this was to be one of the reasons why the disruption of the Whig party was delayed for so long.

Burke had rarely attended Estimates debates in recent years but he was in his seat on 9 February. He heard Fox oppose any increase in the Army Estimates for the coming year in view of the peaceful dispositions of foreign powers. In arguing his case, Fox referred several times to the French Revolution in approving terms. Perhaps Burke was shaken even more when Pitt declared that 'The present convulsions of France must, sooner or later, terminate in general harmony and regular order'. Burke's lengthy speech followed. He admitted that France was now in a state of weakness but 'it was her strength, not to her form of government which we were to attend'. Not only her military strength in the future but the contagion of her democratic principles were dangers against which the English state should arm itself. He refuted the widely held notion that the French Revolution could be judged in the same terms as the Glorious Revolution of 1688. The latter was an aristocratic revolution which defended the constitution, not the work of a gang of demagogues to level property and destroy all the established hierarchies in society. He regretted that he and Fox differed in opinion on these matters and manfully allowed Fox's opinions to stem from his love of liberty but 'he would abandon his best friends, and join with his worst enemies . . . to resist all violent exertions of the spirit of innovation'. Fox rose and, much to Burke's relief, professed his attachment to the constitution and his opposition to the introduction of democracy into England. Burke seems to have accepted Fox's assurance that 'they could never differ in principles, however they might differ in their application'. The conduct of the two men on this memorable occasion was cautious and conciliatory in the extreme. Even when Sheridan rose and, in an insulting and inflammatory speech, ridiculed Burke's opinions and castigated him as a ministerial hireling, Burke replied with surprising equanimity. His speech was far less acrimonious — and far briefer — than might have been expected. Nothing in his rejoinder changed the essence of what he had come before the House to say: that he would tolerate differences of opinion within the party on the French Revolution, but that he would break with it if it sought to encourage the diffusion of democratic principles at home. Nevertheless, in declaring that henceforward he and Sheridan were 'separated in politics', Burke confessed himself 'concerned to find that there were persons in this country who entertained theories of government, incompatible with the safety of the state', among whom he doubtless regarded Richard Brinsley Sheridan as one of the most irresponsible and most dangerous leaders.[1] Although there was nothing in Burke's speech which suggested that he feared for the Prince of Wales, whose friendship with Sheridan continued unabated, such considerations could not have been far from his mind. Of himself and Fox, Burke wrote two years later: 'The day ended with sentiments *not very widely divided and with unbroken friendship.*'[2] Indeed, as long as the French Revolution did not come to underlie a whole series of political measures at home, it remained a matter of opinion. There was no compelling reason why differences of opinion on this, any more than differences on parliamentary reform, which the party had tolerated for years, should be a matter of serious dissension within the party. Nevertheless, Burke had succeeded in confusing opinions on the French Revolution with opinions on matters of domestic reform. The repeal of the Test Act, for example, upon which Fox had so publicly committed himself (and with Burke's blessing) was shortly to be debated in parliament. Further occasions of dispute within the party might be expected because reforming opinions of the type which Burke so roundly condemned found considerable support among the Whigs. His growing disillusion with the party found public expression when he told parliament that he was 'little disposed to controversies, or what is called a detailed opposition. . . . He was far from condemning such opposition; on the contrary, he most highly applauded it, *where a just occasion existed for it*'.[3]

The debate caused a sensation at the time and a flurry of apprehension

---

[1] The debate is given in *The Parliamentary History*, xxviii. 334–72. Burke's initial speech was 'received with great and general applause' according to *The Annual Register* (1790), 68. His reply to Sheridan 'was received by the loudest applause from the Treasury Bench'. Tom Pelham to his father, Wednesday, Mar. 1790, Ad. MS. 33129, ff. 17–18, Pelham MSS.

[2] Burke to W. Weddell 31 Jan. 1792, *Correspondence of Edmund Burke*, iii. 383–409. (My italics).

[3] *The Parliamentary History*, xxviii. 363. (My italics).

among the leaders of the opposition. They tried to reconcile Burke and
Sheridan, but a long conversation between the two on the evening
after the debate did nothing to heal the breach between them. The
following day, Burke's son had an interview with Sheridan, but only
made matters worse when he tactlessly reprimanded him for his
conduct.[1] Sheridan made a few rather unconvincing gestures of
remorse and said that he had spoken as he did because he felt that
Burke's speech was directed against him personally.[2] Not that Burke
escaped criticism. He was blamed in some quarters for refusing to
conciliate Sheridan after the debate and even the ministerial press
regarded Burke as the intransigent party whose vehemence might lead
Sheridan to quit the opposition.[3] Not that all this troubled Edmund
Burke. He was determined to adhere to the opinions which he had propounded on 9 February and took the unusual course of publishing his
speech, probably to avoid misrepresentation.[4] He embarked seriously
on the composition of his *Reflections* and found that his public reputation had begun to revive.[5] His opinions were noticed at court and he
was, once more, a welcome visitor to Carlton House.[6]

But Burke was misunderstood by his colleagues in the party. They
thought that he was exaggerating the imminence of the danger in
which England stood. They could not grasp the sense of urgency which
he felt. They could understand neither his reasoning nor his conviction
that fundamental social and ethical principles were at stake. So overwhelming did these appear to him that they came to dominate his

---

[1] Elliot to his wife, 23 Feb. 1790, Minto, i. 349–54.

[2] Ibid.; Elliot to his wife 22 Apr. 1790, Minto, i. 357; Fox was astonished at the
day's events and was amazed at Burke's speech, 'such a mixture of good sense and
absurdity'. J. Hare to the Duchess of Devonshire 23 Feb. 1790, *Georgiana . . .
Duchess of Devonshire*, ed. Earl of Bessborough (1955), 169.

[3] *The Public Advertiser*, 12 and 19 Feb. 1790; *The World*, 11 and 12 February
1790; Elliot to his wife 22 Apr. 1790, loc. cit.

[4] *The World* of 2 Mar. 1790 advertised the second edition of the speech. Burke
rarely published his speeches.

[5] *The Public Advertiser* of 16 Feb. 1790 mentioned Burke's forthcoming work
and added that Sheridan was expected to reply to it. For a favourable opinion of the
early drafts of the *Reflections* see Elliot to his wife 22 Apr. 1790, Minto, i. 355–9.

[6] T. MacKnight, *The Life and Times of Edmund Burke* (3 vols., 1860), iii. 305;
Diaries and Letters of Madame D'Arblay, ed. A. Dobson (5 vols., 1904–5), iv. 356.

approach to important political issues at home. He refused to support the motion for the repeal of the Test Act because 'extraordinary things have been said and done here, and published with great ostentation in order to draw us into a connexion and concurrence' with the French Revolution 'upon the principle of its proceedings, and to lead us to an imitation of them'. Fox was acting as the unwitting tool of a subversive faction, 'a very bad example, and of a most immoral tendency'.[1] On 2 March, therefore, when Fox's motion came before the House, the two men proclaimed contrasting opinions concerning the desirability of repeal. Burke's views filled Fox 'with grief and shame' and he spoke of Burke's 'dereliction of principle'.[2] Fox found Burke's violent and unintelligible denunciations of the Dissenters embarrassing because he was hoping that the Dissenters would support the Whigs at the coming election. He thus had no hesitation in dismissing Burke's opinions as both extravagant and unfounded. He could well afford to do so, for in spite of the beginnings of that strident fear on the part of the English governing classes towards the Dissenters which was to be such a potent political force in the following years Fox's position in the party was strong enough to withstand Burke's attempts to influence him. Burke, in fact, continued in political isolation. If his harangues against the French Revolution largely mystified his own party[3] then his unflagging concern with the trial of Hastings provoked that indifference which dismayed and depressed him.[4] It was not long before the altercation of 9 February had been forgotten because it seemed to have little relevance to the routine conduct of the opposition. Rumours of splits and divisions in the party floated around but speculation of this sort was surprisingly limited. Fox and his friends deserve

---

[1] Burke to Bright 18 Feb. 1790, Hyde MSS. Copeland Transcript.

[2] Fox and his friends were astounded by Burke's opposition to repeal. Sir P. Magnus, *Edmund Burke* (1939), 189.

[3] Francis to Burke 19 Feb. 1790, Wentworth Woodhouse MSS., Burke Letters I, printed in *Correspondence of Edmund Burke*, iii. 128–32.

[4] For Windham's weariness with the trial at this time, see *D'Arblay*, iv. 367–71. On 11 May Burke moved resolutions providing for the continuation of the impeachment. He was supported weakly by Fox and Sheridan. *The Parliamentary History*, xxviii. 786–94. On 21 May the House debated Burke's complaint that Scott had libelled him. His extravagant language disgusted the House and earned a rebuke from Pitt. Ibid. 824–47.

some credit for having restrained personal animosities from deepening and for having conducted in a placid, if not dull, political climate, a more vigorous opposition campaign than that of the previous session.[1]

The fact that the opposition found work to do in the session of 1790 relieved its members from the deadly tedium which comes with political idleness. The revival of the opposition was noted with some alarm by supporters of administration, who had presumed that the Whigs would never have recovered after the Regency Crisis.[2] If its tactics over the repeal of the Test Act had caused some little anxiety in the party, the opposition stood on firmer ground when it attacked the Tobacco Excise Bill because on this issue it had the support of powerful manufacturing interests and the sympathy of public opinion.[3] Had the party leaders moved for repeal on 16 April the government might have been defeated, but Sheridan's motion for a Committee to consider petitions against the Act was lost by 191–147.[4] Hardly had this storm blown itself out when the Nootka Sound Crisis burst over the heads of the ministers. The political temperature immediately rose and throughout the month of May the opposition mounted its attack on Pitt's foreign policy. But it was difficult for Fox to criticize Pitt's defensive attitude in the face of Spanish aggression and the opposition lacked that public support which it was to enjoy in 1791 when the Oczacov issue tormented the administration. Although the Whigs charged Pitt with incompetence in that he failed to foresee the impending crisis, it was difficult to work up much enthusiasm over a distant island and it was the question of confidence which came to dominate the Nootka debates. Utilizing the traditional opposition ploy of moving

[1] Sheridan tried to explain away the differences which separated himself from Burke in a moderate speech on 16 Apr. Ibid. 694. *The Public Advertiser* of 19 Feb. 1790 stated that the events of 9 Feb. did not warrant the attention they had received.

[2] E.g. Earl of Hardwicke to P. Yorke (n.d. Apr.–June 1790), Ad. MS. 35392, ff. 163–4, Hardwicke Papers.

[3] Adam presented a petition from the tobacco manufacturers of Glasgow on 23 Feb., *The Parliamentary Register*, xxviii. 133–5. On 8 Feb. Sheridan declared that he spoke for the tobacco manufacturers, ibid. xxvii. 483.

[4] It was admitted by several speakers during the debate that a motion for repeal might have come nearer to success. The government's narrow escape worried the ministerial press: see *The Public Advertiser* on 19 and 20 Apr. 1790.

for papers, Grey, on 12 May, reprobated 'the idea of granting a blind and unlimited confidence to any minister' and argued that confidence should be 'founded on a review of the past conduct of government'. Ministerialists, on the other hand, asserted that because the executive was ultimately responsible to parliament for its actions, the House should not interfere too closely in the day to day conduct of business.[1] Yet again, however, much of the force of the opposition's case was lost through the factious behaviour of Fox. Although he professed to support the government, he did his best to harry proceedings and hold up business.[2] Although the Nootka Sound crisis sharpened the edge of political debate and brought members to town, it was not the happiest of issues for the opposition. The feeling was strong that national pride and honour were at stake and the Whigs did not wish to appear unpatriotic.[3]

Notwithstanding the opposition's failure to weaken Pitt seriously on his handling of foreign policy, the divisions in the party and the events of 9 February were concealed beneath a greater sense of purpose. Dissensions were studiously avoided, for this was, after all, election year.[4] Personal quarrels at Westminster seemed for a time of less importance than the more pressing business of cultivating constituencies and winning seats in the attempt to retrieve the losses of 1784.[5] Yet there could be no denying the perceptible hardening of feeling in the country against the French Revolution. The tumults in the Austrian Netherlands of 1789–90 were popularly supposed to owe much to French interference, and the continuing violence and instability inside France led many to view with apprehension the proliferation of reforming societies in England whose contacts with French societies

---

[1] *The Parliamentary History*, xxviii. 794–807.

[2] See, for example, the debate of 6 May, ibid. 770–81.

[3] On the Nootka Sound crisis, see J. Holland Rose, *William Pitt and the National Revival* (1911), 565–85; J. M. Norris, 'The Policy of the British Cabinet in the Nootka Sound Crisis', (1955), *E.H.R.* lxx.

[4] Sheridan went out of his way during the debate of 16 Apr. to deny all rumours that there were any disagreements between himself and Portland (*The Parliamentary History*, xxviii. 694). Fox managed to restrain his enthusiasm for the French Revolution and only during the Nootka Sound debate of 20 May did he voice his opinions strongly (ibid. 815–23).

[5] For the general election of 1790, see Appendix 1.

were exaggerated out of all due proportion.[1] Thus the meeting
arranged at the 'Crown and Anchor' on 14 July to celebrate the
anniversary of the fall of the Bastille appeared to be indisputable proof
that there existed in England not only a dangerous but an influential
faction whose subversive intentions must be carefully guarded against.[2]

Transactions such as these were regarded with dismay by Edmund
Burke; his feelings were outraged. But Burke was never a would-be
aristocrat, terrified by the rumblings of insubordination. To depict
him thus is to make a mockery of the man and of his career. He knew
that the spirit of revolution had scarcely begun to spread in England.
He knew that Fox was no democrat. He knew that the people were
hardly capable of making responsible political judgements for themselves. But, given leaders who could organize the masses and fill their
heads with atheistic propaganda, then the people might be roused to
pull down the fabric of the state as they had done, in Burke's view, in
France. The meeting at the 'Crown and Anchor' on 14 July 1790
convinced Burke that Sheridan threatened to become just such a leader.
The danger was even greater because the Whig party was being
undermined by Sheridan, seduced away from the principles of Rockingham and the Glorious Revolution and led to adopt those of France.
Fox — and the Prince of Wales — were not safe from the contamination. What was to become of Whig principles when the party presses
poured out a stream of French propaganda? The aristocracy must be
made aware of the danger, and the great lords must stamp out the
spread of French principles in the party.[3] On this point, Burke need
not have worried. Men like Fitzwilliam were fully alive to the danger,
but they were unwilling to submit the party to another public dispute
and they hoped that the passage of time would resolve the problems
which beset the party. Fitzwilliam expressed great confidence in
Burke's forthcoming work and hoped it would go forth into the world
'to correct its erroneous mode of viewing and reasoning upon the art

---

[1] Veitch, *Genesis of Parliamentary Reform*, 117, 148–50. *The Public Advertiser*,
earlier sympathetic to the French Revolution, was by now completely hostile.

[2] The meeting was attended by, among others, Sheridan.

[3] These sentiments were expressed by Burke's son in a letter to Fitzwilliam of
29 July 1790, N.R.O. A. iv. 71, Burke Letters. Richard says that 'I know I speak
his sentiments'.

of government'.[1] Burke, toiling away at the drafts and revisions of the *Reflections*, entertained similar expectations. He wanted his doctrines to be of service to the lords of the party, the Prince of Wales and even the King.[2]

In reality, my Object was not France, in the first instance, but this Country. I dont much fear from the faction here who correspond with those who resemble those on the other side of the Water—but no man living is intitled after all that has happened to despise men that mean ill on account of their apparent want of power.[3]

Although he continued to feel that he did not know enough about the affairs of France, he proceeded with the publication of the *Reflections*, confident that he had not misrepresented the situation in that country. On the contrary, 'in most of my Statements, I have rather shot short of the mark than beyond it'.[4]

The *Reflections* was a remarkable production for a politician whose career had seemed to be drawing to an undignified conclusion. In spite of the contempt and the disappointments which he had suffered, Burke was able to set aside personal considerations in what he hoped would prove to be the service of his party and the public. His analytical insight into the fundamental principles of the French Revolution, his grasp of the crude reality underlying apparently innocent libertarian theories, the bold and clearly drawn conclusions which emerged from his study of the Glorious Revolution, clothed in persuasive, yet supremely passionate, language, give the *Reflections* an electrifying power which was felt by his contemporaries. Other writers of the period such as de Lolme seem, by comparison, flat, pedestrian and narrowly circum-

---

[1] Fitzwilliam to R. Burke jnr. 8 Aug. and 15 Sept. 1790, Wentworth Woodhouse MSS., Burke Letters 1.

[2] Burke to Weddell 31 Jan. 1792, loc. cit.

[3] Burke to Calonne 25 Oct. 1790, P.R.O. P.C.I./126/298, Copeland Transcript. For further evidence on this point, see R. Burke jnr. to Fitzwilliam 29 July 1790, loc. cit.; Burke's speech in the Commons on 11 May **1791**, *The Parliamentary History*, xxix. 418. See also Burke's letter to Francis of 20 Feb. 1790 (*Correspondence of Edmund Burke*, iii. 140), where he states, 'I intend no controversy with Dr. Price, Lord Shelburne, or any other of their set. I mean to set in full view the danger from their wicked principles and their black hearts. I intend to state the true principles of the constitution in church and state, upon grounds opposite to theirs.'

[4] Burke to Windham 27 Oct. 1790, Ad. MS. 37843, ff. 19–20, Windham Papers.

scribed. No doubt much of the book was highly contentious through being cleverly overdrawn. It cannot be said to have provided a correct analysis of the Revolution because it concentrated too exclusively upon political problems and because Burke's sympathies were irresistibly drawn towards the preservation of historical tradition and prescriptive privilege. But the constitutional principles which he expounded were immediately acknowledged by many of his readers, although few of them would yet have shared his sense of the urgency of the danger with which England was faced. There was now no escaping the controversy which Burke had opened upon the subject of the French Revolution and upon the basic principles which underpinned the British constitution.

The general thesis of the *Reflections* was unexceptionable to ministerialists, and the government press rang with his praises.[1] Burke must have been deeply gratified by the warm reception which the court afforded his book.[2] In the hearts of those members of the Whig party who were beginning to evince apprehension at the proliferation of reforming societies, the *Reflections* struck a chord. It confirmed their axiomatic belief in the hereditary principle and reiterated what they considered to be the fundamental principles of the British constitution. Burke played upon their fears and upon their aristocratic prejudices. His brilliant exposition of the nature of French principles and his demonstration that the British constitution could find no place for them tended to confirm and exacerbate the growing fear of reform. By refusing to discriminate between the different shades of reformers, by banding them all together as equally dangerous to the fabric of the state, Burke introduced an ideological factor into discussion of the French Revolution which could not be concealed indefinitely. The reformers in the Whig party were furious with the book, though their anger could not disguise their admiration. Some of the praise which the more conservative members of the party heaped upon Burke was tempered with restraint.[3] The opposition press found the *Reflections*

---

[1] As early as 2 Nov., *The Public Advertiser* began to publish a series of extracts from Burke's book. At the same time, the paper made every attempt to detach Burke from the opposition by exaggerating the depth of the split in the party.

[2] *D'Arblay*, iv. 435–6.

[3] E.g. Lord John Cavendish to Burke 14 Nov. 1790, Wentworth Woodhouse MSS., Burke Letters 1, printed in *Correspondence of Edmund Burke*, iii. 171–2.

useful for some purposes but, on the whole, it condemned Burke's opinions, rebuked him for inconsistency and finally disclaimed his views.[1] The rumour that Sheridan intended to compose a reply to Burke was looked upon with alarm in the party lest this precipitate Burke's separation from the opposition.[2] The crucial element in the situation was Fox. If he were to espouse the opinions of Sheridan, then, and only then, members of the party might be forced to reconsider their loyalty to him.[3]

The *Reflections* had been published on the very eve of the new session of parliament. Burke, in fact, had exerted himself to produce it at this time so that the book would achieve a maximum effect on the party. In truth, the opposition was then in a sorry condition. After its exertions in the election campaign of 1790, the texture of the party had once more loosened. Its connection with the Prince of Wales, although weakening, was still an active source of disunion.[4] The Prince was being assisted by a few persons in the party, including Adam, in a scheme to contract a loan from Antwerp to repair his depleted finances.[5] It is possible that Sheridan was half-hearted in his support of the scheme, for rumours were circulating to the effect that the Prince was cooling towards him.[6] Renewed speculation concerning relations between Sheridan and Portland continued long into the new year. Discussion focused upon the likelihood of the two men dividing the party between them, each leading one of its factions.[7] The ministerial press was delighted to find its foe in such a sorry situation and put it about that the 'deluded nobles' of the party, and even Fox, were

[1] *The Morning Chronicle*, 13 and 17 Dec. 1790, 22 Jan., 8, 9, 21 Feb. 1791. See also the comments in *The Public Advertiser*, 15 and 22 Nov. 1790; *The Gazetteer*, 2 Nov. 1790.

[2] The Bishop of Peterborough to Grafton 7 Dec. 1790, Grafton MSS., vi. f. 741, Bury St. Edmunds and West Suffolk Record Office.

[3] Elliot to his wife 5 Dec. 1790, Minto, i. 369–71.

[4] The Prince's anxiety to improve relations with his family (the result of his financial distress) is shown in his letter to the Duke of York of 10 Aug. 1790, Aspinall, *Correspondence of George, Prince of Wales*, ii. 84–85. Something of a reconciliation took place in July 1791, ibid. 172–6.

[5] Portland to Fitzwilliam 29 Dec. 1790, Wentworth Woodhouse MSS., F. 115a.

[6] *The Public Advertiser*, 26 Nov. 1790.

[7] Ibid. 20, 28 Dec. 1790, 1 Jan. and 28 Feb. 1791.

under such a cloud that they would soon retire from politics.[1]

There seemed to be nothing in the political scene to console the opposition. The Convention ending the dispute between England and Spain had been signed on 28 October but it was not significantly controversial. The new session opened a month later but no plans had been concerted for an opposition campaign against Pitt. As Windham put it:

> Of the business that we are to meet upon I am as ignorant as need be, and don't at all know what the right judgement is about Pitt's proceedings, or what the points on which principally he is to be attacked . . . Pitt will come out with new lustre from all the present measures, and heap new confusion on his oppositionists.[2]

The parliament opened disastrously for the Whig party and it seemed that Pitt did not need to lift a finger if he wished to see the opposition humbled. Farcical mishandling of the tactics to be adopted on the election of a new Speaker on 25 November was matched by weakness of numbers on the debate on the Address five days later and no division was attempted.[3] But it did seem that real efforts were being made to hold in check the disruptive elements within the party. Sheridan's restraint towards Burke and his moderation on the subject of the French Revolution were both commented upon in the press.[4] And Fox's conduct at this time — particularly the unobjectionable speech he made at the Whig Club on 7 December — indicates that, at last, he was beginning to learn from his impulsive mistakes of the previous session and trying to avoid provoking unnecessary controversy within the party.[5]

Notwithstanding the caution of Fox and his friends, it was clear that

[1] Ibid. 15, 23 Nov. 1790, 12 and 14 Jan. 1791.   [2] *Windham Diary*, 211–12.

[3] It had been intended that Elliot should stand against Addington or, at least, that a protest should be entered against Addington's election. Neither was done, the latter because Fox was late in coming down to the House. Elliot to his wife 5 Dec. 1790, Minto, i. 369–71; Burke to Elliot 29 Nov. 1790, Osborn Collection, Copeland Transcript (partly given in Minto, i. 364–8).

[4] *The Public Advertiser*, 3, 7 and 10 Jan. 1791; *The Morning Chronicle*, 1 and 3 Jan. 1791.

[5] *The Morning Chronicle*, 8 Dec. 1790. The ministerial press noticed the moderation of Fox as early as Sept.: *The Public Advertiser*, 17 Sept. 1790.

the party showed much more enthusiasm for the debates on the Nootka Sound question than it did for those on the impeachment. The continuation of the trial was threatened by the issue of the abatement of an impeachment by a dissolution of parliament. Fox saw no useful purpose in debating this question and is not surprising that Burke had recourse to the ministers for that succour and encouragement of which his friends had for so long deprived him.[1] While the abatement of the impeachment was being debated in parliament, Burke remained in close contact with the ministers and found that his trust in them had not been misplaced. With Adam's kindly assistance, Dundas was prevailed upon to influence the ministerialists in the House of Lords, where strong opposition to the continuation of the impeachment had been expected.[2] Burke cannot have been impressed with the support he received from his colleagues in the opposition and he was thus led into that amicable intercourse with the ministers — and especially with the amiable Dundas — which was to bear such bitter fruit for the party in the months ahead.[3]

[1] See Fox's speech on 9 Dec. 1790, *The Parliamentary History*, xxviii. 933.

[2] Burke had tried to obtain ministerial support at the beginning of the session but he confessed himself dissatisfied with Pitt's response to his requests. Burke to Elliot 29 Nov. 1790, Minto, i. 364–8. On 30 Nov., Burke raised the matter in parliament. Pitt gave him vague assurances of sympathy (*The Parliamentary History* xxviii. 900–1). But it was with Pitt's concurrence that Burke brought the matter forward on 9 Dec. (ibid. 930–3). For Adam's part in this affair, see Adam to Burke 2 Jan. 1791, N.R.O. A. iv. 57, Burke Letters; Burke to Adam 4 Jan. 1791, Blair-Adam MSS. By Feb. 1791 Burke was obtaining even firmer promises of assistance from the ministers. Pitt to Burke 14 Feb. 1791, Wentworth Woodhouse MSS., Burke Letters 1.

[3] While Burke argued his case from precedent, Fox grounded his arguments upon 'whatever was inconsistent with or subversive of a free constitution'. Debate of 23 Dec. 1790, *The Parliamentary History*, xxviii. 1154. The ministerial press made great play with Fox's notorious indifference to the impeachment: *The Public Advertiser*, 4 Nov., 28 Dec. 1790, 7, 10 Jan. 1791. Burke's separation from his own party was constantly seized on by the government newspapers, who hinted strongly that his political doctrines would find a warmer welcome on the other side of the House (e.g. *The Public Advertiser*, 10, 11, 18 Nov. 1790). While his reputation in these circles was being resurrected, *The Morning Chronicle* attacked him with increasing venom and spite, e.g. on 21 Feb. 1791 it stated that 'the orb which once shone in full splendour, is now hastening to its wane. You have passed the meredian of life, and in a few years you will be among the silent dead.'

Although Pitt was prepared to treat Burke with respect and consideration on matters arising from the impeachment, he was baffled and, at times, annoyed with Burke's vehement denunciations of French principles and subversive reformers. On these subjects Pitt was no nearer to Burke's position than Fox.[1] At this time, Burke's thinking on the French Revolution was developing rapidly. The venom of his hatred of the Civil Constitutions of the Clergy was equalled only by his fear of the military power of France. In January 1791 he had arrived at the conclusion that nothing short of military intervention could subdue 'these madmen' in France and it was to Pitt that Burke looked as the man to perform this service to humanity.[2] Although copies of his *Letter to a Member of the National Assembly* duly found their way into the hands of the ministers, there is nothing to suggest that the cabinet was in any way impressed by Burke's ideas on the state of Europe.[3] In his heart, Burke had no illusions about his own position.

I am a private man, totally destitute of authority and importance in the state, and am perhaps not perfectly well with those who possess its powers.[4]

While the rebuffs and disappointments which Burke suffered at the hands of his own party had not drawn him into intimate relations with the ministers, it was beginning to be clear that he was probably closer to them than he was to Fox on several of the most important questions

---

[1] During the debate on Tooke's petition on 5 Feb. 1791, Pitt reprimanded Burke for his language and Burke ridiculed Fox for his apparent leniency to Tooke. *The Parliamentary History*, xxviii. 1210–21.

[2] The first part of Paine's *Rights of Man*, which was published in Feb., was intended, and received by Burke, as a reply to the *Reflections*. Burke to Trevor Jan. 1791, *Correspondence of Edmund Burke*, iii. 182–6; Burke to the Comtesse de Montrard 25 Jan. 1791, ibid. 191–6.

[3] The *Letter* (printed in *Burke's Works*, 2 vols., 1834, i. 476–91) was completed on 19 Jan. 1791 but was not published until the following month. For Lord Grenville's cold and brief acknowledgement of the work, see Grenville to Burke 23 Mar. 1791, Wentworth Woodhouse MSS., Burke Letters 1.

[4] Burke to the Comtesse de Montrard 25 Jan. 1791, loc. cit. Burke and Portland had attended a levee on 3 Feb. at which George III congratulated Burke on the *Reflections*. In addition, he conveyed to Burke his warm approval of the work, through the Duke of Clarence. Burke to the Duke of Clarence 8 Feb. 1791, Wentworth Woodhouse MSS., Burke Letters 1.

of the day. He was offended by the eulogy on universal religious toleration which Fox pronounced in the Commons on 1 March and he rose to contest Fox's opinions. Yet he spoke with remarkable equanimity and the temperature of the debate remained low. Pitt stood aloof from these exchanges, confessing that he fully agreed neither with Burke nor with Fox.[1] Thus nicely did the situation hang. The best possible commentary on Burke's connection with the Whig party at this time was provided by Burke himself during the first debate on Pitt's Russian policy on 29 March. He refused to consider this issue as a party question because Pitt had so generously lent his assistance on the impeachment.[2]

The session had been unpropitious for the opposition until the Oczacov crisis erupted and shook the ministry of Pitt to its very foundations.[3] The opposition attained a unity of purpose which was perhaps the more impressive when contrasted with the internal faction-fighting which had weakened the Whig party's campaign in the winter of 1788–9. Party meetings provided the party leaders with the preliminary contacts which effective parliamentary tactics demanded, and the division figures reveal that the Whigs were dividing at full strength and attracting the independent vote, too.[4] The leaders of the party took this opportunity to groom some of their abler young members. Men like Whitbread and Grey first made their mark on politics

[1] *The Parliamentary History*, xxviii. 1364–76.

[2] Ibid. xxix. 75–76. 'In the part he should take, or in the opposition he should give ... he disclaimed all party considerations whatever.' He complimented Pitt, who 'had acted so honourably upon a great constitutional question, in which he himself and his reputation, and in which responsibility was immediately concerned, that it had done away all acrimony from his mind and he should never, while he remained in that House, make use of any personal asperity upon any occasion' towards Pitt.

[3] 'The administration of Mr. Pitt had never encountered so rude a shock.' *The Annual Register* (1791), 107. On the Oczacov Crisis, see J. Holland Rose, *Pitt and the National Revival* (1911), 613–24; J. Ehrman, 'The Younger Pitt and the Oczacov Affair', *History Today* (July 1959).

[4] For the important party meeting on 27 Mar., see *Windham Diary*, 219. The highest minority figure was 173 on 12 Apr. The *Morning Chronicle* of 13 Apr. printed a list of 25 M.P.s who would have voted against Pitt if they had been present. The list of the minority printed by the same paper on 15 Apr. identified 33 county members, only some of whom were members of the Whig party.

during the Oczacov crisis when the lucidity of their reasoning, the fire of their oratory and the passion of their denunciations of ministerial policy rivalled the excellent performances in the debates of Sheridan and Fox. Many of the censure and information motions were moved and seconded by these younger members. This was clearly official policy for, on 12 April, Grey admitted to the House that he spoke as the mouthpiece of the party.[1] Party jealousies were quickly forgotten. All sections of the opposition supported the assault on the ministry, ably led by Fox and his young friends. Only Burke remained unmoved. But Burke's strictures on the French Revolution seemed curiously irrelevant to the only thing that mattered: that Pitt's ministry seemed to be tottering to its destruction amidst the failure of his foreign policy.

Since the Regency Crisis, Pitt had seemed to command an almost unprecedented political dominance. While it is true that his relations with Thurlow had worsened, the Lord Chancellor was no longer in the same intimate relationship with the King after George III had learned of his suspicious conduct during the Regency Crisis, and this knowledge served only to stiffen Thurlow's hostility to Pitt and his obstructiveness to ministerial measures in parliament.[2] Although there were rumblings of discontent from within the cabinet on certain issues, especially the Nootka Sound question, these never assumed serious proportions[3] and Pitt was quite easily able to brush aside such objections as there were to the elevation of Grenville to the Lords in November 1790.[4] Now Thurlow could be watched and the govern-

---

[1] *The Parliamentary History*, xxix. 175.

[2] Lord John Campbell, *Lives of the Lord Chancellors* (10 vols.), vii. (1857), 259. In the session of 1789 Thurlow did nothing to help the government in the Lords save obstruct its measures. By the end of 1789, according to Pitt, Thurlow expected to be dismissed. Pitt to Rose 8 Nov. 1789, G. Pellew, *The Life and Correspondence of Henry Addington* (2 vols., 1847), i. 98–99.

[3] J. M. Norris, 'The Policy of the British Cabinet in the Nootka Sound Crisis', 574; Thurlow to Hawkesbury 30 May 1790, Ad. MS. 38192, f. 149, Liverpool Papers; Richmond to Pitt 16 Oct. 1790, P.R.O. 30/8/171, Pitt Papers, quoted in Olsen, *The Radical Duke*, 212–13.

[4] Pitt to the King 20 Nov. 1790, Aspinall, *Later Correspondence of George III*, i. 501–2; Pitt to Hawkesbury 23 Nov. 1790, Ad. MS. 38192, f. 75, Liverpool Papers; Richmond to Pitt 24 Nov. 1790, P.R.O. 30/8/171, quoted in Olsen, op. cit., 214–18.

ment peers could be rallied whenever the Lord Chancellor cared to show his intransigence. Can it be true, in view of the fact that Pitt's position in the cabinet was indisputably strengthening, that it was fear of disrupting the cabinet which led him to change his Russian policy in 1791 ?[1] Leeds, Camden and Thurlow opposed Pitt but none of them was particularly influential by this time and Pitt used the plea of cabinet unity only in his attempts to dissuade the Duke of Leeds from resignation.[2] Nor is there any evidence to show that the King disagreed with Pitt's policy and, of course, there was no obvious successor to Pitt within the cabinet. His position in the cabinet, therefore, was unchallengeable. It was doubtless other factors which led him to reverse his policy. The knowledge that the Prussian King had begun to waver in his initial support of Pitt's bellicose attitude towards Russia may have counted for something. An even weightier factor may have been the very evident public distaste for diplomacy which tended to involve England in a war in a distant region of Europe where the country's interests could scarcely be regarded as important.[3] On this issue, public opinion was behind the opposition and it made effective use of its opportunity to berate the ministry. According to some reports, Pitt began to fear that the strength of the opposition's numbers was causing some rats to desert the sinking ship and thus he reacted accordingly.[4] It was, perhaps, a combination of considerations such as these which led to Pitt's diplomatic turnabout. One thing should be remembered. The opposition, and especially Fox, attributed his reverse solely to the exertions of the Whig party, and this delusion was to be an important element in the party struggles of 1792.

The crisis reached its culmination in parliament on 12 April when the opposition divided at 173, leaving the ministers with a majority of 80. Although there was a tendency for ministerial majorities in the

---

[1] This was the opinion of Holland Rose (*Pitt and National Revival*, 618), for which no evidence was adduced and which has been frequently repeated since, especially by D. G. Barnes, *George III and William Pitt* (Stanford, 1939), 231.

[2] Only Grenville had both reservations about Pitt's policy and any real political weight, but he chose not to exercise the latter.

[3] Ehrman, op. cit., 464.

[4] *The Political Memoranda of Francis, Duke of Leeds*, ed. O. Browning (1884), 154.

eighteenth century to decline after the government had been run fairly close, this did not happen during the Oczacov Crisis. On 15 April the majority climbed to 92 and the minority figure was reduced to 162. Thereafter, the ministry was safe. Pitt, indeed, remained more secure than he had been during the Regency Crisis. To have brought Pitt down — and here was the heart of the matter — would have been to install Fox and the Whigs in office, and the independent members, who might have been anxious to cast a warning vote against Pitt, were not willing to bring him down. With the Easter recess fast approaching, members were beginning to leave town, and it was a notorious fact of eighteenth-century parliamentary life that the independents rarely attended the House in large numbers for the last few months of the session. Even Fox realized — and had the courage to admit — that he could run Pitt no closer than he had done on 12 April. Although he was gratified with the division figures of that date, he predicted that the division on 15 April would be less favourable to the opposition.[1]

During the Oczacov debate of 15 April, Fox, possibly provoked by certain remarks made by Pitt, entered into a comparison of the present state of France with its conditions under the *ancien régime* 'for the purpose of showing that those who detested the principles of the revolution had reason to rejoice in its effects'. He concluded his peroration with the famous panegyric on the French Revolution, 'considered altogether, as the most stupendous and glorious edifice of liberty, which had been erected on the foundations of human integrity in any time or country'.[2] The eulogies upon the French Revolution in which Fox indulged from time to time had begun to cause disquiet in the highest reaches of the party. Portland shared Burke's apprehensions that Fox was trying to commit 'a considerable majority of those who compose it [the party] in both Houses & of nine tenths of those who are consider'd to belong to it out of doors' to his opinions.[3] But

---

[1] Fox to Mrs. Armistead (n.d. Apr. 1791), Ad. MS. 47570, ff. 184-5, Fox Papers.

[2] *The Parliamentary History*, xxix. 248-9. For Pitt's remarks, see 243-4.

[3] Portland to Fitzwilliam 21 Apr. 1791, Wentworth Woodhouse MSS., F. 115d; Tom Grenville to Fitzwilliam 28 Apr. 1791, ibid. Portland was already worried about the democratic propaganda which was appearing in the party newspapers. Fitzwilliam to Adam 20 Apr. 1791, Blair-Adam MSS.

Portland and others like him were content to allow time to unravel the problems which they were as yet unwilling to face. They and others in the party felt that by agitating their contrasting views on the French Revolution, Fox and Burke would only succeed in driving each other to extremes and in weakening the party still further. 'They did not hold it necessary to separate from their great leaders on account of mere speeches. . . . They considered it as more just to wait until the direct collision of their principles with the public weal of the state should force forward some measure that might be made a test, not of opinions, but of conduct.'[1] Yet Burke was determined to challenge what appeared to him as Fox's persistent attempts to publicize his own views and to commit the party to them before the disagreement could spread any further. He well knew that 'several of our best friends are Very uneasy at Fox's conduct' but that they placed considerations for the welfare of the party above the larger dictates of social order and the preservation of the constitution.[2]

Burke had attempted to reply to Fox on 15 April but he had been compelled to give way to the question. He therefore determined to speak on the Committee stage of the Quebec Bill when he could speak as often as he liked and which had been arranged for 20 April. At the last minute, Pitt postponed the debate and contacted Burke. It is not clear whether or not a meeting took place but it is certain that Burke confided his fears to the ministers. The prospect of being silenced in the debate was worrying him and he tried to convince Pitt that by discussing general principles of government he would not be speaking out of order.[3] Perhaps Fox heard of these soundings and it may have been this knowledge which led to the famous conversation between himself and Burke a few hours before the debate on 21 April. But Burke remained deaf to his pleadings. This time, Fox's magic did not work, for Burke's fear of the spread of democratic principles in England had now left him indifferent to the fortunes of the party.[4]

---

[1] *The Annual Register* (1791), 114–15.

[2] R. Burke jnr. to O'Beirne 6 May 1791, Wentworth Woodhouse MSS., Burke Letters 1.

[3] *The Annual Register* (1791), 116; Lord Grenville to Burke 20 Apr. 1791, Wentworth Woodhouse MSS., Burke Letters 1.

[4] Tom Grenville was almost certainly the 'common friend' referred to by *The*

That his motives did not include personal animus against Fox is attested by the friendliness of their discussion. The two men walked to the House together, where they found that Sheridan had moved to postpone the debate. In the brief discussion which followed their arrival at the House, Fox and Burke maintained their ground, voicing their determination to declare their principles of government at a future date, and to do so, if necessary, at the expense of their friendship. There were some rather ominous rumblings of hostility against Burke from the opposition benches which led him to ask the Speaker for protection during the coming debate.[1]

Between 21 April and 6 May little was done to reconcile Burke and Fox. The latter, far from well at this time, slipped away to Newmarket to refresh himself at the races.[2] Burke, quietly ruminating at Beaconsfield, remained impervious to the pleas and the arts of persuasion which Fitzwilliam could muster. He saw clearly enough that it was too late for reconciliation, that 'It is impossible to ascertain what declarations imply future conduct'.[3] Portland, who was stolidly convinced of 'the superiority of F.'s talents & the recitude of his Heart and Head', tried to delude himself into believing 'that this Crisis, (alarming as it is), may be productive of good'.[4] Others were less sanguine. Tom Grenville realized that 'if the debate takes place, however it is managed on Charles's side the mischiefs of misrepresentation will I am persuaded be sufficient to answer all the purposes our *adversaries wish*'.[5]

Annual Register in its account of this conversation. In Grenville's opinion, Burke's determination to speak out arose from the growing popularity of Paine's work and the recent votes of the Unitarian Society which condemned Burke's writings. Its proceedings, reported in *The Morning Chronicle* of 15 Mar., were also reported directly to Burke in an insulting letter of 16 Apr. from H. Wisemore, Wentworth Woodhouse MSS., Burke Letters 1.

[1] *The Parliamentary History*, xxix. 359–64.

[2] Rolleston to Mrs. Armistead 26 Apr. 1791, Ad. MS. 47568, ff. 261–2, Fox Papers.

[3] Fitzwilliam to R. Burke jnr. (n.d. May 1791), Wentworth Woodhouse MSS., Burke Letters 37; Grenville to Fitzwilliam 28 Apr. 1791, loc. cit. Burke's attempt to influence Portland against Fox, half-hearted as it was, is outlined in Minto, i. 376–8.

[4] Portland to Fitzwilliam 26 Apr. 1791, loc. cit.

[5] Grenville to Fitzwilliam 22 Apr. 1791, Wentworth Woodhouse MSS., F. 115d.

The Morning Chronicle of 4 May anxiously expressed the wish
'that no altercation will occur on the subject of French politics
that might in its effects weaken the present virtuous and formidable
minority'.[1]

This most famous debate has often been described, but its importance
is such that it will bear a further examination. Burke rose immediately
to inform the House that the doctrine of the rights of man 'imported
from a neighbouring country' could never be preached or applied
without mischief resulting. These doctrines were the total antitheses
of those upon which not only the British but also the American constitution rested. Thus he made the point that the Whigs of the 1770s had
fought for the principles of 1688 in defending the colonists, not for
those of Tom Paine. French principles were now circulating in England
yet Burke remained 'perfectly convinced that there was no immediate
danger to the constitution . . . the body of the country was perfectly
sound' yet he had 'knowledge and conviction' that dangerous plots
existed. Despite interruptions and points of order, he managed to conclude his oration, whereupon Fox rose to reply. He remarked upon the
irrelevance of Burke's speech to the matter in hand and adverted to the
manner in which it was delivered 'which he must consider as a direct
injustice to him'. Furthermore, he accused Burke of 'manifest
eagerness to seek a difference of opinion, and anxiety to discover a
cause of dispute' upon theoretical matters. He reiterated his admiration
for the French Revolution, 'one of the most glorious events in the
history of mankind', and predicted that the French constitution could
'be improved by experience, and accommodated to circumstances'.
Yet these differences of opinion between himself and Burke had
nothing to do with the business in hand and should not have been
raised during the debate. 'Instead of seeking for differences of
opinion on matters entirely topics of speculation, let them come to
matter of fact, and of practical application.' Yet Fox then proceeded
to do exactly what he had just rebuked Burke for doing. He
maintained that the rights of man were 'the basis and foundation of
every rational constitution, and even of the British constitution itself',

---

[1] *The Morning Chronicle* of 29 Apr. 1791 denied that Fox had ever committed
himself to definite views on the French Revolution.

and charged Burke with having entertained similar opinions in the past.

Burke's rejoinder and the events which followed are among the most famous and the most moving of all parliamentary occasions. He 'commenced his reply in a grave and governed tone of voice'. He protested against the personal animus which Fox had injected into the discussion and against the dead set which had prevented him from proving several of his assertions respecting France and the French constitution. He proceeded to expand upon some of his earlier arguments, remarking that 'monarchy was the basis of all good government and the nearer to monarchy any government approached, the more perfect it was and vice-versa'. He then went on:

It certainly was indiscretion, at any period, but especially at his time of life, to provoke enemies, or give his friends occasion to desert him; yet if his firm and steady adherence to the British constitution placed him in such a dilemma, he would risk all, and, as public duty and public prudence taught him, with his last words exclaim 'Fly from the French constitution', (Mr. Fox here whispered, that 'there was no loss of friends'). Mr. Burke said Yes, there was a loss of friends — he knew the price of his conduct — he had done his duty at the price of his friend — their friendship was at an end.

And, at this point, according to a multitude of witnesses, Fox broke down and wept bitterly. A few minutes later, he rose again, and, after he had composed himself, protested that their friendship could not be at an end and that they might act together as before on other questions. He denied Burke's insinuation that he had condoned the introduction of French principles into England yet he admitted that when the *Reflections* was published 'he condemned that book both in public and private, and every one of the doctrines it contained'. His tone became harsher when he went on to demonstrate that Burke had formerly been a strong advocate of reform and that his present declarations seemed inconsistent with his former behaviour. He reiterated his view that the British constitution rested upon the rights of man and that the French constitution, though capable of improvement, was not different in substance. The Whig party had been formed to defend the principles of the British constitution. There was now dispute over the true nature of those principles. He hoped that Burke would come to understand his own errors and return to the fold.

> The right. hon. gentleman has said that he shall lose my friendship; but this I assure him he shall not lose mine. He has also said, he should lose that of the friends about him, because he stands up for the constitution of this country. I, however, hope that my friends are as fond of that constitution as the right. hon. gentleman is, and that the example of France will make them cautious not to run into the same errors, and give the same provocation to the people.

This sort of specious manœuvring was hardly likely to impress Burke. It left him 'at a loss to understand what was either party or friendship', and he protested against these 'pretences of friendship'. Pitt concluded the debate in a most interesting manner. He had earlier defended Burke against those who wished to rule him out of order. He now congratulated Burke upon his warnings about the danger to the constitution and promised that 'he would cordially cooperate with [him] in taking every possible means to preserve it'. Pitt's motives are usually difficult to understand but he can hardly have been unaware of the political advantages to be gained by exacerbating the quarrel between Fox and Burke.[1]

The memorable drama of the events of 6 May should not be allowed to obscure the vital issues which were raised during the Quebec debates. Perhaps, too, the tragedy which accompanied the proceedings of that day needs to be re-examined because the friendship between Fox and Burke had, at least since 1783, been more a matter of assertion than of fact. While there can be no doubt that Burke felt his exclusion from the party very keenly after 6 May,[2] he realized that great issues and principles overrode personal considerations. The unforgettable debate of 6 May served to raise these issues and principles so that in future they could not be ignored by the Whig party. At first glance, the struggle between Fox and Burke rested upon questions of personal consistency but more fundamental problems were at issue.

---

[1] The debate is given in *The Parliamentary History*, xxix. 364–401. There is a slightly, but not materially, different account in *The Parliamentary Register*, xxix. 318–53.

[2] See Burke's pathetic remarks during the debate on 11 May in *The Parliamentary History*, xxix. 403, 417–18, 426.

What was to be the declared policy of the party towards the French Revolution and towards reform at home? Beneath this, there lay the most crucial question of all. What was the nature of the British constitution? In short, was that constitution which it was the party's purpose to defend 'founded upon the wisdom of antiquity, and sanctioned by the experience of time', or was it, as Fox said on 6 May, founded upon the doctrine of the rights of man?[1] If Fox committed the party to the latter opinion, then he was, in Burke's view, not only departing from the principles of the Rockingham Whigs but unwittingly laying England open to dangers which had destroyed the fabric of French society. Although Burke retained his belief in the idea of party, he had convinced himself that the Whig party was acting as the vehicle for doctrines which struck at the root of those upon which the party, and the British constitution, rested.[2]

If he had hoped to dissuade the men in the party from embracing French principles, then Burke had significantly failed. The generosity of some of Fox's language towards him should not conceal the real personal triumph which Fox had achieved. By refusing to admit that the differences between himself and Burke amounted to anything more than a theoretical disagreement, and by affirming that his friendship for Burke could not be sundered by such speculative guesswork, he was able to present Burke's separation from the party as the voluntary action of Burke himself — which indeed it was. The impression was given that Burke would be welcomed back into the party when he had changed his opinions. The famous paragraph which appeared in *The Morning Chronicle* of 12 May formally announced Burke's separation, approved of Fox's opinions and vindicated his leadership. If Burke had feared that the political vacuum which had been the result of Fox's lazy leadership of the party might have been filled by Sheridan, and thus open to challenge by himself, then he had misjudged Fox. At just that period when the leadership of the party seemed to be in question, Fox had asserted his authority and imposed his own discipline upon Burke. As Fox saw it, if Burke insisted on raising unnecessary disagreements concerning matters of opinion while the Oczacov Crisis

[1] Fox's opinions are summed up in his speech on 6 May, ibid. 379–80. For Burke's remark see ibid. 403.

[2] Burke's reiterated definition of party was pronounced on 11 May, ibid. 421.

was continuing to embarrass Pitt, then he must suffer the consequences of his obstinacy.[1]

[1] For Fox's indifference to Burke and his reference to the *Letter to a Member of the National Assembly* as 'mere madness', see Fox to Lord Holland 26 May 1791, Ad. MS. 47571, ff. 1–2, Fox Papers, printed in *Fox's Memorials*, ii. 363–5. The debates on the Quebec Act came at an extremely delicate time during the Oczacov debates. *The Morning Chronicle* of 25 May 1790 asserted that Pitt was helping to foment the dissension within the opposition to distract attention from his own difficulties. The opposition press blamed Burke for the affair and castigated him as a ministerial hireling. Only in the government press did Burke find support and protection.

3. *The Decline of the Whig Party*

May 1791–*February* 1793

I. The Growth of the Schism in the Party
May 1791–May 1792

The secession of Burke from the Whig party might have remained nothing more than a memorable biographical incident had not events in Europe unleashed political forces which effected a realignment of political groupings in England. The months which followed the Quebec debates were to show that Burke's eclipse in the 1780s had been merely a pause before what was to be the greatest period in the career of the philosopher-statesman. If Burke had died before the French Revolution there is every possibility that the split in the party would still have occurred. But because it was Burke who provided an interpretation of that Revolution in traditional terms which Englishmen could appreciate, even if they could not agree with it, then the struggle for power within the opposition was to be a struggle for and against the principles which Burke believed to be at issue. It was Burke, moreover, who was to take the lead in the attempts which were made to destroy the Whig party. The great philosopher of party found himself in the painful dilemma of trying to destroy the party because it was ostensibly dedicating itself and its energies to the propagation of evil principles — principles which were the very antitheses of the sacred Whig principles which the party had pledged itself to uphold and defend.

After the drama surrounding the Quebec debates, the rest of the session inevitably seemed something of an anti-climax. Further debates on Oczacov revealed that Pitt could be brought down only in the event of a Russian declaration of war.[1] The opposition unwisely introduced measures of its own late in the session when they attracted little interest

[1] The divisions in the Commons on 25 May and 2 June were 208–114 and 170–75. The opposition peers did not attempt a division after the debate of 8 June.

and even less support.[1] Only Fox's Libel Act provoked a high level of debate and discussion.[2] Before the session had ended, attention was beginning to focus upon events across the Channel, where spectacular scenes were soon to be enacted which furnished astonishing confirmation of the soundness of the opinions which Burke had been voicing for so many months. The revolt of the slaves in St. Domingo was watched with great concern in England but it was the flight to Varennes which riveted the minds of Englishmen to events in France as nothing had yet done.[3] The flight and recapture of the French royal family set in train a series of developments which served only to intensify English anxiety for the safety of Louis XVI and the peace of Europe. Earlier hopes that France might have transformed herself into a peaceful, constitutional kingdom were shattered at one blow. The dramatic events which followed the flight to Varennes hardened English feeling against the French Revolution and caused a perceptible reaction of sentiment against the political societies at home. The change in the public mood was sensed even by the reformers who nevertheless persisted, albeit with the utmost caution, with their arrangements to celebrate the second anniversary of the fall of the Bastille.[4] The ugly scenes enacted at Birmingham shortly afterwards showed how high the reaction was flowing among the lower classes of society.[5] Rising

[1] The reform of the Scottish burghs came forward on 28 May when Fox persuaded Sheridan to defer the matter until the following session. *The Parliamentary History*, xxix. 636–41. The Enquiry into Public Income and Expenditure was debated in an empty House on 3, 6, 7 and 8 June.

[2] The Act was closely modelled upon Burke's bill of 1771, but Fox did not acknowledge the fact, J. Prior, *Memoir of Edmund Burke* (2 vols., 1826), ii. 157.

[3] *The Public Advertiser*, 28 June 1791; Miss Farren to Sir Charles Hotham late June 1791, A. M. Stirling, *The Hothams* (2 vols., 1918), ii. 254; Lady Malmesbury to Lady Elliott 26 July 1791, Minto, i. 390.

[4] Veitch, *Genesis of Reform*, 180–3. Fox was reluctant to allow Sheridan to attend the banquet at the 'Crown and Anchor' but, as usual, Sheridan ignored his leader's instructions. Fox to Lord Holland 26 May 1791, *Fox's Memorials*, ii. 363–5. The Whig Club decided not to attend the dinner. P. Yorke to the Earl of Hardwicke 8 July 1791, Ad. MS. 35392, ff. 212–13, Hardwicke Papers.

[5] On the whole, the reaction of the ministerial press and government supporters to the Birmingham riots was to commend the loyalist spirit of the rioters while condemning their violence. See W. Laprade, *England and the French Revolution* (1909), 40–51; *The Morning Chronicle* of 11 Aug. defended Priestley and deplored the riots.

public anxiety concerning the spread of innovating principles was reflected in the Whig party. The leaders were alarmed and distressed at the deepening divisions in the opposition on the subject of the French Revolution which was being exacerbated by the pressure of events outside human control. Fox's principles were confused with those of the wildest reformers, notably by the ministerial papers, which accused him and others of rejoicing in the humiliation of the French royal family.[1] Fitzwilliam had already been disturbed by the restlessness of the Sheffield reformers and his fears were shared by Loughborough, who was already proclaiming the need for 'Some Measures . . . to check the insolent propagation of [subversive] doctrines by those Meetings which have been the primary Cause of the riot'[2] As usual, Portland could not bear to discuss the differences which were now seriously endangering the unity of the party, still less could he bring himself to try to resolve them.[3]

The Quebec debates had not significantly changed Burke's position in the party. His friendship with Fox was now totally dissolved but he 'appears to retain his attachment to most of his old *particular* friends'.[4] Nevertheless he was separated from the life of the opposition and had no future intercourse with the Whigs save, as Lord Holland put it, not unjustly, 'for the purpose of disuniting them'.[5] He disliked attending parliament because it distressed him to vote against the wishes of Portland and Fitzwilliam and because the occasional debates on the progress of the impeachment brought him into rather chilly contact with Fox.[6] On the other hand, the kindness, and, to a point, the protection which Pitt had extended to Burke during the Quebec debates did much to

[1] T. L. O'Beirne jnr. 25 July 1791, Wentworth Woodhouse MSS., Burke Letters 1; *The Public Advertiser*, 29, 30 June 1791.

[2] Loughborough to Fitzwilliam 1 Aug. 1791, Wentworth Woodhouse MSS., F. 115a.

[3] T. L. O'Beirne to R. Burke jnr. 25 July 1791, loc. cit.

[4] Mr. Elliot of Wells to Sir Gilbert Elliot 16 May 1791, Minto i. 378–80; *Windham Diary*, 226.

[5] *Memoirs of the Whig Party during my Time* (2 vols., 1852–4), i. 11.

[6] Burke to Weddell 31 Jan. 1792, loc. cit.; on the impeachment debate of 27 May, for example. Fox and Burke clearly had had little or no prior consultation and thus they adopted different lines of argument which did nothing to assist the progress of the impeachment. *The Parliamentary History*, xxix. 641–51.

confirm the growing amity between the two men. But there were, as yet, no signs that the ministers had begun to take seriously Burke's passionate warnings about the French Revolution.[1]

Developments in France during the summer of 1791 filled Burke with alarm and apprehension until he could no longer bear to act the part of a mere observer while the French monarchy and the hereditary orders of French society were plunging into an abyss from which they could never return. And this while the kings and courts of Europe remained indifferent to the contagious spirit of subversion which could topple their thrones and throw the continent into chaos.[2] Not without some encouragement, he renewed his entreaties with the ministers to come to 'some decision in the foreign system as far as it regards France — Surely a step may be taken with great safety, great dignity and great effect'.[3] Nobody would listen to his warnings and it was with a growing sense of desperation that he put the finishing touches to *The Appeal from the New to the Old Whigs*, which he published on 3 August 1791.

He had begun to compose the pamphlet after the Quebec debates. By the stand he had taken during May 'I have lost some few friends . . . but I have not lost my spirits, nor my principles, and I have rather increased my inward peace. I have spoken the sense of infinitely the majority of my countrymen, and that also of my late party (at least I think so), though, from deference to some persons, they do not think it necessary to speak out so clearly'.[4] In the writing of the *Appeal*

It was not my plan to go deeply into the abstract subject, because it was

---

[1] For Pitt's sympathetic attitude towards Burke during the Quebec debate of 11 May, see *The Parliamentary History*, xxix. 404. Ministers defended the impeachment in the Lords on 16 and 31 May and in the Commons on 27 May. Ibid. 514–545, 660–4, 641–51.

[2] Burke to the Chevalier de Rivarol 1 June 1791, Wentworth Woodhouse MSS., Burke Letters 1, printed in *Correspondence of Edmund Burke*, iii. 206–16.

[3] Bland-Burges to Burke 26 June 1791, Wentworth Woodhouse MSS., Burke Letters 1; Burke to Dundas 1 July 1791, Morgan Library MSS. Copeland Transcript; Lord Buckinghamshire to Lord Grenville 30 June 1791, H.M.C. *Dropmore*, ii. 112–13.

[4] Burke to the Marquis of Bouillé 13 July 1791, Wentworth Woodhouse MSS., Burke Letters 1, printed in *Correspondence of Edmund Burke*, iii. 216–28.

rather my desire to defend myself against the extraordinary attacks of some
of my late political friends . . .[1]

Burke had been mortified at the reception with which the party
had greeted his *Reflections*. Instead of reaffirming their fidelity to the
principles of the Whig Party which he had elaborated in the book,
some members of the opposition had set on foot a dangerous campaign
which had for its aim the adoption of Paine's principles as the creed of
the party. The growth of agitation out of doors had alarmed him but,
even more, the attempt of Fox during the Quebec debates to discredit
Burke and to prove his inconsistency with the former doctrines of the
party proved beyond all doubt that the *Reflections* had failed in their
purpose. Yet Burke knew that many members of the opposition could
not approve of all that Fox had said and done and that there might still
be time to save the party from acting as the vehicle for the dissemination of French principles. But the situation was too urgent for the
niceties of political discrimination. Thus he represented the whole party
'as tolerating, and by a toleration, countenancing those proceedings' so
that he could 'stimulate them to a public declaration of what every one
of their acquaintance privately knows to be . . . their sentiments'.[2] By
this time, he had come to the conclusion that

There is no way left but for the weighty men of all parties to declare themselves, not only in favour of our constitution, which the others will do hypo-
critically when they are driven to it, but to declare against the French businesss,
which cuts off that faction by the roots. If they will not do this, the Dissenters
will infallibly triumph.[3]

And so, if the *Reflections* had memorably restated what many contemporaries believed to be the fundamental principles of the British
constitution, the *Appeal* denied any claim that the notions entertained
by the new Whigs could ever be accepted as party doctrine.[4]

[1] Burke to C. C. Smith 22 July 1791, Copeland Transcript of MS. in Princeton
Library.

[2] Burke to R. Burke jnr. 5 Aug. 1791, Wentworth Woodhouse MSS., Burke
Letters 1, printed in *Correspondence of Edmund Burke*, iii. 924–8.

[3] Burke to R. Burke jnr. 25 July 1791, ibid. Burke Letters 1, printed in *Correspondence of Edmund Burke*, iii. 220–3.

[4] The *Appeal* is printed in *Burke's Works*, i. 492–536; *The Public Advertiser* of
11 Aug. 1791 said that the book proved that the New Whigs had no connection
with Old Whig doctrine.

Burke's unconditional declaration of war on the new Whigs, together with his questioning of their status in the party, dismayed the Whig grandees.[1] 'It is most lamentable to think of the construction which will be given ... & of the general bad effect it will produce' mourned the Duke of Portland. He refrained from giving public expression of his private approval of Burke's work and feared that Burke had so exaggerated his case that the whole of the party was 'involved in the general censure' which Burke had bestowed upon the new Whigs.[2] Fitzwilliam told the author of the offensive book that he would have preferred to express his sentiments more tactfully. There might be 'an envious, mischievous individual or so' in the party and Fox might be careless in his language at times but he was sound at heart.[3] Such dispiriting comments could not repress Burke's rising jubilation. 'Not one word from one of our party. They are secretly galled. They agree with me to a title; but they dare not speak out for fear of hurting Fox. . . . They leave me to myself; they see that I can do myself justice.'[4] The returning confidence of the old campaigner can best be attributed to his conviction that 'it was the general opinion that I had not wandered very widely from the sentiments of those with whom I was known to be so closely connected'.[5] He had already shown his determination to cut his remaining ties with the party by refusing further financial aid from the kindly Fitzwilliam and once more he expressed a wish to retire from politics.[6] He was inclining ever more strongly to the view that 'The cause is tried in France' and that the only method of saving Europe was for a coalition of European sovereigns to destroy revolutionary France. As far as the party was concerned, he had

---

[1] For the futile, last-minute attempt by Portland and Loughborough to suppress the publication of the *Appeal*, see Loughborough to Fitzwilliam 1 Aug. 1791, loc. cit.

[2] Portland to Laurence 26 and 30 Aug. 1791, Portland MSS. P.W.F. 6240, 6241.

[3] Fitzwilliam to Burke 18 Sept. 1791, Wentworth Woodhouse MSS., Burke Letters 1, printed in *Correspondence of Edmund Burke*, iii. 333–5.

[4] Burke to R. Burke jnr. 18 Aug. 1791, ibid. Burke Letters 1, printed in *Correspondence of Edmund Burke*, iii. 265–80. On 10 Aug. he had written to Richard that 'even Fox did not differ from me materially, if at all, and that I was sure the rest, for the greater number, heartily agreed and without any limitation'. Ibid. Burke Letters 1, printed in *Correspondence of Edmund Burke*, iii. 236.

[5] Burke to Weddell 31 Jan. 1792, loc. cit.

[6] Burke to Fitzwilliam 5 June 1791, loc. cit.

now done all he could. He was now to embark upon courses of action
which were absolutely irrelevant to party politics, which could receive
no countenance from his former colleagues and which rendered him
insensible to any considerations for the welfare of the party which he
may, until now, have continued to embrace.[1]

Burke now occupied himself first with the cause of the *émigrés* and,
later, with the problem of Ireland. He sent his son to the *émigré* court
at Coblence to act as his informant and representative. He was soon
made aware of the disapproval of the English cabinet. Notwithstanding
preliminary rebuffs, Burke had several interviews with the ministers at
which he strove vainly to persuade them to abandon their policy of
neutrality. If they did so, then Austria and Prussia would probably
follow their lead.[2] If the ministers refused to do this, they might at
least make a declaration of support for the *émigrés* and the French
monarchy which might influence the French to spare the doomed
Louis XVI.[3] But as early as 18 August Burke had confessed his failure
to budge the ministers from their neutrality and, although the long and
weary interviews continued throughout September, he never succeeded
in convincing them that Europe stood in deadly peril from the French
Revolution.[4] All that these meetings achieved was to render relations

---

[1] Burke to Fitzwilliam 28 Sept. 1791, Wentworth Woodhouse MSS., F. 115a. In
the winter of 1791–2 nothing passed which might have brought Burke into more
intimate relations with the members of the party. He met Portland occasionally but
their conversation was usually 'quite remote from any thing, which could touch
upon any of those points upon which either of us should find ourselves embarrassed'.
Portland strongly disapproved of Burke's independent initiatives in foreign policy.
In particular, he viewed Richard Burke's mission to Ireland with the greatest
misgivings and he was apprehensive lest it became 'a new subject of discussion and
of obloquy'. See Burke to R. Burke jnr. 1 Jan. 1792, Wentworth Woodhouse MSS.,
Burke Letters 1.

[2] Burke to R. Burke jnr. 18 Aug. 1791, Wentworth Woodhouse MSS., Burke
Letters 1, printed in *Correspondence of Edmund Burke*, iii. 265–80; R. Burke jnr. to
E. Burke 10 Sept. 1791, ibid. Burke Letters 10.

[3] Burke to R. Burke jnr. 18 Aug. 1791, loc. cit.; Burke to the Queen of France
ante 20 Aug. 1791, ibid. Burke Letters 10G.

[4] Burke to R. Burke jnr. 18 Aug. 1791, loc. cit.; Dundas to R. Burke jnr. 20
Sept. 1791, Wentworth Woodhouse MSS., Burke Letters 1, printed in *Corres-
pondence of Edmund Burke*, iii. 335–6; Lord Grenville to E. Burke 23 Sept. 1791,
N.R.O. A. iv. 47, Burke Letters; Burke to R. Burke jnr. 26 Sept. 1791, Wentworth

between Burke and the ministers — and especially Dundas — more cordial than they had yet been.[1]

The passionate industry which he expended first upon one cause and then another is some illustration of the despair which overwhelmed Burke. He had been rejected by the party, ignominiously expelled from its activities. He had failed to draw from the lords of the party that condemnation of French principles and of the French faction in the opposition for which he had so ardently worked. Most recently, he had failed to convince the ministers of the impending crisis which was certain to strike in the near future.

I shall finish my *Thoughts*, and I shall write my letter to Weddell. Then I think there is an End for ever of my doing anything in the business.[2]

He could see plainly that the party grandees were in a difficult and painful situation and he could sympathize with them in their unhappy dilemma, but Burke placed far and above the delicate balances of internal party groupings the simple fact that Fox and his friends were 'propagating French doctrines, which seek not to destroy absolute monarchy but totally to root out that thing called an *Aristocrate*'. The old desire for peace and repose, the old lingering wish to escape from the pains and problems of public life tantalized him once more. Only the impeachment, the great work of his life by which he wished to be remembered, continued to bind him to a life of public service. But if he could not retire, at least he could work in isolation. He wished to have nothing to do either with the ministry or with the opposition.[3]

Woodhouse MSS., Burke Letters 1, printed in *Correspondence of Edmund Burke*, iii. 341–9.

[1] Burke was informing Dundas of the dispositions of the party leaders and conveying other important political information to him. Dundas to Burke 26 Sept. 1791, Wentworth Woodhouse MSS., Burke Letters 1; Burke to Dundas 30 Sept. 1791, Murray Papers, Copeland Transcript.

[2] Burke to R. Burke jnr. *ante* 1 Nov. 1791, N.R.O. A. xiii. 2, Burke Letters.

[3] Ibid.; Burke to Fitzwilliam 21 Nov. 1791, Wentworth Woodhouse MSS., F. 115a, printed in Magnus, *Edmund Burke*, 343–9. Burke did maintain his contacts with the ministers at this time. In Dec. he presented the ministers with a copy of *Thoughts on French Affairs* (printed in *Burke's Works*, i. 563–80), which advocated externally aided counter-revolution to destroy the French Revolution. For other contacts, see J. King to Burke 11, 12 and 18 Nov. 1791, N.R.O. A. iv. 42, 40, 39;

But the affairs of Ireland drew him inevitably into renewed contact
with the ministers. The mission of Burke's son, Richard, to assist the
Catholic Committee in its agitation against the laws which debarred
Roman Catholics from holding high offices in the government of
Ireland, was at first looked upon kindly by Pitt, who appeared to be
willing to discuss Irish affairs with Richard.[1] Yet the rising tide of
agitation in Ireland, the alarmism of the Lord-Lieutenant and the
outcry which the mission evoked among ministerial supporters in both
countries left the English government in a cleft stick. Pitt and Dundas
became distinctly less affable towards the Burkes.[2] Although Edmund
warned his son that the mission was both difficult and dangerous,
Richard did not succeed in allaying the fears which his mission aroused
among the Ascendancy. While he was in Ireland, from January to
April 1792, Richard accomplished nothing and the situation and the
prospects of that country seemed no brighter than before.[3] Once more,
Burke had failed to rouse the English ministers to heed his warnings
and to take his advice. Although he remained on friendly terms with
them, it seemed that their respective opinions remained as far apart
as ever.[4]

While Burke was restlessly searching for the solutions of problems
which transcended party, the opposition was passing the winter of

Burke to J. King 12 Nov. 1791, ibid. A. iv. 43; R. Burke jnr. to R. Burke snr. *ante*
19 Dec. 1791, N.R.O. A. xi. 1, Burke Letters.

[1] Pitt saw Richard about the mission on 9 Oct. 1791 and expressed himself
willing to hold further meetings. R. Burke jnr. to Pitt 8 Oct. 1791, Wentworth
Woodhouse MSS., Burke Letters 8; Pitt to R. Burke jnr. 13 Oct. 1791, N.R.O. A.
iv. 34, Burke Letters.

[2] Lord Grenville to Dundas 29 Oct. 1791, H.M.C. *Dropmore*, ii. 221–2; Dundas
to R. Burke jnr. 25 Dec. 1791, Wentworth Woodhouse MSS., Burke Letters 1,
printed in *Correspondence of Edmund Burke*, iii. 365–6; Westmorland to Pitt 1 and
14 Jan. 1792, C.U.L. 69586, ff. 1038, 1043; Hobart to Buckingham 30 Jan. 1792,
Court and Cabinets, ii. 203–5.

[3] Dundas to R. Burke jnr. 20 Jan. 1792, Wentworth Woodhouse MSS., Burke
Letters 1: 'the Irish Government are not more satisfied with you than you are with
them'.

[4] Camden and Dundas had both congratulated Burke warmly on the *Appeal* and
had approved its sentiments. Camden to Burke 5 Aug. 1791, Wentworth Woodhouse
MSS., Burke Letters 1, printed in *Correspondence of Edmund Burke*, iii. 228–9.
Dundas to Burke 12 Aug. 1791, Wentworth Woodhouse MSS., Burke Letters 1.

1791–2 in a deceptively calm and harmonious fashion. Its unprofitable association with the heir to the throne continued to weaken as the Prince gradually repaired his relationship with his family.[1] At the same time, William Adam was attempting to place the finances of the party upon a more secure footing. He had found that routine party expenses, especially the cost of having messengers available to send out division notes, had gradually accumulated during the last three sessions until a deficit of £150 had accrued. He provided for such contingencies in the future by setting aside an annual sum of £200 from the funds of the party.[2] Meticulously, he wished to clear away existing arrears before the new session opened. In particular, large sums remained outstanding to the newspapers. But Adam's approaches to Portland to assist in the payment of such debts were coldly received. The Duke lectured him on his handling of the press and reprimanded him for the appearance in the party papers of many offensive paragraphs which had proved 'highly injurious' to the party and 'very promiscuous to the Community at large'.[3] It had, indeed, been clear to Burke for some time that the organs of the party were in the hands of those he described as the French faction and there were soon to be signs that this fact was beginning to cause Portland serious disquiet.

To add to the relaxed and almost somnolent political scene, affairs on the continent were more stable than they had been for some time. Louis XVI's acceptance of the new constitution in September appeared to inaugurate a new era in which the fruits of the Revolution might still be secured without undue violence. As the winter passed peacefully, the reformers in England were correspondingly stilled, 'almost ashamed of their bad taste', remarked Burke.[4] The country was lulled into a mood of placid contentment. If this were not enough, while Pitt dreamed of fifteen years of peace, the rising wealth of the country

[1] The Queen to the Prince of Wales 30 Aug. 1791, Aspinall, *Correspondence of George, Prince of Wales*, ii. 189–90; *The Public Advertiser* of 10 Jan. 1892 renewed the cry that the Prince was on the point of quitting his political friends. The marriage of the Duke of York in Sept. 1791 had not weakened links between the Princes and the opposition because Adam and Portland were busy arranging his finances.

[2] Adam to Fitzwilliam 4 Sept. 1791, Wentworth Woodhouse MSS., F. 115e; Fitzwilliam to Adam 8 Sept. 1791, Blair-Adam MSS.

[3] Portland to Adam 10 Sept., 1791, Blair-Adam MSS.

[4] *Correspondence of Edmund Burke*, Burke to Dr. Dodge 29 Feb. 1792, iii. 420–3.

underlined the boundless optimism with which the governing classes of England faced what appeared to be a halcyon future. Few years can have opened more auspiciously, yet closed more gloomily, than 1792.

Burke was not the only politician to have grave reservations about the contemporary scene. It is a sign of his maturing political judgement that Fox was now aware that the problems in the party could no longer be allowed to drift and that the dissonant elements in the opposition must be welded together more thoroughly. He knew well that many of the most influential members of the party disapproved of his sympathy for the French Revolution and he therefore made some attempts to moderate his language and to cloud over his opinions in a shroud of ambiguity.[1] But he was unable to discipline either himself or his followers as completely as the gravity of the situation in the party demanded. He told Fitzwilliam in March that, although there were differences of opinion between them, party unity need not be endangered by differences of emphasis or of application of principle. Only on the subject of the abolition of the slave-trade was Fox adamant and uncompromising in his standpoint. He blamed the Northites in the party for entertaining opinions which were 'very different' from those of the Whig party on religious toleration. On the crucial issue of parliamentary reform, Fox hedged, declaring that 'I am more bound by former declarations and consistency, than by any strong opinion I entertain in its favour'. He even admitted to Fitzwilliam that 'the part which you have taken on the question' might be 'upon the whole the most manly and judicious'. Fox declared his anxiety lest the *ancien régime* be re-established in France, yet admitted that 'The *present* state of the country alarms me very much'. While regretting the public disputes to which the party had recently been subjected, he remained 'firmly convinced that the existence and union of our party is useful to the country, and as such that it is our duty to maintain it by every exertion of effort'.[2]

---

[1] *The Public Advertiser* of 6 Oct. 1791 commented upon the 'new Fox' as depicted in the opposition press.

[2] Fox to Fitzwilliam 16 Mar. 1792, N.R.O. Box 44, no. 9, ff. 1–5. See also Fox's eulogy on monarchy in a debate on 7 Mar. 1792, *The Parliamentary History*, xxix. 1007. And it was in public that Fox declared his dislike for the second part of Paine's *The Rights of Man*. Elliot to his wife 24 Mar. 1792, Minto, ii. 1–3.

Although the activities of the party were rather more restrained than usual,[1] the spirit and the mood of Fox and his friends could not be repressed completely. In spite of the warnings which had been dealt out to Adam, *The Morning Chronicle* pledged its attachment to the new French constitution of September 1791 and condemned the dangerous champions of counter-revolution.[2] Plans for reform continued to circulate within the party and they found influential support. Sheridan once again agitated the reform of the Scottish burghs and in this he received the explicit and public approval of Fox. Fox, indeed, appeared concerned to present reform as a matter consistent with the traditional doctrines of the Whig party.[3] The essential Fox remained unchanged. He found it difficult to dissimulate his true feelings and opinions. With his impulsive and mercurial temperament, he could not resist the opportunity of scoring a mark in debate or the temptation to deliver tirades against despotism in general.[4] Thus his specious attempts to heal the divisions in the party were doomed to failure because they were the crude stratagems of party politics and because Fox did not find it easy to present a double face to the world.

Yet such restraint as he had been able to exercise was to be of crucial significance in preserving party unity. The growth of political societies in March presented quite a new force in domestic politics which stiffened the fears and confirmed the anxieties of the conservative Whigs in the party.[5] The London Corresponding Society brought the working classes into politics for the first time. There was something alarming about the avidity with which they devoured cheap literature

---

[1] Even *The Public Advertiser* of 9 Feb. admitted that the Whig Club meeting of 7 Feb. was innocuous. For the formation of a new informal party club to preserve unity between all sides of the party, see Elliot to his wife 24 Mar. and 5 Apr. 1792, Minto, ii. 1–3, 5–8.

[2] *The Morning Chronicle*, 22 Oct. 3 Nov. and 30 Dec.

[3] See the debate of 18 Apr. 1792, *The Parliamentary History*, xxix. 1196–9.

[4] He declared before the Commons on 9 Feb. that blind confidence in a minister was 'more subversive than any of the wildest schemes that the wildest of modern reformers could ever have devised'. ibid. xxix. 804. See also the debates on 17 and 20 Feb. 1792, ibid. 848, 885.

[5] For this reform agitation, see Veitch, *Genesis of Reform*, 189–96; Brown, *The French Revolution in English History*, 55–74; H. Butterfield, 'Charles James Fox and the Whig Opposition, 1792', *Historical Journal* (1949), ix. 3, 301–3.

— especially the popular editions of Paine — and something threatening in the attempts of the societies to concert their activities on a national scale. The emerging industrial towns threw up movements for reform in social and economic circumstances which men like Portland and Fitzwilliam could not begin to understand. And this inability drove them to adopt a rigid and repressive view of all such proceedings.[1] There can be little room for surprise, therefore, when they reacted so violently to the formation of a society within the ranks of the Whig party itself which avowedly sought to encourage and to lead the agitation which they deplored and feared so deeply.[2]

The formation of the Association of the Friends of the People was not the prank of Holland House legend, nor was it a really surprising development. During the last two sessions, the Oczacov debates had provided the opposition with a façade of unity. The younger members of the party, who were more radically inclined than the Whig aristocrats, had played a prominent role in the opposition's campaign against Pitt, seemingly with the concurrence of all sections of the party. Many of these younger members supported the movement for the reform of parliament. Until March 1792 there had been nothing to indicate that the party could be torn apart on this subject, a subject on which it had long been able to tolerate divergent opinions. Further, the lords of the party had acquiesced in the enquiry into the alleged abuses committed by ministerial supporters at the Westminster election of 1788, which was noisily demanded by the same younger members. Such acquiescence led to the fatal miscalculation made by Grey and Lauderdale. Their Association arose, in fact, from that deceptive unity which the party had maintained in the previous months and from the unwarranted confidence of the Friends of the People that they could carry the party with them. They did not appear to have noticed that the country was

[1] Portland to Fitzwilliam 6 Apr. 1792, Wentworth Woodhouse MSS., F. 31a; Butterfield, op. cit., 301–3.

[2] There had been hints in the press that some such move on the part of the reformers in the Whig party was on foot. Butterfield, op. cit., 303 n. 38; *The Public Advertiser* of 3 Apr. observed that Portland and Fitzwilliam 'have lately discovered some alarming symptoms of intended secession'. And before the news of the formation of the Association had been published *The Morning Chronicle* of 12 Apr. 1792 had predicted a motion for the reform of parliament before the end of the session.

already stirring, for they assumed that it was incumbent upon themselves to go to the country, to rouse the people to support them and, thus assured of public support, to reform parliament. Only thus would the aristocracy be saved from the fruits of its blind fear of radical reform. They failed to appreciate that the Whig aristocracy was already appreciably more anxious at the spread of reform movements than they had been earlier.[1]

The news of the formation of the Association was greeted with alarm. The ministerial papers sought rather to outlaw its members than to aggravate the gaping wounds in the side of the Whig party. The Association was thus presented to the public as a gang of levellers and republicans, leading dangerous military plots which were dedicated to the overthrow of property and the destruction of the constitution. On the other hand, the other reforming societies did not trust the Association and refused to defer to its leadership of the reform movement. The Friends had thus failed in their initial purpose but, perhaps more important, they had failed to make reform respectable. They had succeeded only in rousing a storm of protest such as to call into question their own political future and which tore open the fissures existing in the Whig party.[2] In the opposition, the reformers were suspected of trying to oust Portland from the leadership and it was widely feared that they would arouse forces which they could not control.[3] Everything now turned upon Fox. Would the Man of the People lead the reform movement in the country? It was certain that only he commanded the prestige sufficient to challenge Portland's position in the party. On the other hand, he was the only member of the party who might yet bring the hasty reformers to their senses.

Although both his position in the party and the exact nature of his reforming inclinations were subjects of the widest speculation, Fox's alarm and annoyance at the Association cannot be questioned. Neither

[1] On the formation of the Association, see Butterfield, op. cit., 302–4; P. J. Brunsdon, 'The Association of the Friends of the People' (unpublished M.A. dissertation, Manchester, 1961), 203–7; for the Holland House legend, see Lord Holland's *Memoirs*, i. 13–15; *Journal of Lady Elizabeth Holland* (2 vols., 1908), i. 101.

[2] Butterfield, op. cit., 307–8; Brunsdon, op. cit., 49–54.

[3] E.g. Fitzwilliam to Carlisle 31 Oct. 1792, H.M.C. *Carlisle*, 698–9; Elliot to his wife 14 Apr., 1 May 1792, Minto, ii. 11–15, 16–19.

he nor those closest to him joined the Association. In fact, he had attempted, with the aid of Tom Pelham, 'to put an end to a scheme so very injurious to us as a party'.[1] He was fully aware of the delicacy of his position.[2] The revival of parliamentary reform placed him 'in the disagreeable dilemma of either changing his former conduct on the same question, or differing with a great part of those who act with him, and, indeed, with the most weighty and respectable part of his support'.[3] Fox's ardour for parliamentary reform had been little in evidence during the last few years and his only wish now was to keep such potentially divisive questions hidden as discreetly as possible. What Fox wanted was to keep the party united at a time when Pitt was still embroiled in continental difficulties and while rumours about his relationship with Thurlow were puzzling the political world. He seems to have felt that a great opportunity to overthrow Pitt was at hand and his anger at the Association was all the more bitter then, for it weakened the party and allowed Pitt to seize the initiative once more.[4]

Fox's opinions seem to have made themselves felt, for serious attempts were made within the party to close its ranks and, at least, to avoid a public altercation of its differences. The immediate danger was likely to occur during the debate on Grey's notice of a motion to reform the representation, which was to come before the Commons on 30 April. During the preceding days the party leaders met several times and, on the eve of the debate, a meeting of conservative Whigs was held at Burlington House.[5] Those present decided that Grey's

[1] Pelham to Lady Holland 27 Apr. 1792, Ad. MS. 51705, unfoliated, Holland House MSS. On 25 Apr. Fox wrote to Fitzpatrick, saying: 'There are several unpleasant things going forward.' Ad. MS. 47580, ff. 143–4, Fox Papers; and on 3 May he remarked to Lord Holland that 'things here are very very bad'. Ad. MS. 47571, ff. 7–8, Fox Papers. *The Public Advertiser* of 18 May predicted that Fox would shortly quit the radicals in the party.

[2] T. Pelham to Lady Holland 15 June 1792, Ad. MS. 51705, unfoliated, Holland House MSS.

[3] Elliot to his wife 1 May 1792, Minto, ii. 18; see also the remarks of Burke in his letter to William Burke 3 Sept. 1792, Wentworth Woodhouse MSS., Burke Letters 1, printed in *Correspondence of Edmund Burke*, iii. 514–22.

[4] Fox to Adam 3 Sept. 1793, Blair-Adam MSS.; the government press had been circulating stories that Thurlow was soon to retire, e.g. *The Public Advertiser*, 17 Feb. 1792.

[5] *Windham Diary*, 253.

opinions on the desirability of parliamentary reform should not be allowed to stand on record as being those of the party as a whole. The opponents of reform had now effectively thrown down the gauntlet to the Friends of the People. Such uncompromising action jolted the reformers and brought them to realize, once for all, that they could not hope to commit the party to the measures which they proclaimed to be necessary for the salvation of the constitution.

And thus the debate on 30 April was remarkable for the moderation and the caution which were displayed by both wings of the Whig party. Even Sheridan expressed the hope that the question of reform would not be treated as a party issue. Speakers like North and Windham, who opposed parliamentary reform, were careful to garnish their speeches with the most generous praise of the reformers. But it was Pitt who set the tone of the debate and who swung the sense of the House unmistakably against the reformers. His arguments were echoed by speaker after speaker. Although every effort had been made to preserve harmony in the ranks of the opposition, the Friends of the People found that the debate had gone badly for them. Windham had proclaimed that he would unite with any body of men 'who were determined to set their faces against every endeavour to subvert the true principles of the constitution', sentiments which were seconded by Tom Grenville. Grey confessed himself 'anxious and uneasy ... to find those whose good opinion was dear to him, deprecate with such strong expressions of apprehension and alarm, the notice which he had given'. But it was left to Francis to voice the angry frustration which the Associators must have been feeling: 'You look for our principles not in our declarations, but in the supposed views and projects of other men.'[1]

Fox's equivocal attitude in the debate indicates that he was fully aware of the difficulties and dangers of his position. Although he 'had no difficulty in declaring himself a friend to improvement of every kind', and although he defended the Association from the attacks which other speakers had made upon it, 'he should have hesitated before he recommended him [Grey] to take the part he had taken'. In trying to placate both wings of the party, Fox satisfied neither. The conservative Whigs still feared that Fox might declare for the reformers.[2] But he

---

[1] *The Parliamentary History*, xxix. 1300–41; Butterfield, op. cit., 309.
[2] Elliot to his wife 1 May 1792, Minto, ii. 18.

had already failed to restrain them from forming the Association and in the following months he left them very largely to their own resources. In some ways, his refusal to countenance the Association was itself, perhaps, a factor which explains the weakness of that body during the summer of 1792.[1] Yet the most potent weapon which Fox possessed was the ambiguity which continued to accompany his public declarations.

Fox might twist and turn but the party was now the prisoner of events which were to shape its future. Although several reporters gave the lie to widespread fear of revolution, there can be no doubt that the intensification of reforming agitation in May deepened the anxieties of the conservative Whigs and sharpened their suspicion of the Friends of the People.[2] But Fox appears to have felt — at least he behaved — as though the immediate danger to the unity of the party had passed; that he could, once more, afford to indulge those liberal instincts which he had lately tried to suppress.[3] Miscalculation once more led to disaster. The unity of the party was at that very time being threatened by a new and more dangerous challenge than the Friends of the People could ever have been. The ministers, who had been in touch with Loughborough and had received from him secret information concerning the divisions in the opposition, were well placed not only to allay the fears of the propertied classes in the country by adopting measures to quieten the reformers but also to prise open the fissures which were tearing the

[1] Fox may have been responsible for the second, more moderate, declaration of the Association, which was published on 5 May. Butterfield, op. cit., 307. For the divisions and weaknesses of the Association in the following weeks, see Veitch, *Genesis of Reform*, 211–12; Butterfield, op. cit., 304; Elliot to his wife 7 May 1792, Minto, ii. 20–21; Windham to Gurney 2 May 1792, Ad. MS. 37873, ff. 172–4, Windham Papers, printed in *Windham Papers*, i. 100–5.

[2] On the reform movement at this time, see the work of: Butterfield, 'Charles James Fox', 305–6; J. Holland Rose, *William Pitt and the Great War* (1911), 25–26; H. W. Meikle, 'The King's Birthday Riots in Edinburgh, May 1792', *Scottish Historical Review*, vii. 21–27.

[3] See his speech during the debate on his motion to repeal certain Penal Statutes on 11 May (*The Parliamentary History*, xxix. 1372–1403). He delivered a panegyric on the rights of man, extolled the Unitarians and declared that the *Reflections* was a worse libel than Paine's book. He concluded by affirming that there was no danger from the stirrings of the people unless it came from the 'violent high-church spirit in the country'.

Whig opposition apart. Pitt opened a formal communication with Loughborough and suggested that a forthcoming meeting of the Privy Council should be attended by the leaders of the opposition to consider 'measures as the present circumstances may require'.[1]

Perhaps no man was better placed than Loughborough to attempt to cajole the conservative Whigs into a closer and more cordial relationship with the ministers. After the resignation of Thurlow, he was the obvious candidate for the Seals. He was on friendly terms with Auckland, who was close to Pitt, and he had no difficulty in renewing his contacts with the genial Dundas. His opinions, on the subjects of France and domestic reform, were those of the conservative Whigs. None could challenge his influence with the Northite peers, and especially with Malmesbury and Carlisle. Yet his scarcely concealed ambition and his thinly disguised duplicity endeared him to none save those who wished to use him for their own purposes. He was thus badly placed to challenge Fox's influence with the old Whig nobility. Loughborough was perhaps a better judge of the manœuvres of politics than many of his contemporaries. It was not political skill that he lacked. In a sense, it was political skill that led him astray; his crucial weakness was that his mastery of strategy was much less complete than his mastery of tactics. In the tortuous twists and subtleties of that political intrigue in which he revelled, he would lose sight of his ultimate aims and then miscalculate or ignore elements in the situation which a more clear-sighted politician would have used to his own advantage.

In response to Pitt's request, Loughborough lost no time in sounding his friends. He intimated to the ministers that the leaders of the opposition would support a definite measure to pacify the country and one which might enable them to rid their party of those who had joined the

---

[1] Loughborough to Dundas 24 Apr. 1792, Scottish Record Office G.D.1/17/2, Melville Castle MSS.; Pitt to Auckland 1 May 1792, Ad. MS. 35441, f. 512, Auckland Papers, printed in *Auckland,* ii. 401–2. This letter indicates that Auckland had been receiving secret information about the party, almost certainly from his friend Loughborough. The decision to contact Loughborough followed upon a conversation between Pitt and Dundas of which a memorandum survives in the Scottish Record Office G.D.1/17/4, Melville Castle MSS. Auckland transcribed most of it and sent his transcript, with a letter, to Loughborough on 1 May. *Auckland,* ii. 402–4.

Association.[1] By 9 May the ministers had drawn up a Proclamation and they invited Portland to discuss the measure.[2] On 10 May the two men met. Pitt suggested to the Duke that he and some of his principal friends might attend the Privy Council when the Proclamation was to be discussed. Portland thereupon proceeded to canvass his colleagues, but, although they concurred in Pitt's recognition of the urgent need for strong government action, their attendance at the Privy Council might be 'misrepresented and misunderstood'. As Portland put it, when writing to Pitt on 13 May: 'We may act in concert though not in conjunction.'[3] The Proclamation might have been issued at this stage had not two delaying factors intervened. On 15 May Thurlow opposed, and nearly defeated, a ministerial finance measure in the Lords. While Pitt was persuading the King to rid himself of his Lord Chancellor, some of the conservative Whigs were struck with pangs of conscience about the Proclamation. They suddenly realized that it was 'too personally hostile to our old friends'.[4] Nor could they conceal their deep-rooted and long-nourished suspicion both of Pitt and his motives. Their apprehensions may have been dispelled in part by the willingness evinced by Pitt and Dundas to change some of the offending passages in the Proclamation and, thus amended, it was published on 21 May.[5]

The Proclamation was to be debated in the Commons on 25 May and there seemed every prospect that a direct collision between the two wings of the opposition would be unavoidable. To complicate Portland's

[1] Dundas to Loughborough (n.d. May 1792 — probably 5 May), Scottish Record Office G.D.1/17/3, Melville Castle MSS.; Loughborough to Auckland 4 May 1792, C.U.L. 69586, f. 1080.

[2] Pitt to Portland 9 May 1792, ibid. f. 1085; Portland to Pitt 9 May 1792, ibid. f. 1084.

[3] Portland to Pitt 13 May 1792, P.R.O. Pitt Papers, 168; the Duke sought Fox's advice about these overtures but Fox 'saw no danger to warrant any unusual measure'. (Elliot to his wife 14 May 1792, Minto, ii. 23–25.) Portland's refusal to attend the Privy Council was regarded by Lord Grenville as 'an additional proof of the decisive influence Fox possesses' over the conservative Whigs. Grenville to Buckingham 15 May 1792, *Court and Cabinets*, ii. 207.

[4] Elliot to his wife 17 May 1792, Minto, ii. 25–28. This was not a stratagem of Fox. North, in fact, raised this difficulty.

[5] Portland to Pitt 24 May 1792, C.U.L. 69586, f. 1090; Lord Holland, *Memoirs*, i. 15–16; Elliot to his wife 26 May 1792, Minto, ii. 32–33; *The Morning Chronicle*, 23, 24 May 1792.

problems further, Dundas had already begun to tease Loughborough by offering him the Seals and by speaking of coalition.[1] Loughborough told Portland of these important developments on 24 May but the Duke refused to return an answer until he had contacted Fox and Fitzwilliam.[2] If these offers were made public, Portland's position in the party would become impossible, for they would only serve to aggravate the dissensions in the Whig party. The conciliatory behaviour of Charles James Fox saved both Portland from added embarrassment and the party from further convulsions. At Fox's instigation, a meeting of party leaders took place on the evening of 24 May at which he was clearly determined 'to prevent things going to extremities to-morrow in the debate, and to soften, at least, all personal asperity. . . .'[3] After the meeting, Portland penned a note to Pitt, warning him not to expect too decided a support from the opposition benches during the debate.[4] And, although the members of the party aired their different views on the Proclamation in the Commons on 25 May, every effort was made to preserve the impression of party unity.[5] Later the same day, Portland, immensely gratified by the party's forbearance, wrote to Loughborough, rejecting the ministerial offer as 'utterly inadmissible'.[6]

Although the first direct challenge to the unity of the Whig party had been overcome, events had already gone too far and had acquired a momentum of their own which demanded far more than a temporary stifling of internal differences if the unity of the party was to be preserved. Loughborough was hungry for the Seals and could be relied upon to aggravate the schism in the party by lending all of his political

[1] See p. 91.

[2] Portland to Loughborough 25 May 1792, Portland MSS. P.W.F. 9220; Butterfield, op. cit., 311.

[3] Elliot to his wife 24 May 1792, Minto, ii. 30–32; Butterfield, op. cit., 310; Fox to Adam 20 May 1792, Blair-Adam MSS.

[4] Portland to Pitt 24 May 1792, C.U.L. 6958[6], f. 1090.

[5] Grey denied that 'their general concurrence of sentiment was at an end', and Windham declared that 'When this debate was at an end . . . they should act as cordially to-gether as if no such difference had ever existed'. The report of the debate in *The Parliamentary Register*, xxxiii. 457–89, is rather more complete than that given in *The Parliamentary History*, xxix. 1476–1514.

[6] Portland to Loughborough 25 May 1792, loc. cit.

arts in the cause of coalition. Although the Friends of the People had wilted before the constitutional reaction which followed the publication of the Proclamation, Fox had not disavowed the Association. The future of its members within the party was to be for many months an irksome and problematic issue. The conservative Whigs had already demonstrated their willingness to lend their support to the government on matters of internal security and there was no reason why co-operation on one issue might not lead to co-operation on others. Such considerations did not, even yet, take account of England's relations with foreign powers. Isolation and neutrality remained, much to the disgust of Burke, the corner-stones of English foreign policy during May, when France was already at war with the allies.

The party had found itself divided on the question of parliamentary reform in the spring of 1792. If it continued to be a serious political issue, Elliot could only predict 'a total separation of the party'. He was troubled already at the prospect of coalition, but thought it

unlikely, not to say impossible, that either *half* shall, with any advantage to the public, or credit and comfort to themselves, form any new connection, or have a share in any administration. . . . I do firmly believe it to be impossible, at least in the present circumstances. What is to happen in this eventful world a twelvemonth hence, my eyes are too short-sighted to conjecture.[1]

II. The Struggle for the Whig Party, May 1792–February 1793

The swift and surprising political developments of April and May had revealed to the opposition the pressing need for restraint and for vigilance if the unity of the party was to be preserved. The Proclamation had not yet dispelled all fears for the safety of the country entertained by the conservative Whigs and thus Fox had to trim his sails and confound those who wished to depict him as a democrat.[2] The session was drawing to an end and with it the danger that the party might destroy itself through public discussion of reform. But already a new threat

[1] Elliot to his wife 31 May 1792, Minto, ii. 34–35.

[2] For Fox's solicitousness for party unity, see his letter to Adam of 28 May 1792, Blair-Adam MSS. *The Morning Chronicle* presented Fox as a moderate at this time and he left his opinions on reform vague.

to the unity of the party had emerged, that of coalition. Dundas had already hinted in April that the ministers might be interested in some such arrangement with the conservative Whigs. He had vaguely indicated to Loughborough that as many as four cabinet places might be put at the party's disposal, to say nothing of seats at the Privy Council and other honours. The Duke of Portland rejected the offer, yet confessed: 'I have bestowed much more thought upon it than I should have thought necessary.'[1] In fact, Loughborough had known from the beginning that 'the chief departments c'd never come in question' and that Dundas had not intended his remarks to be taken as a formal overture.[2] Yet it was not long before Loughborough's campaign for coalition came to be assisted by Burke, who had been sorely disappointed by the fact that Portland's co-operation with the government in May had not led to a firmer arrangement.

Since his son's disastrous mission to Ireland, Burke's communications with the ministers had almost lapsed. Only on matters arising from the impeachment did he seek their aid. Although he pressed his opinions on the French Revolution and domestic reform upon some of his old friends in the opposition, his views were disregarded and he was distressed at the failure of the party to expel the reformers from its ranks.[3] When the possibility of a coalition first emerged from the crisis of April and May 1792, Burke began to take a more direct part in politics. He saw that Portland must himself take the initiative in instigating coalition and impressed upon him the desirability of Loughborough's acceptance of the Seals. Portland, however, 'determined nothing, because I believe the larger plan occupied his thoughts'.[4] Burke saw, too, that Fox's influence with the Duke must be surmounted

---

[1] Butterfield, 'Charles James Fox', 311 and 330 postscript; Portland to Loughborough 25 May 1792, loc. cit. Portland rejected the offer ostensibly on the grounds that the posts held out were too few, their patronage insufficient and their influence on policy inadequate.

[2] Loughborough to Portland (n.d. — late May? — 1792), Portland MSS. P.W.F. 9220.

[3] Burke to Weddell 31 Jan. 1792, loc. cit.; Elliot to his wife 9 Apr. 1792, Minto, ii. 8–11; Burke to Laurence 13 Apr. 1792, *Maggs Catalogue* (spring 1918), 365 (118). Part of this letter is given in *Sotheby's Catalogue* (1881), 53. Copeland Transcript.

[4] Burke to Loughborough 27 May 1792, Campbell, *Lives of the Lord Chancellors*, vi. 343.

and thus, at a meeting at Burlington House on 9 June, he urged Portland and Fitzwilliam to bring Fox to a specific declaration of his opinions. At the same time Burke convinced them, if only for a short period, that coalition was a necessary measure. Their concurrence in his views meant that negotiations with the ministers could proceed.[1]

The basic motives of the individuals concerned remained unchanged throughout the two separate negotiations for coalition which took place during the summer. In the first, Loughborough acted as an intermediary between the party and the ministry. On 14 June he saw Pitt and Dundas who professed themselves friendly to the idea of coalition. But a further interview on 25 June revealed that, although lines of communication should remain open, there was then too much hostility in ministerial circles towards the inclusion of Fox in any arrangement. The second negotiation centred on the unfortunate Duke of Leeds. Portland told him that Pitt would be willing to surrender the Treasury to a 'Third Party', thus allowing both himself and Fox to serve in the same administration without raising the problem of precedence between them. And at Portland's request, Leeds spoke to George III about the reconstruction of the government, when he found, to his astonishment, that the King knew of no such arrangements. The wearying and intricate manœuvres for which these exchanges are famous should not obscure the fact that if the motives of the participants can be unravelled from the maze of baffling half-truth and deception, then light can be thrown upon the problem of coalition, its practicability, its desirability and its necessity.

The complicated events of the summer had several important effects, not the least of which was the fact that they left the Whigs even more suspicious of Pitt than they had hitherto been. Their distrust of him was not without its justification. For Pitt did not tell the King of the first negotiation. He did not obtain the royal permission to open negotiations with a party which had for so long been considered to be hostile to the throne. At no time did Pitt raise the issue of coalition with George III, although he confidently asserted that the King

---

[1] *The Diaries and Correspondence of James Harris, First Earl of Malmesbury* (4 vols., 1884), ii. 453–4; see also a letter from William Burke which reflected Edmund's views closely: William Burke to Portland 8 June 1792, Wentworth Woodhouse MSS., Burke Letters 1 (incomplete copy).

would raise no objections.[1] Further, Pitt and Dundas had predicted that the inclusion of Fox in a responsible situation would not prove to be an insuperable obstacle. But they were forced, or so they said, to break off the first negotiation on the grounds that Pitt's friends had raised a storm of opposition to the proposal. It would, indeed, have been surprising if Pitt had been unaware of the opinions of his friends about Fox. Other observers had noted that, on this problem, the movement for coalition must flounder.[2] There were still further objections. One difficulty lay in the respective situations of Pitt and Fox. Neither would ever accept a position inferior to that of the other. Since detailed proposals were never thoroughly discussed by the parties concerned, it is not surprising that so many problems were left unexamined at this time. The most likely explanation of his conduct is that Pitt was not willing to consider coalition seriously but that he was intent upon aggravating the divisions in the Whig party and, perhaps, detaching some of its members. At the same time, the glowing reports which Loughborough passed around to the Whigs concerning the willingness of the ministers to come to some arrangement with them confused the situation further. At the height of the second negotiation, Pitt could congratulate himself that there were 'very strong indications that even without any regular treaty, all serious hostilities from any but the violent set are at an end — I think it may soon lead to some marks of Honor but not at present to any other arrangement'.[3] There were, indeed, several motives which might have led Pitt to strengthen his administration, but there were none which would have led him inevitably into a coalition. In the House of Lords, with the solitary exception of Grenville, the ministry was weak in debating talent.[4] Even more, the prestige of the administration had been falling. By detaching some of its most vocal opponents and by persuading them to

[1] *Malmesbury Diary*, ii. 459–61; William Elliot to Sir Gilbert Elliot 19 June 1792, Minto, ii. 41–44.

[2] William Elliot to Sir Gilbert Elliot 29 June 1792, Minto, ii. 44–52.

[3] Pitt to Bishop Pretyman 22 July 1792, East Suffolk Record Office, Pretyman MSS., T. 108/42, Ipswich. The ministerial press disliked the prospect of coalition and insisted that Pitt would not change his situation in the near future. E.g. *The Public Advertiser*, 4 Aug. 1792.

[4] Bland-Burges to Auckland 10 July 1792, *Auckland*, ii. 414–17; Storer to Auckland 10 Aug. 1792, ibid. 428–30.

lend the weight of their support to the government, Pitt might well feel that he was only doing what any politician would have had the sense to recognize as expedient.[1] There was no immediate threat of subversion in the country at large during the summer as Pitt was very well aware, for the Proclamation had done its work well. But it was recognized that domestic tranquillity was a delicate bloom and that in times of crisis it could be preserved only by the constant exertions of the gentlemen of the counties. These exertions would be the more successful for being the product of unity. At all costs, the party strife of Westminster must not be translated to the country at large while democrats and atheistic republicans were lurking underground, awaiting their chance to strike. Unity of class interest may therefore have been a remote and indirect, yet still a significant cause of the sudden emergence of coalition as a political issue. Finally, Pitt may have felt that his cabinet could well benefit from the infusion of new blood and fresh vigour. The Seals were vacant and the days in office of Stafford and Camden were clearly numbered. Pitt may therefore have wished to detach some individuals, but there is nothing to show that he considered a party coalition as a serious possibility.[2]

These negotiations become even more of a political charade when they are considered from the point of view of the conservative Whigs, who were never agreed on the most fundamental of the conditions which must be attached to a junction with the government. There was, in the first place, the strange triumvirate of Burke, Loughborough and Malmesbury. Although his thinking influenced the attitudes of the other two men, Burke's ideas were curiously ill-digested. Nor did he participate quite as keenly as might have been expected in the political manœuvres of the summer for which he had done much to provide the initial momentum. He rightly dismissed Portland's visionary dream of 'a large coalition system' as 'utterly impracticable'. Yet, until the end of June he believed that Fox's inclusion in an arrangement with

---

[1] Carlisle to Loughborough 29 July 1792, Campbell, *Lives of the Lord Chancellors*, vi. 345; Burke to W. Burke 3 Sept. 1792, Wentworth Woodhouse MSS. Burke Letters 1, printed in *Correspondence of Edmund Burke*, iii. 514–22.

[2] Sheffield to Lady Webster 21 July 1792, Ad. MS. 51845, Holland House MSS., unfoliated. For Pitt's offer, in early July, of the post of Governor-General of India to the Whigs, see *Malmesbury Diary*, ii. 469.

the ministry was both desirable and possible. He could not see that it was impossible for Pitt and Fox to sit in the same cabinet and he does not seem to have considered seriously what the attitude of the King, the Whig party at large or the friends of Pitt might be to all these speculative proposals. By the end of June, he had resigned himself to the probable failure of the negotiations, whereupon he declared that all systematic opposition should cease and that the Friends of the People should be disavowed by the lords of the party. In his view, Loughborough ought to take the Seals and open the way into the ministry for the rest of the party.[1] This overlooked the fact that Loughborough was unwilling to satisfy his ambitions unless the Seals were made part of a larger arrangement.[2] Most curious of all, Burke trusted Loughborough. The latter showed his lack of insight by his persistence, until August, in the belief that Pitt might be willing to leave the Treasury.[3] Loughborough was unwillling to imperil the negotiations by acting the part of an honest mediator between government and opposition. And thus he did not tell Pitt what the Whig lords were agreed upon: namely that there must be a new prime minister and that he, Pitt, must make room for another. By acting in this manner, Loughborough was defeating his own purposes and failing to take advantage of what few political counters he possessed.[4] He was thus to be placed at a severe disadvantage when others began to manipulate the political game which he had mismanaged so thoroughly.

While men like Malmesbury and Carlisle were willing to follow the policies of Burke and Loughborough in relation to coalition, Portland, Fitzwilliam and the Whig lords adopted ideas which made coalition even more difficult to accomplish. They had assented to these negotiations in a fit of enthusiasm while they had been swayed by the oratory of Burke, but they were never more than reluctant participants in the complicated political moves of the summer. Their distrust of Pitt was endemic. They did not wish to act with him in the government and

---

[1] Burke to Loughborough 13 June 1792, Campbell, op. cit., vi. 344–5; *Malmesbury Diary*, ii. 466–7; *D'Arblay*, v. 92.

[2] Loughborough to Burke 13 June 1792, Wentworth Woodhouse MSS. Burke Letters 1.

[3] Loughborough to Carlisle 1 Aug. 1792, H.M.C. Carlisle, 696–7.

[4] Loughborough to Burke 13 June 1792, loc. cit.

they were pleased when the negotiations ultimately failed.[1] They were prepared to place more stringent conditions before the ministers as the price of a coalition. Power and patronage must be evenly distributed between the new ministers and the old. There must be 'a large coalition system', not merely the accession to office of a few individuals. Portland laboured under no illusions about the difficulty of achieving coalition but 'if Pitt meant what we did *bona fide*, a coalition was a most desirable measure'.[2] He understood, too, that Pitt must be included in such an arrangement but insisted that he surrender the Treasury to a neutral third party. Fox would not, could not, honourably accept a position inferior to that of his great rival. Portland and many others could not conceive of a coalition unless Fox were part of it. Their insistence ruined the chance of success in the first negotiation.[3]

Fox had remained mysteriously in the background during the month of June while this negotiation was taking place. But it was he who seized the initiative from Loughborough and whose motives predominated during the second negotiation. It was at Fox's behest that Portland contacted Leeds in the first instance, and it was Fox who guided and advised the Duke during the tricky soundings which led up to Leeds's farcical interview with George III.[4] Portland himself was innocent of any premeditated trickery. In this, he was Fox's instrument. He fell in so readily with Fox's schemes because he never doubted Fox's sincerity and because, on the issue of coalition, at least, the opinions of the two men were not widely dissimilar.[5]

---

[1] *Malmesbury Diary*, ii. 467–8; Portland to Fitzwilliam 27 June 1792, Wentworth Woodhouse MSS., F. 31a. For Windham's suspicion of the ministers, see Windham to Adam 25 July 1792, Blair-Adam MSS. Elliot was averse to joining the government (*Malmesbury Diary*, ii. 455–7). Portland's reluctance to take office was only overcome by the efforts of Malmesbury and Fitzwilliam (ibid. 459–61).

[2] *Malmesbury Diary*, ii. 458–61.

[3] Ibid. ii. 454–5; William Elliot to Sir Gilbert Elliot 11 June and 11 July 1792, Minto, ii. 40–41, 52–57.

[4] Portland to Fox 21 July 1792, Ad. MS. 47561. f. 112, Fox Papers; Fox to Portland 21 July 1792, ibid. f. 117, printed in *Fox's Memorials*, iv. 286–7; Portland to Fitzwilliam 22 July 1792, N.R.O. Box 44/8, ff. 1–2; Fox to Portland 26 July 1792, Ad. MS. 47561, ff. 122–3, Fox Papers, printed in *Fox's Memorials*, iv. 289–90; *Malmesbury Diary*, ii. 470.

[5] Portland to Loughborough 17 Aug. 1792, Portland MSS. P.W.F. 9223; Fox to Portland 21 Aug. 1792, Ad. MS. 47561, ff. 130–1, Fox Papers.

Almost as soon as Burke had raised the issue of coalition in early June, Fox had impressed upon Portland that 'it should appear they had not acceded to Pitt's Ministry but went to it on fair and even conditions to share equally with him all the power, patronage, etc.'[1] Fox thus seemed willing to discover the possibility of negotiating a coalition but at this stage he did not set out his conditions too closely. Indeed, he initially proposed impossible conditions and by retreating from them demonstrated to Portland and the other conservative Whigs his apparently sincere desire to come to an acceptable arrangement. He insisted at first that Pitt should be excluded from a coalition ministry, but he later watered down this impossibly rigid condition to a demand that Pitt leave the Treasury.[2] It was widely believed, therefore, that he seriously intended to come to terms with Pitt. He was thus able to present Pitt, and the undeniably shady propositions which Pitt made to the conservative Whigs, as insincere and treacherous.[3] Fox's role in the second negotiation has already been mentioned. His motives in this mysterious affair are difficult to grasp. One of his primary intentions was to bring before the King the knowledge that the opposition was willing to negotiate an honourable arrangement and thus to secure the King's goodwill for a future occasion.[4] He also wished to reveal to the King Pitt's caballing with members of the Whig party.[5] Fox was still convinced that Pitt's ministry was on the point of collapse and that his attempts to detach individuals and to destroy the Whig Party were merely a reflection of Pitt's desire 'to prevent any hearty co-operation against him at a juncture in which he must feel himself so vulnerable'. The second negotiation, therefore, served Fox's purpose of demonstrating to Pitt that his hopes of dividing the party were illusory and that stiff terms would be the condition of any coalition between the government and the opposition. This might put an end to Pitt's increasingly dangerous attempts to weaken the party.[6]

[1] *Malmesbury Diary*, ii. 459.   [2] Ibid. 461–3, 468–9, 472–3.
[3] Fox to Portland 21 Aug. 1792, Ad. MS. 47561, ff. 130–1, Fox Papers; Fox to Portland 21 July 1792, loc. cit.
[4] Portland to Fox 21 July 1792, loc. cit.
[5] Fox to Portland 26 July 1792, loc. cit.
[6] Fox to Portland 21 July 1792, Ad. MS. 47561, f. 117, Fox Papers, printed in *Fox's Memorials*, iv. 286–7, c.f. the remarks of Edmund Burke in a letter to his son of 22 Aug. 1792 (N.R.O. A. xiv. 63, Burke Letters): 'Fox is convinced, that the

The unity of the party in April and May had survived, in part at least, thanks to Fox's recognition of the need for moderation. The second challenge to party unity had been resisted largely through his own skilful tactics. He was thus able to outmanœuvre Pitt and Loughborough partly because coalition was not at that time a practicable possibility but also because he used to the full such advantages as his position gave him. His incontestable influence with Portland was exercised discreetly. If Loughborough's acceptance of the Seals was contingent upon a coalition, then Portland's attitude to the ministry was of the first importance. Fox did not scorn the prospect of coalition. Rather he secured his own influence among the conservative Whigs by revealing Pitt as the person who would shrink from an honest arrangement. Fox was aided, moreover, by the fact that the conservative Whigs were divided on the subject of coalition and that there was never continuous pressure from them, Loughborough and his friends excepted, forcing Fox to involve himself too closely in negotiations. He was aided, too, by the deep-rooted suspicion of Pitt which preoccupied Portland and his followers and which the events of the summer served to confirm. There were other factors, too, which allowed Fox to dominate the political scene in the summer of 1792. The ambiguous status in the party of the Friends of the People was, in the last analysis, a matter which made men like Fitzwilliam shrink from the idea of a coalition, for the latter could never seriously entertain the prospect that Sheridan and his friends might occupy important government posts. Fox's relation to them was, at best, cloudy and imprecise and there was no certainty that he would have agreed to become part of an arrangement without their inclusion.[1] And Fox's participation in a coalition was never considered to be less than indispensable by the conservative Whigs.[2] This was a weapon which Fox did not hesitate

King is tired of Pitt, and has no Objection at all to him, that he feels himself on very elevated and very strong Ground.'

[1] *Malmesbury Diary*, ii. 465; W. Elliot to Sir Gilbert Elliot 29 June 1792, Minto ii. 44–52.

[2] In addition to their reluctance to break old friendships and their desire to retain the services of one of the most talented men of the day, the conservative Whigs may have feared that if they entered the ministry without Fox 'it would be foolish to leave him to head the discontents of the country'. Lord Sheffield to Lady Webster 21 July 1792, Ad. MS. 51845, Holland House MSS., unfoliated.

to use whenever he found it convenient to do so. His opinions on the French Revolution, on Reform, on the abolition of the slave-trade and on the repeal of the Test Act would require detailed discussion, a daunting affair, since a compromise would have to be reached not only between the Whigs and Pitt, but between Fox and the conservative Whigs. These discussions never began, for there seemed every reason to minimize as much as possible the disunion in the party.[1]

Fox's role in the tactical manœuvres of the summer had been a crucial one, but if he succeeded in his subtle attempts to counteract the dangerous moves made by Pitt and Loughborough the exact content of his victory is not immediately apparent. He had, for a time, at least, fought off the campaign to weaken and destroy the Whig party but there was nothing to indicate that such a campaign might not recur. He had consolidated his influence over the Duke of Portland, but the issue of coalition had now been raised and had attracted powerful support within the party. The Friends of the People were still a group distinct and outlawed by the conservative Whigs and, although Fox had impressed the latter with his ostensibly moderate attitude towards coalition, he had not done anything to close the rift in the party.[2] Much was to depend on future events. If the political societies were to revive, and if their activities once more became an issue in politics, then Fox could not hope to prevent the divisions in the party from deepening and he might not be able to forestall the renewal of co-operation between the lords of the party and the government. But if any man could keep the party together, then that man was Charles Fox. His motives and his beliefs were misunderstood by contemporaries and it is by no means easy to disentangle the public from the private man. It is dangerous to credit Fox with more deliberation than his personality

---

[1] *Malmesbury Diary*, ii. 459–61.

[2] In reply to Carlisle's query concerning the relationship of the Friends of the People to the party, Fox said that 'it ought to be our duty to prevent such a separation, if possible'. He admitted that, in principle, he supported the notion of coalition but 'there should be a really new Administration, in which pretensions are not to be considered by the criterion of present possession'. This, and similar pronouncements by Fox, suggest that he was attempting to satisfy the desires for office of men like Carlisle, by encouraging them to hope for office in a Whig administration. Carlisle to Fox 23 July 1792, *Fox's Memorials*, iii. 22–23; Fox to Carlisle 25 July 1792, H.M.C. *Carlisle*, 696.

would have allowed and, at a time when politics were in a peculiarly fluid state, it is misleading to attempt to construct a systematic philosophy when Fox himself never adhered to one. But Fox's mind contained a roughly shaped frame of reference within the bounds of which his ideas and his prejudices worked. His distaste for Pitt emerges even from the equivocal statements which he made during the summer. His refusal to consider serving under Pitt was too strident and too insistent to cohere with his general intention of assuming a conciliatory attitude towards the government. He distrusted Pitt's every move, as he had done in the past, and credited him with the worst possible intentions. He saw at an early stage that Pitt's contacts with the party had but one purpose and that was to weaken the opposition. Fox felt sure that Pitt might yet be brought down and replaced by a Whig administration, and it was partly to repel Pitt's overtures that he manipulated Portland so successfully during the second negotiation. Fox's role, as he himself saw it, was to preserve the unity of the party and to continue to try to overthrow Pitt by the parliamentary means which had caused the government so much embarrassment during the last two sessions of Parliament. Although he simulated an enthusiasm for coalition, he laid down conditions which could not possibly be fulfilled and his real attitude towards coalition was most probably contained in his confidential remark to his nephew, that he disliked new connections and preferred to remain as he was.[1] There is no reason to suspect that he had changed his opinions on reform or on the French Revolution but he was unwilling to face the implications which these opinions would necessarily carry with them. If Fox was the essential link which continued to hold the two wings of the party together, it might reasonably be asked whether his private opinions led him to sympathize with the radical or the conservative groups within the party. In some ways this is the vital question concerning Fox's conduct in 1792. But it was a question which Fox himself was not prepared to face. The real purpose of his policy during the summer of 1792 was to keep the party together and thus avoid having to make a choice between the two wings into which it was now divided. This explains his constant attempts to mini-

---

[1] Fox to Lord Holland 20 Aug. 1792, Ad. MS. 47571, ff. 111-12, Fox Papers, printed in *Fox's Memorials*, ii. 366-8.

mize the differences within the party, to present himself to the conservative Whigs as a friend to coalition, to strengthen his influence over the Duke of Portland and to reveal to the King and to Pitt that the party was not disunited, indeed, that it still presented a threat to Pitt's ministry, while, at the same time, its leaders were responsible men who would be ready to serve their country should they be requested to do so. By exaggerating the weakness of the government — and in this the conservative Whigs were possibly more strident than Fox — he hoped to convince men like Carlisle and Loughborough that their individual ambitions might be at hazard if they joined Pitt's shaky administration, only to be turned out of office shortly afterwards by a confident opposition party. It was to be several months before Fox found himself compelled to join forces with one of the two wings but there was nothing inevitable in the decision he ultimately made and, in the autumn of 1792, many confident voices predicted that he would soon return to respectable opinions and leave the reformers in the party.[1]

Artifices of deception and mysteries of ambiguity concealed from many of those most intimately concerned the true state of the Whig party. Portland and Fitzwilliam felt certain that Pitt had been trying to dupe them during the previous months. Both had been ready to test his sincerity and to explore the possibility of coming to an arrangement with the government which, in their view, was chronically weak and its members incompetent. 'They have no principle. They know not what *party* is, but for the desire of annihilating it, and suppose favours emoluments and Patronage a compensation for the loss of Consistency and Character'.[2] Both Portland and Fitzwilliam were ready to place their trust in Fox. Indeed, they appeared anxious lest Fox be exasperated by the activities of Loughborough's clique to the point where he might quit the party in disgust and declare his allegiance to the Friends of the People.[3] They felt confident that the growing crisis in France of August and September 1792 would demonstrate beyond all doubt that Fox's opinions and theirs on the French Revolution were not so widely separated and that he would quickly adopt their own views on

[1] Edmund Burke believed this. Burke to R. Burke jnr. *post.* 24 Aug. 1792, Wentworth Woodhouse MSS., Burke Letters 1.
[2] Portland to Burke 12 Sept. 1792, ibid.
[3] Ibid.; Fitzwilliam to Carlisle 31 Oct. 1792, H.M.C. *Carlisle*, 698–700.

the urgent need for action on the part of the English government. They never doubted that Fox's inclusion in a coalition cabinet was an absolute condition of any arrangement with the ministers.[1]

The uneasiness of the circle around Loughborough, however, strongly indicated that the many problems and difficulties attending the arrangements for a coalition had not been clarified. Were the Friends of the People still to be regarded as members of the opposition, and what was the exact nature of Fox's connection with them? Did Fox wish to insist upon the inclusion of some of their number in an arrangement with the government? Was Fox willing to serve in the same cabinet as Pitt or was he demanding the first place for himself, or perhaps for Portland? What of Fox's opinions on France, on parliamentary reform and the repeal of the Test Act? Would it be possible to satisfy Fox's party proclivities on the subject of patronage and the disposal of places? On some of these subjects Fox had given equivocal assurances but others had not even been mentioned. There had been talk of suspending systematic opposition but Fox's intention was clearly to bring Pitt down and to form a party administration. But Loughborough summed up the fears of many: 'We are to consider whether that triumph is a thing to be wished for or dreaded. I confess I should consider it a public duty to prevent it rather than promote it'.[2]

The conservative Whigs and Fox were holding the party together because they were refusing to admit the existence of intractable problems which, if revealed, could do no other than benefit the government and a few individuals in the opposition. Events at home and abroad in August and September made it impossible for these problems to go ignored for an indefinite period and allowed Loughborough and Burke to renew their machinations. Lord Loughborough had remained in close touch with Dundas during the summer, although the negotiations he had helped to instigate had collapsed in ignominious failure and had harmed rather than helped to advance the cause of coalition. He realized that the immediate prospects of achieving a coalition were not high

[1] R. Burke jnr. to Edmund and Jane Burke Aug. 1792, Wentworth Woodhouse MSS., Burke Letters 1; Portland to Loughborough 23 Aug. 1792, Portland MSS. P.W.F. 9225; Fitzwilliam to Carlisle 31 Oct. 1792, loc. cit.

[2] Loughborough to Carlisle 1 Aug. 1792, H.M.C. *Carlisle,* 696–7; Carlisle to Loughborough (n.d. autumn 1792), Campbell, *Lives of the Lord Chancellors,* vi. 345.

and he reconciled himself to the task of acting as mediator between the conservative Whigs and the government. He was assisted in this by the willingness of ministers to consider offering honours of a minor sort to the conservative Whigs and it was Loughborough who carried their proposals to the Whigs and who returned their answers. The creation of an English peerage for Stormont was, in fact, Loughborough's own idea.[1] For two months he sounded the leaders of the opposition about the possibility that one of their number might accept the vacant Governor-Generalship of India.[2] It was through Loughborough that the ministerial offer of a Garter to Portland was conveyed in July. The Duke found the offer tempting and his refusal to accept it was accompanied by signs that he did not wish to sever the contacts with the government which had been established during the previous months.[3] He naturally became the man whom the ministers most wished to impress with signs of their confidence. Thus, even before North's death on 5 August, his Riband was being spoken of as intended for Portland but once again he resisted the offer.[4] More successful than these stratagems was the election of Portland to the office of Vice-Chancellor of Oxford University, a post of great public prestige and one subject to political considerations. The ministers did everything, short of lending their official support to the Duke's candidature. They suggested his name, countenanced his nomination and watched the progress of the election anxiously. Portland was clearly delighted

---

[1] Dundas to Loughborough 26 and 30 June, 19 July 1792, S.R.O. G.D.51. 1/17/6, 7, 8, Melville Castle MSS.

[2] *Malmesbury Diary*, ii. 468–9; *Windham Diary*, 257–8; Fox to Portland 21 July 1792, Ad. MS. 47561, f. 117, Fox Papers, printed in *Fox's Memorials*, iv. 286–7.

[3] Portland asked Fox's advice but returned his answer to Loughborough before Fox had replied. He told Loughborough that 'it would be misunderstood by many & especially by many of those who look up to me', 21 July 1792, Portland MSS. P.W.F. 9221. The Duke regarded his refusal as consistent with his co-operation with the ministry on the Proclamation in May and he refused to go further. 'It is an additional act in affirmance of our Claim to public confidence.' Portland to Fitzwilliam 22 July 1792, N.R.O. Box 44/8, ff. 1–2. Fox's hostility to the offer was grounded on the view that it would, if accepted, provoke fresh divisions at a juncture when Pitt 'must feel himself so vulnerable'. Fox to Portland 21 July 1792, Ad. MS. 47561, f. 117, Fox Papers, printed in *Fox's Memorials*, iv. 286–7.

[4] Pitt to Lord Grenville 22 July 1792, H.M.C. *Dropmore*, ii. 294; Dundas to Loughborough 29 Aug. 1792, S.R.O. G.D.51. 1/17/13, Melville Castle MSS.

and flattered to be put forward. In the election he defeated the other candidate, the Duke of Beaufort, and the installation which took place in early October marked the return to public respectability of the conservative Whigs.[1]

These marks of favour were undoubtedly regarded as political necessities of the first order by the ministers. They had been sorely embarrassed at the interview of the Duke of Leeds with George III, 'a measure which could not possibly produce any one good Consequence', and they were at pains to bring the conservative Whigs to understand that ministerial changes might take place only with 'caution and reserve'.[2] At the same time, they were aware of the suspicion with which they were regarded by the Whig lords and they were anxious to dispel it.[3] Dundas made it plain to Loughborough that the idea of a coalition must be dropped, although friendly contacts should be maintained between government and opposition, and he hinted that Loughborough himself was welcome to take the Seals whenever he felt able to do so.[4] But Loughborough would not take office unless his acceptance was part of a wider arrangement and, in the middle of September, he confessed that there was little hope of coalition: 'I have for some time dismissed the subject from my thoughts'.[5]

The impasse which had been reached in the relations between government and opposition could not endure the impossible strains to which party alignments in England were subjected by the mounting crisis on the continent. The September Massacres horrified English opinion and hushed the reformers into an abject silence, but there were as yet no indications of a Royalist spirit at work in the country.[6]

[1] Dundas to Loughborough 8 Aug. 1792, S.R.O. G.D.51. 1/17/9, Melville Castle MSS.; Dundas to Loughborough 15 Aug. 1792, S.R.O. G.D.51. 1/20/1; Pitt to Grenville 9 Aug. 1792, H.M.C. *Dropmore*, ii. 299–300; Portland to Laurence 22 Aug. 1792, Portland MSS. P.W.F. 6243.

[2] Dundas to Loughborough 21 Aug. 1792, S.R.O. G.D.51. 1/17/11, Melville Castle MSS.

[3] Dundas to Loughborough (n.d. 1792), S.R.O. G.D.51. 1/20/9.

[4] Dundas to Loughborough 29 Aug. 1792, S.R.O. G.D.51. 1/17/13.

[5] Loughborough to Burke 15 Sept. 1792, Wentworth Woodhouse MSS., Burke Letters 1.

[6] According to Portland, Fox had been disgusted by the events of Aug. in Paris. Portland to Loughborough 23 Aug. 1792, loc. cit.; *The Morning Chronicle* of 12 Sept. 1792 condemned the Massacres.

Although the sympathies of the cabinet were partisan, it adhered to a policy of neutrality in the war between France and the allies.[1] The failure of the English government to take action goaded Edmund Burke to fury. His representations with the ministers were abruptly dismissed and he was told that the government would tolerate no further interference by the Burkes in the affairs of Ireland.[2] To his disappointment, the ministry would do nothing to help the *émigrés* who were flowing to England in rapidly increasing numbers. Burke began to suspect that the ministers themselves would soon be responsible for countenancing the spread of French principles in England if their conduct did not change.[3] Yet he desperately needed the support of Pitt and Dundas if the impeachment were to continue and therefore he swallowed the bitter pill of Shore's appointment to the post of Governor-General of Bengal.[4] Burke realized that the fate of Europe depended upon Pitt's ministry. He could do no other, therefore, than pledge himself to its support, 'whether you stand alone, whether you aggregate some portion of the minority to you, or whether you blend and amalgamate the whole into one mass'.[5]

Even before the September Massacres had lent added urgency to the problems in the Whig party, Burke had changed his earlier view that Fox might be won back to respectable opinions and that a coalition might be negotiated which included Fox. Burke saw that Portland was falling increasingly under the influence of Fox, that Fox would not

[1] The reforming societies feared that Pitt would go to war on the side of the allies. Butterfield, 'Charles James Fox', 316–17. J. T. Murley, 'The Origin and Outbreak of the Anglo-French War of 1793' (unpublished D.Phil. dissertation, Oxford, 1959), 42–45.

[2] Burke to Grenville 18 Aug. 1792, Wentworth Woodhouse MSS., Burke Letters 10, printed in *Correspondence of Edmund Burke*, iii. 503–11, and in H.M.C. *Dropmore*, ii. 463–6; Lord Grenville to Burke 6 Sept. 1792, Wentworth Woodhouse MSS., Burke Letters 1. On Ireland, see Dundas to R. Burke jnr. 1 Aug. 1792, ibid., and Richard's notes of a conversation with Pitt in Sept., ibid., Burke Letters 8d.

[3] Burke to Grenville 19 Sept. 1792, ibid., Burke Letters 1 (copy), printed in *Correspondence of Edmund Burke*, iv. 5–8.

[4] Burke to Dundas 8 Oct. 1792, ibid., Burke Letters 1; Dundas to Burke 19 Oct. 1792, N.R.O. A. iv. 32, Burke Letters.

[5] Burke to Dundas 8 Oct. 1792, loc. cit.

break with the reformers in the party and that he had no real interest in a coalition which left Pitt at the Treasury. Coalition was now necessary as a union of forces against Jacobinism at home and abroad. Because Fox could never agree to this, Burke saw that the conservative Whigs must separate from Fox if a coalition were to be made.[1] The progress of the campaign on the Continent, Brunswick's defeat at Valmy, the subsequent retreat of the Prussian Army and the series of reverses culminating in the dramatic French victory at Jemappes on 6 November[2] provoked an upsurge of popular feeling in England which both encouraged the activities of existing political associations and gave birth to new ones.[3] The reaction of the government was fraught with political implications of the first importance. Ministers did not fear direct rebellion. What they dreaded was French interference in domestic affairs and the prospect, much overrated by contemporaries, that she might rouse the societies to armed rebellion.[4] The contamination of French principles was spreading to every community in the land and, therefore, propaganda, loyal addresses and government edicts were all inadequate to deal with the situation.[5] The crisis could be met only if 'the magistrates and gentlemen of the country' were active in their localities, if they informed the government of republican movements, if they assisted the government in their suppression, and if they strove to mount a loyalist reaction in defence of the constitution.[6] Here,

---

[1] Edmund and Jane Burke to William Burke 3 Sept. 1792, Wentworth Woodhouse MSS. Burke Letters 1, printed in *Correspondence of Edmund Burke*, iii. 514–522.

[2] *The Morning Chronicle* exulted in the French victories, e.g. 10 Oct. 1792.

[3] On the subject of the agitation of the societies at this time see, *inter alia*, Brunsdon, 'The Friends of the People', 105–14; Murley 'Anglo-French War of 1793', 57–59. 162–77; Butterfield, 'Charles James Fox', 317; Holland Rose, *Pitt and the Great War*, 62–69; Veitch, *Genesis of Reform*, 220–30.

[4] For the (limited) activities of French secret agents, see Murley, op. cit., 62–85, 161–2, 180; Grenville to Auckland 6 Nov. 1792, *Auckland*, ii. 464–7.

[5] For the government's propaganda system in England and Scotland, see Long to Dundas 10 Oct. 1792, Arniston Letter Book no. 75, Arniston MSS. There was, at this time, much talk and expectation of forthcoming government measures. Even Adam was alarmed at the extremism of the reformers and wished to found a moderate, reforming newspaper. Sir R. Adair to Adam 12 Oct. 1792, Blair-Adam MSS.

[6] The government was doing little. Its first official action was the circular letter of 25 Nov. See Veitch, op. cit., 235.

then, was an overwhelming case for coalition. The lords and gentlemen of the Whig party must co-operate with the government in stem-
ming the flow of democratic republicanism in a crisis which could not
afford the luxury of party political warfare. The ministry's parliamentary majority was not in danger but the palpable weakness of Pitt
and his colleagues in allowing the country to come near to being
overrun by the Jacobins could only be overcome if government
received a voluntary accession of strength and thereby revived its
flagging morale and reputation.[1]

The crisis of October and November brought Edmund Burke to
a further intervention in the affairs of his country, and indeed, in those
of Europe, although he well knew that he had 'no connexion of interest
with either ministry or opposition'.[2] He had long preached that the
French Revolution presented a direct military threat to Europe and
that this threat could have been allayed had military intervention been
used earlier. At the root of all his actions lay the conviction that there
was now little hope of preventing the French dominating the continent
and England as well, and for this the supineness of ministers was responsible.[3] He saw Pitt on 7 November but could not shake the neutrality
which had been proclaimed in July. Despairing of the attitude of the
ministry, he turned to the conservative Whigs. He reiterated his plea that
they should separate from the reformers, 'for otherwise this false appearance of union is itself a source of the greatest distraction'. The conservative Whigs should assure ministers of their decided support 'in a line of
measures against the doctrinal arms of France' with a view to bringing
them 'to act in a very different sort of spirit from any that they had
hitherto Shewn'.[4] Burke was assisted in his self-appointed duty by
Loughborough, who was by this time in close consultation with

[1] For charges of neglect and weakness from one friendly to ministers, see
Buckingham to Grenville 8, 15 Nov. 1792, *Court and Cabinets*, ii. 326–8, 333. That
the ministers were genuinely alarmed at this time is indisputable. See Butterfield,
op. cit., 330 postscript; Murley, op. cit., 177–9.

[2] Burke to R. Burke jnr. 2 Nov. 1792, Wentworth Woodhouse MSS., Burke
Letters 1, printed in *Correspondence of Edmund Burke*, iv. 24–29.

[3] Burke to R. Burke jnr. 17 Oct. 1792, Wentworth Woodhouse MSS., Burke
Letters 1, printed in *Correspondence of Edmund Burke*, iv. 19–24; Burke to Fitzwilliam 29 Nov. 1792, ibid. Burke Letters 1.

[4] Burke to Fitzwilliam 29 Nov. 1792, ibid. Burke Letters 1.

ministers, and there was open talk of his receiving the Seals.[1] A further supporter of the idea of a coalition was Windham, who was on intimate terms both with Fox and with the conservative Whigs.[2] This triumvirate met several times on 11 and 12 November. Wisely, they accepted for the present the fact that Portland was implacable on the subject of coalition and they adopted as their aim the suspension of 'active opposition, for the purpose of changing the Ministry, or even for disabling it in its operations'.[3]

Burke and Windham met Pitt on 13 November. They hinted that strong measures in the present crisis would meet with the approval of the conservative Whigs but Pitt required 'more certain and definite assurances of support from the heads of the party before the meeting of parliament'.[4] To ensure that these were obtained, Pitt formally offered the Seals to Loughborough on 18 November.[5] Burke and Windham toiled away at the task of pushing the conservative Whigs into a closer arrangement with the government but, by 20 November, their failure had become apparent.[6] The lords of the party held views which were different in many respects from those of the two propagandists of coalition. Although Portland had withdrawn his previous objections to the allied invasion of France, and although he could not 'see with indifference the strides which France is making to universal domination & disorder', his opinions on the desirability of interference in the continental war, which Burke and Windham were preaching, remained ambiguous. And although he approved of the interviews

[1] Dundas to Loughborough 13 Oct. 1792, S.R.O. G.D.51. 1/20/4–9, Melville Castle MSS.

[2] *Windham Diary*, 266–7.

[3] Portland to Fitzwilliam 17 Oct. 1792, Wentworth Woodhouse MSS., F. 31a; Burke to Fitzwilliam 29 Nov. 1792, ibid. Burke Letters 1. Burke to R. Burke jnr. 18 Nov. 1792, ibid. Burke Letters 1, printed in *Correspondence of Edmund Burke*, iii. 523–30 (incorrectly dated Sept. 1792).

[4] Burke to Fitzwilliam 29 Nov. 1792, loc. cit.; Butterfield, op. cit., 320–1.

[5] Pitt to Dundas 15 Nov. 1792, Aspinall, *Later Correspondence of George III*, 1. 630 n.1; Pitt to Loughborough 17 Nov. 1792, Campbell, *Lives of the Lord Chancellors*, vi. 346; Pitt to Grenville 18 Nov. 1792, H.M.C. *Dropmore*, ii. 335–6.

[6] Burke to Fitzwilliam 29 Nov. 1792, loc. cit.; Burke to R. Burke jnr. 18 Nov. 1792, loc. cit.

with the ministers which had taken place he was not prepared to allow Loughborough to accept the Seals.[1] Tom Grenville and Fitzwilliam were prepared to follow Burke and Windham to the point of suspending systematic opposition, but they evinced alarm at the talk of war against France. War, they held, would provoke distress and arouse the people, thus diminishing their resistance to contamination from French principles.[2] The autumn crisis, therefore, had not reduced the significance of the divisions among the conservative Whigs while, as Pitt observed, 'there still appears to be too much uncertainty in their conduct'.[3] As the King put it, they were indeed 'much less fixed in their resolution to support' government than Burke and Windham had calculated. He was henceforward rather exasperated with them.[4] Burke retreated to the peace of Beaconsfield, and Windham, his burst of energy exhausted, plunged 'through doubts and perplexities into a sort of repose'.[5]

Not for the first — or the last — time it was upon Fox that the continuation of the precarious unity in the party depended. The savage occurrences in France of former months had depressed and discouraged him. But his real sympathies should not be obscured by what he told Portland and others. His disgust at the September Massacres had been matched by his exultation on hearing the news of the retreat of the

---

[1] Portland to Loughborough 23 Nov. 1792, Portland MSS. P.W.F. 9230; Portland to Fitzwilliam 17, 27 Oct. 1792, Wentworth Woodhouse MSS., F. 31a; Portland to Loughborough 16 Nov. 1792, Portland MSS. P.W.F. 9229.

[2] Tom Grenville to Fitzwilliam 15, 17 and 24 Nov. 1792, N.R.O. Box 44. The details of the measures advocated by Windham and Burke were: republican publications should be suppressed, the country should be placed in a posture of defence and be prepared to assist the allies. Windham to Fitzwilliam 17 Nov. 1792, N.R.O. Box 44.

[3] Pitt to the King 25 Nov. 1792, Aspinall, *Later Correspondence of George III*, i. 630. Pitt and Windham met on 24 Nov. Loughborough saw Pitt on the following day to tell of his refusal of the Seals. *The Public Advertiser*, 28 Nov. 1792; *Windham Diary*, 267.

[4] The King to Pitt 26 Nov. 1792, Aspinall, *Later Correspondence of George III*, i. 630 n.2.

[5] Burke to Loughborough 28 Nov. 1792, Wentworth Woodhouse MSS., Burke Letters 1 (copy).

allies.[1] Yet his opinions were still ambiguous. Windham and Lough-borough, for example, found themselves unable to tell Pitt very much about them and Portland persisted in putting the story around that Fox was horrified by what the French were doing.[2] Even the ministerial press carried reports that Fox was drifting away from the radicals in the party.[3] In reality, Fox saw nothing alarming in the state of Europe after Jemappes and he regarded the impending English law against aliens as 'abominable'.[4]

But Fox could not conceal his opinions now that the Seals had been offered to Loughborough, when overtures with the ministry had been renewed and while Portland and others were desperate to obtain his advice.[5] Before the end of November, his letters and his conversations indicated beyond all doubt that he did not believe Europe to be threatened by the French, 'that the danger to this Country chiefly consisted in the growth of Tory principles', that he was cheered by the failure of the allies and 'extremely chagrined and exasperated' by the initiatives which had been taken by Burke and Windham.[6] Some traces of ambiguity and deception remained but Fox, at bottom, was losing the will and the desire to simulate his real feelings and opinions in a situation which was allowing him less room for manœuvre.[7] The impossibility of his position weakened his political grasp. He convinced

[1] Fox to Lord Holland (n.d. Sept. 1792), Ad. MS. 47571, f. 16, Fox Papers, printed in *Fox's Memorials*, ii. 370–1; 12 Oct. 1792, ibid. f. 18, printed in *Fox's Memorials*, ii. 371–5; Fox to Mrs. Armistead 7 Oct. 1792, ibid. 47570, ff. 189–90.

[2] Pitt to Grenville 18 Nov. 1792, H.M.C. *Dropmore*, ii. 335–6; Windham to J. C. Hippisley 28 Mar. 1793, Ad. MS. 37848, ff. 59–66, Windham Papers, i. 113–120; Fitzwilliam to Carlisle 31 Oct. 1792, H.M.C. *Carlisle*, 698–700.

[3] *The Public Advertiser*, 24 and 27 Sept., 4 and 27 Oct. 1792. It is interesting that Carlisle, who was unusually suspicious of Fox, acquitted him of any love for parliamentary reform. Carlisle to Fitzwilliam 19 Oct. 1792, N.R.O. Box 44.

[4] Fox to Lord Holland 23 Nov. 1792, *Fox's Memorials*, ii. 378–80.

[5] Tom Grenville to Fitzwilliam 17 Nov. 1792, loc. cit.; Burke to Fitzwilliam 29 Nov. 1792, Wentworth Woodhouse MSS., Burke Letters 1.

[6] Ibid.; Portland to Fitzwilliam 30 Nov. 1792, Wentworth Woodhouse MSS., F.31a; Burke to Loughborough 28 Nov. 1792; Campbell, *Lives of the Lord Chancellors*, vi. 347–8; Loughborough to Burke 30 Nov. 1792, Wentworth Woodhouse MSS., Burke Letters 1; Fox to Lord Holland 23 Nov. 1792, loc. cit.

[7] Portland to Fitzwilliam 30 Nov. 1792, loc. cit.; Fox to Adair 26 and 29 Nov. 1792, *Fox's Memorials*, ii. 257–9, 259–63.

himself that he could not restrain the lords of the party from suspending opposition. In a fury of frustration Fox determined to bring Pitt down by 'a violent and hostile opposition'. He made no further attempts to paper over the yawning chasms in the party and seemed to enjoy flouting the feelings and wishes of some of its most influential members.[1] To add to his problems, the revival of the activities of the Friends of the People in early November was accompanied by violent and extreme language such as to worry even Grey. The problem of their status in the party must inevitably be raised once more, in a situation which would allow Fox little hope of bridging the gap in the party as he had done for the last six months.[2] And while the reformers in the party were becoming significantly less moderate, the conservative Whigs feared so strongly the forces which the Friends of the People might arouse that some of their number participated in the loyal Associations.[3] Not that their alarmism should be exaggerated. They did not believe that revolution in England was imminent. They wished merely to safeguard the country from the possible spread of the democratic contagion.[4] The Proclamation which was issued by the government on

[1] Burke to Fitzwilliam 29 Nov. 1792, loc. cit.; Anstruther to Windham 30 Nov. 1792, Ad. MS. 37873, f. 181–2, Windham Papers.

[2] Grey to Dalrymple 7 Nov. 1792; Tierney to Grey 29 Oct. and 4 Nov. 1792, Grey MSS., University of Durham; Black, *The Association*, 248; *The Morning Chronicle* (e.g. 22, 26 Nov. 1792) had thrown off the mask and had declared Fox's attachment to parliamentary reform. The paper gave publicity to the Association's activities, including the connections of some of its members with France (20 Nov. 1792). Yet Fox himself was against bringing forward reform proposals at this time, whereas the Friends of the People decided in early Nov. to introduce a motion for parliamentary reform during the coming session. Tierney to Grey 5 Nov., 15 Nov. 1792, Grey MSS.

[3] J. Anstruther to Windham 30 Nov. 1792, loc. cit.; A. Mitchell, 'The Association Movement of 1792–1793', *Historical Journal* (1961), iv(1), 59; for a rather different view of the loyal Associations, and one which lessens their importance as a means of suppressing sedition, see D. Ginter, 'The Loyalist Association Movement of 1792–1793 and British Public Opinion', *Historical Journal* (1966), ix(2), 179–90. The best account of the loyal Associations is that by Black (*The Association*, 233–74).

[4] Portland to Windham 30 Nov. 1792, Ad. MS. 37845, f. 7, Windham Papers; W. Elliot to Sir Gilbert Elliot 19 Nov. 1792, Minto, ii. 73–75; J. Anstruther to Windham 30 Nov. 1792, loc. cit. It is difficult to emphasize strongly enough the

1 December was therefore looked upon by them as a necessary pre-
cautionary measure, not the less welcome for being long overdue.

The Proclamation ordered the embodiment of the Militia, a matter
which could only be justified on the pretext of insurrection and on
condition that parliament be assembled within fourteen days. Fox's
anger knew no bounds:

> If they mention danger of *Insurrection,* or rather as they must do to legalise
> their proceeedings, of *Rebellion,* surely the first measure all honest men ought
> to take is to impeach them for so wicked and detestable a falsehood. I fairly
> own that, if they have done this I shall grow savage, and not think French
> *lanterne* too bad for them. Surely it is impossible — if anything were impossible
> for such monsters, who, for the purpose of weakening or destroying the honour-
> able connection of the Whigs, would not scruple to run the risk of a civil war.
> I cannot trust myself to write any more, for I confess I am too much heated.[1]

Fox spent 1 December with Portland at Burlington House, where
Fitzwilliam met them in the evening. Fitzwilliam reported Fox's
sentiments as follows:

> I by no means like him: He would be ready to defend Holland, beyond that I
> think he would not stir one step: his object is to direct our attention to the
> internal measures of Govt.: the breach of Law in calling out the militia &
> calling of Parlt. in an unusual manner, & upon false pretences etc.[2]

On 4 December Fox attended a meeting of the Whig Club at which he
denounced the loyal Associations. His violent condemnation of the only
bodies which, in the views of the lords of the party, might save the
country might well suggest that Fox saw no danger from the French

---

feelings of the conservative Whigs towards the government at this time. Whilst
wishing to support it in the present crisis, its proven incompetence in allowing the
danger to get out of hand made several of the Whigs think very carefully indeed
before they would seriously consider union with such a set of supposedly inept
ministers.

[1] Fox to Portland 1 Dec. 1792, Ad. MS. 47561, ff. 133–4, Fox Papers, printed in
Fox's Memorials, iv. 291–2. See a similar letter from Fox to Adam of the same date
in the Blair-Adam MSS.

[2] Lord Fitzwilliam to Lady Fitzwilliam (n.d.) letters of late 1792 to early 1793,
N.R.O. Box 45. Even the normally alarmist Fitzwilliam was sceptical of the validity
of Pitt's reasons for calling parliament and was well aware that, except for a few
sporadic and widely separated outbreaks of violence, the country was quiet.

and that his anger at Pitt's latest manœuvres left him insensible to pleas of party unity.[1]

Events were set in train by Pitt, who requested that the conservative Whigs should approve the King's speech. Portland expressed himself particularly satisfied with the passages relating to internal security. The die was cast.[2] There was no reconciling Fox with the Whig Lords. He thought the alarm was 'totally groundless' and was affronted by their remarks that Pitt had not gone far enough and that he had acted at too late a date. They regarded the opening of the Scheldt as sufficient motive for aiding the Dutch — a point which Fox could not accept. On 12 December, the eve of the debate, the party leaders met and agreed not to divide the Houses of Parliament on the following day as a mark of their support of Pitt's internal policy. When Fox heard of this, 'he with an oath declared *that there was no address at this moment Pitt could frame, he would not propose an amendment to, and divide the House upon*'.[3]

The debates of 13 to 15 December dispelled any hopes that may have been entertained that the party might still have held together in spite of its chronic divisions. Fox went further than he might have done. Not only did he proclaim to the world the opinions he had expressed in private. He committed himself to opposing the aliens Bill and promised to maintain the cause of reform by persisting in his efforts to repeal the Test Act and by reviving his exertions to secure the reform of parliament. His undoubtedly sincere desire to avoid a European war led him to propose the recognition of the French republic. By attacking ministerial policy at home and abroad, he only threw into clearer relief his own opinions and thus demonstrated their incompatibility

[1] *The Morning Chronicle*, 5 Dec. 1792; Butterfield, 'Charles James Fox', 327–9; J. Watkins, *Memoirs of Sheridan* (2 vols., 1817), ii. 165.

[2] Pitt to Loughborough 7, 9 Dec. 1792, Campbell, *Lives of the Lord Chancellors*, vi. 346.

[3] *Malmesbury Diary*, ii. 473–5; Elliot to his wife 13 Dec. 1792, Minto, ii. 79–82; on 11 Dec., Fox wrote to Mrs. Armistead (Ad. MS. 47570, ff. 191–2, Fox Papers). 'I am not very sanguine about the *continuance* of our union because I see so many persons on both sides so maliciously set upon breaking it, but one must hope for the best.' A few hours before the debate on 13 Dec., he wrote: 'I am afraid there will not appear so much Union as I had hoped, but still it will not be so bad as I once feared, & possibly things may mend.' (Ibid. ff. 193–4.)

with those of the conservative Whigs. Although the Whig lords contributed half a dozen 'charity votes' to the minority on 13 December, and although Tom Grenville gave Fox an equivocal support in the debate, it did not go unrecognized that Fox relied almost entirely on the radicals in the party for votes and speeches.[1] The distress which he felt at the ending of his private and political friendships with the Whig lords was offset by the fact that he took for granted the righteousness of his own conduct. The fact that his momentous decision had been made strengthened his determination to uphold his opinions and to fight once again the struggle for liberty which he imagined the Whig party of the age of North to have conducted.[2] These debates widened the split in the party by making it public, by making political loyalties contingent upon voting behaviour, by making conduct a test of opinions. When allowance has been made for the six 'charity votes', the four followers of Lansdowne and the three independents who voted with Fox, there remain thirty-seven members of the party who voted with Fox in the division of 13 December. Contemporaries were thus justified in regarding the strength of the conservative Whigs at something over one hundred.[3] In the following months, however, it was to become apparent that Fox could summon over sixty members to vote in the minority. For the present his following was negligible and he did not divide the House again before the holidays.

The awful clarity with which Fox had propounded his provocative ideas convinced several of the more prominent conservative Whigs

[1] On 15 Dec., the violence of Courtenay and M. A. Taylor received the condemnation it deserved. Five other speakers supported Fox, all of them Friends of the People. For a hostile discussion of the 'charity votes', see *Malmesbury Diary*, ii. 476.

[2] 'Let no man be deterred by the dread of being in a minority', 13 Dec. 1792. *The Parliamentary History*, xxx. 24. The old social routine, which had done so much to keep the party together, was crumbling at this time. See *Malmesbury Diary*, ii. 479; for the Duke of York's hostility to Fox, see Wilkins, *Mrs. Fitzherbert and George IV*, 293; see the bitter speeches made by Sheffield and Stanley on 14 Dec., *The Parliamentary History*, xxx. 81–82. Fox confided his distress to Mrs. Armistead in his letters of 15 and 18 Dec. Ad. MS. 47570, ff. 195–6, 197–8, Fox Papers.

[3] *Malmesbury Diary*, ii. 482–3; Dundas to the King 20 Jan. 1793, Aspinall, *Later Correspondence of George III*, i. 645–6; Elliot to his wife 18 Dec. 1792, Minto, ii. 84–85; this latter is the most reliable estimate. See Appendix 1. Fox was depressed with his 'miserable' division. Fox to Mrs. Armistead 15 Dec. 1792, loc. cit.

that the time had come when Portland could no longer delay issuing a declaration of separation from Fox. If he did not do so, then they would fall under the stigma of unpopularity under which Fox was now labouring, and their reputations and influence would suffer. It was both dangerous and unnecessary to allow the voting behaviour of some of Portland's kinsmen to create the impression that the conservative Whigs shared Fox's views, an impression which Fox's newspapers were spreading. The conservative Whigs did not want coalition; they wished to support government as a separate body. Unless Portland made some such declaration as they were suggesting, the party would disintegrate and its members go over to the ministry as individuals.[1]

During the three weeks which followed the opening debates of the session, the leading conservative Whigs sought to bring Portland to make a public declaration of his separation from Fox.[2] Their efforts were fruitless. The party was not destroyed. Behind the intrigue and the contradiction which characterized these proceedings lay several factors which explain why Loughborough was forced to enter the government alone. Fox retained his close friendship with Portland and exercised continuously that unchallengeable influence which had already done much to keep the party together. Whenever the conservative Whigs exerted pressure upon Portland, Fox was ready to counter-act their influence and to dissuade Portland from entering upon courses of action which might presage dangerous and unintended consequences.[3] Not that Portland needed very much persuasion.

[1] *Malmesbury Diary*, ii. 476–9; Elliot to his wife, 18 Dec. 1792, Minto, ii. 84–85; *The Public Advertiser* of 20 Dec. 1792 reported rumours that Portland, Spencer and Rawdon were being considered for the post of Lord-Lieutenant of Ireland.

[2] Windham to Hippisley 28 Mar. 1793, loc. cit.; *Malmesbury Diary*, ii. 476–98; Minto, ii. 84–98; Portland to Fitzwilliam 29/30 Dec. 1792, Wentworth Woodhouse MSS., F.31a.

[3] Fox saw Portland on 16 Dec., shortly after Elliot and his friends had been with him. *Malmesbury Diary*, ii. 478–9. As Burke noted with exasperation, Fox condemned the loyal Associations on 17 Dec. and joined one on the following day. *Observations on the Conduct of the Minority* in *Burke's Works*, i. 615–16. *The Public Advertiser*, 20 Dec. 1792, commented on Fox's moderate speech on that occasion. Fox was quick to contest Elliot's assertion in the Commons on 28 Dec. that he had Portland's authority to declare the party to be divided. Portland to Fitzwilliam 29/30 Dec. loc. cit.: *Malmesbury Diary*, ii. 492–3; Elliot to his wife, 29 Dec. 1792, Minto, ii. 96–98.

Although he lacked the political arts of Fox, he was no less unwilling to put an end to the party. Coalition was out of the question. His duty was to do what he could to defend the constitution. He might thus support ministers on particular measures directed towards this end. He was uneasy at much of Fox's conduct but he believed that Fox's motives, unlike those of some of the conservative Whigs, were pure and that he had at heart only the best interests of his country. The crisis might pass and it might then once more be possible for the party to act together. There seemed to Portland no adequate reason which might justify a separation from Fox and he had no intention of issuing or making the declaration which the conservative Whigs were demanding.[1] Even Windham had reservations about separating from Fox. If Portland did leave him, then he would be seduced by the republicans and might become their leader, a dangerous and powerful adversary. Windham did not, as Malmesbury says, believe that an 'irreperable breach' with Fox was necessary at this stage.[2] He was closer to Portland than any of the other conservative Whigs except Fitzwilliam. He kept Portland informed of their activities and impressed upon him the fact that they spoke only for themselves and not for the body of the party.[3] On more than one occasion during these confusing days, he acted as Portland's confidant and seems to have assisted the Duke in his attempts to keep the conservative Whigs at bay.[4]

Political tension within the party eased on 4 January when the delayed Christmas recess at last allowed politicians to leave town for three weeks. The news that Fitzwilliam was in complete agreement with Portland on the subject of a separation from Fox discouraged

[1] Portland to Fitzwilliam 29/30 Dec. 1792, loc. cit.; Portland to Loughborough 27 Dec. 1792, copy in the Portland MSS. P.W.F. 9231.

[2] *Malmesbury Diary*, ii. 481.

[3] Portland to Fitzwilliam, 29/30 Dec. 1792, loc. cit.; Windham to T. W. Coke 21 Dec. 1792 quoted in A. M. Stirling, *Coke of Norfolk and his Friends* (2 vols., 1912), i. 390–2.

[4] *Malmesbury Diary*, ii. 494–5; Portland to Fitzwilliam, 29/30 Dec. loc. cit.; on 15 Dec. Windham denied that he and Fox were divided by 'a difference that amounted to principle' (*The Parliamentary History*, xxx. 100–1), but on 4 Jan. he announced that he was no longer in systematic opposition to ministers (*The Parliamentary History*, xxx. 214–16).

further attempts to influence the Duke, and the pressure on him slackened.[1] By this time, the ministers had ceased to hope that Loughborough could bring Portland to declare a more whole-hearted support of administration and they renewed their initiatives on 9 January by offering Loughborough the Seals. He and Malmesbury made one final effort to influence the Duke by writing to him on 12 January. Portland did not reply and on the eighteenth Loughborough at last made his decision to accept the Seals.[2] If Loughborough had been tortured by the prospect of taking office as an individual, he must have congratulated himself when his action was almost immediately justified by events on the continent. The news of Louis XVI's death-sentence was received in England on 21 January, that of his death on the 24th. Nothing since the September Massacres had impressed public opinion in England so much and Loughborough's ostensibly patriotic action needed no apology. In terms of the internal politics of the Whig party, events seemed to vindicate Loughborough's decision even more thoroughly.[3]

The success of the loyal Associations had been so much resented by the reformers in the Whig party that in December, led by Grey and Erskine, they founded the Association for Preserving the Freedom of the Press. Its activities at first seem to have centred upon Erskine's defence of Paine but the failure of Erskine forced the Association to generalize its complaints against the loyal Associations.[4] The Association was closely connected with the Friends of the People and many members were common to both. The date and circumstances of its formation, however, and the membership of men like Tooke gave it

---

[1] Portland to Fitzwilliam, 29/30 Dec. 1792, loc. cit. Malmesbury commented that 'much depended' on Fitzwilliam's views, *Malmesbury Diary*, ii. 496. See also ibid. ii. 497–8.

[2] Ibid. ii. 498–500; Loughborough to Burke 19 Jan. 1793, Wentworth Woodhouse MSS., Burke Letters 1.

[3] 'How miserable have these Frenchmen by their wild extravagant & unfeeling cruelty stained the noblest cause that ever was in the hands of Man.' Fox to O'Brien 23 Jan. 1793, Ad. MS. 51467, Holland House MSS.

[4] *The Morning Chronicle* of 5 Dec. 1792 announced the formation of a new society. For the Association, see Black, *The Association*, 253–5; Brunsdon, 'Friends of the People', 215–16; the Association first met on 19 Dec. and voted thanks to Erskine for his defence of Paine, *The Morning Herald*, 21 Dec. 1792.

the worst possible reputation.[1] A joint meeting of the two societies was planned for 19 January, a fact which did not fail to have political implications which embarrassed the leaders of the Whig party. The meeting passed resolutions supporting reform and condemning the loyal Associations, toasted the Foxite M.P.s, witnessed a violent harangue on the ministers from Sheridan and heard a lengthy panegyric on Fox. 'My conduct', wrote Loughborough, 'requires no excuse after last Saturday's scene at the Crown and Anchor.'[2] Portland was worried by these developments but thought that the meeting 'may give Chas. F. a very fair opportunity of securing himself to his true friends'.[3] He was at this time under great pressure from the conservative Whigs and the Prince of Wales but persisted in the view that the split in the party was no more than 'a temporary or occasional, separation'.[4] Despite his intrigues, Loughborough entered the ministry alone. There seemed now every reason to believe that the storm had been weathered, that despite its paralysing divisions, the party might hold together yet longer and thus find some opportunity of repairing its damaged fabric.[5]

When parliament assembled after the recess these hopes swiftly disappeared. On 1 February Fox and his followers went to all lengths, short of excusing the execution of Louis XVI, to defend and explain away every action of the French during the last six months. Fox acknowledged the sovereignty of the people and declared that the English crown was elective. The inevitability of war was driving him

---

[1] For Burke's comments on the members, see *Observations*, in *Burke's Works*, i. 616; the Association was discussed in the Commons on 6 May 1793 by Morningington and Whitbread. *The Parliamentary History*, xxx. 869, 884–5.

[2] Loughborough to Carlisle 21 Jan. 1793, H.M.C. *Carlisle*, 701; the meeting is very fully reported in *The Morning Chronicle* of 21 Jan.; *The Public Advertiser* of 22 Jan. dismissed the meeting as a frivolity.

[3] Portland to Fitzwilliam 25 Jan. 1793, Wentworth Woodhouse MSS., F.31a.

[4] The Prince to Portland and Portland's reply of 21 Jan. 1793, Aspinall, *Correspondence of George, Prince of Wales*, ii. 329–36; *Malmesbury Diary*, ii. 503–4.

[5] Loughborough was encouraging the conservative Whigs to expect office. Loughborough to Carlisle, two letters of 21 Jan. 1793, H.M.C. *Carlisle*, 700–1; *Malmesbury Diary*, ii. 501–2; Malmesbury to Elliot 21 Jan. 1793, Minto, ii. 106–7; Elliot to his wife 5 Feb. 1793, Minto, ii. 112.

along the road to pacifism.[1] When the declaration of war arrived on 9 February, certain of the conservative Whigs could be restrained no longer. Accepting Windham's rather hesitant leadership, they met on 10 February and, deciding that a reunion with Fox was impossible, they declared their separation from him. 'As Portland will not call us together, nor act as our chief, we have taken this method of manifesting that we are not individual deserters, but a strong body.'[2] This 'Third Party', as it styled itself, hoped that its action might lead to a restoration of Portland's leadership when he had come to share its views. Portland was surprisingly unruffled at this decisive development and seemed concerned only lest the conservative Whigs declare a suspension of systematic opposition.[3]

The schism in the party was now widening further and the lines of division were to be defined more closely in the following days. During January a proposal had been under discussion in the Whig Club which threatened to divide the party even more deeply and to bring Fox into a closer relationship with the radicals and reformers. Some of the radical members of the Club wished to move a vote of thanks to Fox for his speech of 4 December 1792 which had condemned the loyal Associations. Fox would not countenance the scheme unless it received the approval of Portland. Portland suspected that it hid a vindication of Fox's *general public conduct* and that it had been brought forward by those in the party and in the Whig Club who wished to create fresh dissensions. 'I most solemnly & distinctly protested against it.'[4] But Portland's protests did not prevent the Club at its next meeting, on 5 February, from calling an extraordinary meeting for 19 February to

---

[1] *The Parliamentary History*, xxx. 270–316; comments on Fox's extremism can be found in: Sheffield to Auckland 5 Feb. 1793, *Auckland*, ii. 495–7; MacKenzie to Adam 26 Feb. 1793, Blair-Adam MSS.

[2] Elliot to his wife 12 Feb. 1793, Minto, ii. 113–14; Sheffield to Auckland 22 Feb. 1793, Ad. MS. 34448, ff. 296–7, Auckland Papers.

[3] Elliot to his wife 12 Feb. 1793, loc. cit.; Tom Grenville to Windham 10 Feb. 1793, Ad. MS. 37849, f. 204, Windham Papers, printed in *Windham Papers*, i. 110–12; Windham to Hippisley 28 Mar. 1793, loc. cit.

[4] Fox to Adair 11 Jan. 1793, Ad. MS. 47565, f. 167, Fox Papers; Adam to Portland 14 Jan. 1793, Portland MSS. P.W.F. 45; Adair to Portland 22 Jan. 1793, ibid. 13; Portland to Fitzwilliam 17 Jan. 1793, Wentworth Woodhouse MSS., F.31a.

express its approval of Fox's conduct.[1] The moderate members of
the Club showed consternation and, through Serjeant Adair, attempted
to persuade Portland to approve of a motion of their own, thanking
Fox for his services, but phrased more cautiously than that of the
'restless and pernicious faction' in the Club. Although Fox found
nothing objectionable about this more moderate motion, Portland was
still uneasy. He felt that it intimated a trace of 'disapprobation or . . .
doubt of the propriety of the conduct which others of our Friends &
myself have thought it necessary to pursue for the safety of the
Constitution & the Kingdom' and, in truth, he was unwilling to allow
his name to be used in any declaration made by the Whig Club.[2] But it
was essential that Portland do something about the proceedings of
the Club and he decided to use his influence to support the more
moderate motion. With Fitzwilliam and Fox, the draft of a motion was
prepared and it was this motion which was moved and passed at the
meeting of 19 February.[3]

There were some members of the Club, however, who were unwilling to allow even this watered-down motion to stand on record as
an expression of their own opinions. On the initiative of Edmund
Burke, Elliot, Laurence and a few others formed themselves into a
committee which met frequently in late February and early March at
the St. Albans Tavern. By the date of the next meeting of the Whig
Club, 5 March, a letter of resignation had been written which was
signed by forty-five members of the Club.[4] This letter was read out

---

[1] *The Morning Chronicle*, 6 Feb. 1793. Fox was present at this meeting.

[2] Robert Adair to the Duke of Portland 7 Feb. 1793, Portland MSS. P.W.F. 32;
Serjeant Adair to the Duke of Portland 14 Feb. 1793, ibid. P.W.F. 14: the Duke of
Portland to Serjeant Adair 17 Feb. 1793, ibid. P.W.F. 15; Serjeant Adair to the
Duke of Portland 18 Feb. 1793, ibid. P.W.F. 16.

[3] The Duke of Portland to Thomas Grenville 15 Feb. 1793, Ad. MS. 42058,
ff. 118–19, Thomas Grenville MSS.; Serjeant Adair to the Duke of Portland 19
Feb. 1793, Portland MSS. P.W.F. 17. The meeting was fully reported in *The
Morning Chronicle* of 21 Feb. Fox's speech in response to the motion was moderate.
He declared that the members of the Whig Club were divided only in their opinions
of the best means of preserving the constitution.

[4] Elliot to his wife 2 Mar. 1793, Minto, ii. 120–21; Sheridan ridiculed the letter
as early as 28 Feb. in the Commons (*The Parliamentary History*, xxx. 537). The
letter is given in all the newspapers. It states the grounds of resignation as: (*a*) dis-

at the meeting and accepted. The presence of Portland at the meeting gave the impression that he acquiesced in the resignations and the statement which the Club issued to the newspapers claimed 'good authority for asserting *that the Duke of Portland never will secede, and never will join any public or political party, but in company with Mr. Fox*'.[1]

The resignations from the Whig Club mark the conclusion of one stage in the story of the break-up of the Old Whig party. Fox and Portland had failed to keep the party together, but their failure had not been so considerable as to prevent Portland maintaining a nominal, yet politically significant connection with the Foxite Whigs for another twelve months. At the same time, a 'Third Party' had broken away from Portland which proposed to sever all ties with Fox and advocated a closer understanding with the ministry. Now that Loughborough was on the Woolsack, his ambition and his duplicity would no longer distort the political relationships of the Whig party with the ministers. Nevertheless, the new situation in which the opposition now found itself had given rise to baffling problems, the sheer novelty of which tortured and tantalized the politicians involved in them. For some time there was no general agreement about the real nature of these problems and so it was to be long before there could be any agreed solutions. While the political scene reverberated with news from the Continent, while the future course of the war remained impossible to predict, and while so many elements in the political life of the kingdom were unstable and fluid, the Whig party was necessarily faced with many long months of uncertain and baffling attempts to come to grips with its problems.

---

approval of the resolution of 19 Feb., (*b*) opposition to Fox's parliamentary proceedings from 13 to 15 Dec., (*c*) refusal to concur in the imputations cast upon the loyal Associations, (*d*) refusal to approve opposition to the Aliens Bill, (*e*) disapproval of opposition to the war, and finally 'Much less can we approve of the frequent extenuations and even assertion of the doctrines on which the French Revolution has been effected and on which it is well known that our enemies principally rely for the utter subversion and final subjugation of this kingdom.'

[1] *The Morning Chronicle*, 6 Mar. 1793.

4. *The End of the Old Whig Party*

March–December 1793

I. THE PROBLEM OF PARTY, MARCH–MAY 1793

The alarms and dangers of the winter had disrupted the opposition of former years and had left it in a strange and unprecedented situation. The problems which confronted Portland in March 1793 required solutions such as might determine the whole future of the party. Yet these problems could only be resolved by calling into question the former conduct of the party and the political tenets of its members. Portland was thus not alone in refusing to take decisions which would sacrifice the past and pledge the future of the party until the existing hypothetical and uncertain issues had become urgent political realities. If the war against France was to be settled in one campaign, as was universally expected, there was no need to destroy the party, which might reunite its divided forces at a later date. If the ministers were so palpably dishonest as the events of the summer of 1792 had shown them to be, and if they remained unwilling to negotiate on an acceptable basis, then there was no question of the Portland Whigs entering the ministry. If there was now less to fear from republican agitation at home then there was no urgent need for Portland to commit himself to a firmer support of Pitt's administration than that which he had already promised. Not for the first time, Portland took a middle course between the Foxite Whigs and those who advocated separation from Fox and a closer connection with the ministry. His intention was to maintain the great Whig connection and to prevent its irreparable disruption. Although such conduct might be justified in logic, it was a line of proceeding which left Portland with little room for manœuvre. He occupied a position which left him vulnerable to any shifts of opinion and which relied too heavily upon circumstances which were outside his control.

On two issues — the status of Fox in relation to the party and the connection between the ministry and the conservative Whigs — Portland could appeal to sentiments of party feeling which were not the less powerful for being vague and equivocal. While he shared the uncompromising hostility of the other conservative Whigs towards the Friends of the People, Portland was prepared to allow Fox a greater latitude. He acknowledged that what separated them 'consists in the opinion we entertain of the existence and extent of the danger to which the Constitution has been and continues to be exposed'. The Duke insisted that Fox's conduct, unlike that of Pitt, was inspired by the purest of motives. Indeed, Portland felt that Fox might well be right in his attitude to republicanism at home and in his plea for negotiations with the French.[1] However much he deprecated the line which Fox had chosen to take at the beginning of the session, it was only on these two matters that he and Fox differed. Portland's personal contacts with Fox had convinced him of the undoubted sincerity of Fox's antipathy to the spread of French principles in England and his reluctance to see France occupy the territories of other European powers.[2] And for all the contemptuous references to them in the literature, letters and papers of the time, it is doubtful if serious politicians regarded the Foxite Whigs and their opposition to Pitt during the war as either unconstitutional or unpatriotic. In spite of the reappearance of the so-called 'Patriotic' line of conduct in 1793, an uncompromising ministerialist like Jenkinson could lecture the Commons on the need for 'a constant supply of men to form vigorous and effective administrations . . . a constant supply of men to form vigorous and effective oppositions, for the purpose of watching over the conduct of . . . ministers'.[3] And when Portland brought himself to attend the Lords for the purpose of announcing his support of the principle of the war, he usually found something to criticize and not infrequently added that his support of the war would not 'prevent him from inquiring scrupulously into the conduct of ministers in the way in which they should carry it on'.[4]

[1] Portland to the Prince of Wales 21 Jan. 1793, Aspinall, *Later Correspondence of George III*, i. 650–2.
[2] Ibid.
[3] 6 May 1793, *The Parliamentary History*, xxx. 812.
[4] 12 Feb. 1793, ibid. xxx. 413.

Fitzwilliam, whose distaste for the Foxites knew no bounds, admitted that he was 'generally and systematically in opposition'.[1]

This idea of 'opposition' was perhaps not quite so extraordinary to contemporaries as it appears to posterity. In fact, Portland was merely reverting to the old slogan of 'Men not Measures'. He was forever reminding his friends that the sinister events which had led to the downfall of the Coalition ministry in 1783 had been an outrage of Whig principles. His attitude to the ministers had been underlined on 21 December 1792 when he told the Lords: 'He could not forget the manner in which they came into power; he could not forget the many circumstances in their conduct by which, in his opinion, they had forfeited all title to the confidence of the nation.'[2] It followed, then, that if Portland and the conservative Whigs were to declare an unconditional support of Pitt, then they, by implication, would be denying the principles upon which the Whig party had professed its opposition to the ministry. Nor was this mere logic-chopping. Portland and his friends undoubtedly feared that if they were to enter into closer relations with the ministry, their public reputations would be destroyed and their support would thus be of little avail. Portland, indeed, was far more aware of the sophistries of politics than was Burke and it was to be many months before the Duke admitted that there were causes and priorities which might demand the destruction of the party.

Nevertheless, to men accustomed to the routine of opposition, Portland's conduct was sometimes bewildering, if not unintelligible. Lord Sheffield, who was one of the members of Windham's 'Third Party', aptly summed up their view when he remarked that 'no party can hold men to-gether whose views for the Public Interest are so totally different'.[3] Yet Portland was able to maintain his position because there were many who could not accept Sheffield's over-simplified observation. Such men could not lightly abandon the political habits and personal friendships which had been forged during years of fruitless opposition and party attachment. There was consider-

[1] Fitzwilliam to Richard Burke jnr. 27 Aug. 1793, N.R.O. A. iv. 20, Burke Letters.

[2] *The Parliamentary History*, xxx. 159.

[3] Sheffield to Gibbon 23 Jan. 1793, R. E. Prothero, *Private Letters of Edward Gibbon* (2 vols., 1896), ii. 361–7.

able reluctance to admit that the French Revolution was a matter which should be allowed to divide a party and produce a new alignment. If the old party distinctions were to be lost, then politicians would be divided into two groups of extremists. In lending unconnected support to the ministry on the issue of the war and on those issues which arose from it, Portland felt that he was doing his duty and accepting his responsibilities. For the present, to go further might do more harm than good.

Considerations such as these possessed a certain plausibility but they depended for their force upon the assumption that the war was merely one particular measure, upon which differences might be tolerated. Fox invariably insisted that this was the case. He denied the existence of 'a general difference of opinion' among his friends 'as made it impossible . . . to preserve that connexion in which they had acted so long'. He could point to Portland's speech of 21 December as a proof that 'no essential difference' separated himself from the Duke. Burke, on the other hand, affirmed that 'no public connexion could subsist between them, because they differed systematically and fundamentally'.[1] But it was not clear that Burke was correct. Even Windham had stated that such a difference 'was not a difference that extended to principle' and Frederick North, who usually followed Burke's politics during the war, admitted that the principles upon which the party existed could quite well justify the proceedings of the Foxite opposition.[2] In some ways, then, the very ambiguity of party dogma enabled Portland to maintain a specious unity and deferred for a while the disintegration of the Whig party. And from one point of view, the struggles of 1793 were waged over the fundamentals of the party's doctrine and, among the conservative Whigs, gave rise to a reassessment and reinterpretation of the function of party in the constitution. The pressure of events hurried them into this debate and hastened them towards conclusions which were personally distressing and politically distasteful. It is the progress of this debate and the painful stages by which the conservative Whigs came to their conclusions which form the essential theme of party history in 1793–4.

---

[1] 28 Dec. 1792, *The Parliamentary History*, xxx. 177–9, 181.
[2] 15 Dec. 1792, ibid. xxx. 100; 21 Mar. 1793, ibid. xxx. 595.

While the issues which divided the party were becoming clear, there was still considerable doubt and confusion over the extent of the internal schism. Windham's 'Third Party' was convinced that there was no possibility of reuniting with Fox because the war was not merely a particular issue, 'but that every species of public principle is involved in it'. It was necessary, then to separate from Fox and 'to give a cordial support to the Executive Power against French Principles at home and abroad'. The members of this party felt it desirable to act in a body so that they might avoid the imputation of deserting Portland as individuals. By taking up an unequivocal position in the present crisis, they hoped to impress Portland with the urgency of the situation and to weaken Fox's extraordinary influence over him.[1] But it was to be almost a year before Portland could be persuaded to declare his final separation from Fox, and Windham displayed neither the ability nor the energy which might have rendered the 'Third Party' a real force in politics. Portland and Fitzwilliam could not quickly forget Windham's unwarranted and unauthorized attempt to offer the party to Pitt in the previous November, and Fitzwilliam regarded his latest political manœuvre as 'running the length of something little short of systematic support of the Ministers, or of the court'.[2] The party grandees wished 'to pledge themselves to no support of government or suspension of opposition, except in those particular instances which were effected by and comprehended in the very particular dangers of the times', and they were distressed by Windham's 'determination to set aside for the present, all views of opposition'.[3] Many of the most influential men in the party were unwilling to follow Windham's course of action and his 'Third Party' was therefore disappointingly slender in means, deficient in talent and inconsiderable in numbers. On 10 February — two days before the first meeting of the 'Third Party' — Windham attempted to calculate

[1] Richard Burke jnr. to Fitzwilliam 16 Aug. 1793, N.R.O. A. iv. 19, Burke Letters; Lord Sheffield to Lord Auckland 22 Feb. 1793, Ad. MS. 34448, ff. 296–7, Auckland MSS.; Elliot to his wife 12 Feb. 1793, Minto, ii. 113–14.

[2] Windham to J. C. Hippisley 28 Mar. 1793, Ad. MS. 37848, ff. 59–64, Windham Papers, printed in *Windham Papers*, i. 113–20; Fitzwilliam to Lady Rockingham 28 Feb. 1793, Rockingham MSS., R. 164, f. 14–1, 2.

[3] Tom Grenville to Windham 10 Feb. 1793, Ad. MS. 37849, f. 204, Windham Papers, printed in *Windham Papers*, i. 110–12.

the amount of support it might attract. His master-list of 86 M.P.s, whom he obviously considered to be likely supporters, provides the best possible commentary on the uncertainties of politics in the early months of 1793, when it was frequently impossible to predict the behaviour of politicians, when political groups were shifting their ground and when party alignments were undergoing a gradual change. He included no fewer than 14 M.P.s in his list who actually joined Fox in systematic opposition to the war. And Windham could only conclude that 23 M.P.s out of a list of 86 of those he considered to be the conservative Whigs would join his 'Third Party'. Some of the more doubtful men were whipped in during the following days and a partial list of the 'Third Party' which was drawn up by Lord Sheffield on 22 February adds 7 other names which were not among Windham's 23 and 2 of which were not among the list of 86 names. The men who seceded from the Whig Club in February 1793 were closely connected with Windham, Burke and Elliot, and, indeed, the secession itself was among the first public actions of the 'Third Party'. Yet the list of 45 names which appeared in the *Morning Chronicle* of 6 March includes only 18 M.P.s, 10 of which appear either in Windham's short list or Sheffield's further list. The 'Third Party', therefore, consisted of about 38 M.P.s. But of these 38, only 26 were members of the Whig party. The remaining 12 were independent country gentlemen who occasionally voted with the opposition or, in some cases, were members who had had no previous contact with the opposition. The pressure of war was weakening former lines of demarcation among politicians and rallying the independents in support of the patriotic cause. Windham's 'Third Party' enabled some of them to support the ministers while remaining safely unconnected. But what is more immediately to the point is that, out of an opposition which numbered perhaps 146 in December 1792, Windham's group contained only 26 members. It is not to be wondered at, then, that Windham was disappointed and dejected at the fruits of his efforts. The campaign which Burke, Loughborough, Malmesbury, Elliot and Windham had been fighting since November had palpably failed. Less than one-fifth of the party — and this included few men of ability or influence — could be persuaded to separate from Fox and thus to destroy the Whig party.[1]

[1] Notes in Windham's hand dated 10 Feb. 1793, Ad. MS. 37843, ff. 201–2,

Portland's apparently anomalous political conduct — support of administration while remaining in systematic opposition — found more general acceptance in the party than Windham's 'Third Party' policy. In the House of Commons, 54 M.P.s followed the Duke's course, refusing to vote with Fox but unwilling to commit themselves too closely to a general support of administration.[1] Fitzwilliam described them as those who 'will give support to measures of vigour, even when they cannot approve either the mode by which such a system was introduced, or the principles of the person, who so introduced them: but still thinking the measure right, will support the naked measure, engaging for nothing further'.[2] The Portland Whigs saw that their function as a party in the changed political circumstances had not lapsed. If the door could be kept open until circumstances permitted Fox and his friends to return to the routine of co-operation and political friendship of former years, then the party might yet be saved and it might continue to fulfil its historic functions. Yet this prospect seemed remote. On the one hand there were men like Windham rushing to lend an uncompromising support to the government and on the other there was 'that abominable excrescence', the Association of the Friends of the People, 'coming forward to put themselves at the head of the seditious, the factions, the disorganizers'. For the present, 'the true old Stuff of the Whig Party . . . by exercise of their patience, and their habits of vexation and disappointment', would of necessity, occupy middle ground between the two extremes.[3] And so, in the interests of a specious unity, Portland proclaimed to the world his rejection of Windham's politics by attending the Whig Club meeting of 5 March. Although he had strongly disapproved of the resolution of 19 February he had been unable to control those proceedings of the Club which had prompted 45 of its members to register their public separation from Fox by signing Burke and Elliot's letter of resignation. On 5 March this letter was read to the company. Sheridan could scarcely conceal his jubilation at the resignations, and Fox toasted 'The Duke of Portland

---

Windham Papers; Lord Sheffield to Lord Auckland 22 Feb. 1793, loc. cit. See Appendix 2 for details and lists of the 'Third Party'. For Fox's contempt for this party, see *The Parliamentary History*, xxx. 549.

[1] See Appendix 3.   [2] Fitzwilliam to Lady Rockingham 28 Feb. 1793, loc. cit.
[3] Ibid.

and the Whig Interest'. Well might Elliot feel that the game had been lost and Portland with it. 'I give him up completely now, as this is direct duplicity and open hostility with us.'[1]

The Duke of Portland's anxiety to maintain some connection with Fox may have been inspired by a further motive. As the weeks passed, it was apparent that Fox could command a larger following than the events of December had led observers to expect. By the end of February, the size of the Foxite party was beginning to emerge more clearly. Fox was supported by about 60 members of the Old Whig party.[2] This was not far short of one half of the opposition — a fact which may have confirmed Portland's reluctance to separate from Fox. By the end of the session of 1793, the Foxite opposition included no fewer than 66 members of the old Whig party and there were, in addition, a further 15 to 20 M.P.s who voted with Fox fairly regularly, many of whom were independent country gentlemen. This substantiates the conclusion which was drawn from the analysis of Windham's 'Third Party' — that whether politicians liked it or not, the war was effecting a shift of political alignments. In particular, it was drawing independents into a more definite relationship with both the ministry and the opposition and thus tending to strengthen rather than to confuse the essential cleavage of opinion between the ministry and the Foxite Whigs, a cleavage which could not be entirely concealed even by the equivocal postures of the Portland Whigs.

The Foxite opposition included an unusually high proportion of newer M.P.s who were enthusiastic for radical reform and who could be easily led by men like Sheridan and Francis. M.P.s of this type had entered parliament after 1784 and had failed to assimilate the aristocratic notions of the Rockingham Whigs. At the feet of Fox they had acquired their political education and had picked up the opposition catch-phrases, particularly the denunciation of the corrupt influence of the crown. But the antidote to this influence, in the minds of men like Charles Grey, was not reliance upon the aristocracy, but an appeal of the people. When they formed the Association of Friends of the People in April 1792 they were trying to save the aristocracy from the con-

---

[1] *The Morning Chronicle*, 6 Mar. 1793. Elliot to his wife 7 Mar. 1793, Minto, ii. 121–2.

[2] See Appendix 4.

K

sequences of its fear of reform, but they were also undermining the creed of the Old Whig party. Since then they had been outlawed by the party chiefs and had become indifferent to the unity of the party. But now the events of the winter had brought Fox into a much closer relationship with them and their activities were to be of direct consequence in determining the future role of Fox in the party.

Yet the Foxite opposition was not entirely a reforming party. About one half of its members did not support parliamentary reform and even William Adam spoke against Grey's motion in May 1793.[1] Nevertheless, it was the reformers who were generally the most vocal in the House and in the country, and who invariably led the lively attacks on Pitt's diplomatic and repressive policies. Although they were castigated as Jacobins and smeared with the taint of republicanism, they were animated with a sense of martyrdom and inflamed with the conviction of self-righteousness. The hopelessness of their parliamentary position did not deter them from exploiting the customary techniques of the opposition. Routine opposition was left entirely in their hands, even while measures were under discussion which might perhaps have allowed the Portland Whigs to co-operate with them. That such co-operation was not forthcoming was keenly resented by Fox. During the debate on the Third Reading of the Bill to renew the charter of the East India Company:

he should again object to that part of the bill which went to the creation of new offices in the gift of the crown, in order that those with whom he had formerly concurred in a vote for reducing the influence of the crown, might have an opportunity of delivering their sentiments. . . . If they still concurred with him in the opinions they had formerly professed, it became them, like men who acted from a sense of duty, unbiased by any temporary motives, to maintain those opinions by their votes on the present occasion.

When his appeal fell upon deaf ears Fox was furious and was rightly reprimanded by Pitt for his 'ungoverned and angry words'.[2] Indeed, routine opposition was a thankless task in the conditions of 1793. To have held up supplies would have confirmed the popular view of the Foxites as unprincipled traitors and, in consequence, there was rather less opposition to routine business than in previous years. Such debate as there was usually called into question the purity of Pitt's motives

[1] See Appendix 4.   [2] 24 May 1793, *The Parliamentary History*, xxx. 939–44.

and kept up the cry against the rising influence of the crown. The helpless frustration which occasionally swept over the Foxites led them to direct much of their attack upon their old associates rather than on Pitt. 'Their friends', remarked Sheridan, 'treated them with a sort of French fraternity, and did them more real injury than their open enemies.' To the opposition, the Portland Whigs were little better than dupes of the ministers, 'the very set of men their principles must make them detest'.[1] In this state of mind, they were indifferent to any consideration of party interest such as that which was tantalizing the Duke of Portland. As for Burke and Windham, the Foxites regarded them as little better than creatures of Pitt, and were never tired of railing at Burke for the apparent inconsistency of his conduct. The impeachment of Warren Hastings was the last means of co-operation which remained and it is hardly surprising that the Foxite managers gave little of their attention to this tiresome proceeding.[2]

In his more nostalgic moments, Fox occasionally lamented the dis-unity in the party and hoped that at some future date co-operation would be restored. Such anticipation was little better than wishful thinking. It is true that he did not run the lengths of some of his radical friends. He did not join the Association for the Liberty of the Press, and his speeches at the Whig Club were notable for their restraint.[3] Nevertheless his political conduct cannot be described as conciliatory. His *Letter to the Electors of Westminster* is an explicit defence of his own conduct since the beginning of the session. As one of the few published works of Fox, as an appeal to the people and as a fairly dispassionate reiteration of his opinions, the pamphlet is of some im-portance. Its opening sentence speaks more loudly of his growing indifference to the party than pages of polemic would have done:

To vote in small minorities, is a misfortune to which I have been so much accustomed, that I cannot be expected to feel it very acutely.[4]

[1] 18 Feb. 1793, *The Parliamentary History*, xxx. 452, see also 528; Grey to Lady Melbourne (n.d.). Countess of Airlie, *In Whig Society* (1921), 19–21.

[2] Grey to Burke 7 June 1793, Wentworth Woodhouse MSS., Burke Letters 1. See the debates of 30 May, 6, 7 and 12 June 1793, *The Parliamentary History*, xxx. 965–94; *The Morning Chronicle*, 4 Mar. 1793.

[3] E.g. on 19 Feb. 1793, reported on 21 Feb., *The Morning Chronicle*.

[4] The letter was published on 26 Jan. Although its price was one shilling, a fourth edition was advertised in *The Morning Chronicle* as early as 31 Jan. 1793.

After nine years of monotonously dull opposition, Fox's restless energy flooded to the surface now that the political game was quickening. As in the days of Rockingham, great causes were once more at stake and Fox was convinced of Pitt's malevolence. Not uncharacteristically, Fox assumed that all virtue was to be found among those who agreed with his opposition to Pitt's policy and from this there followed his intransigence towards the Portland Whigs. Although he did not admit that the reunion of the party was impossible, he made it clear that few concessions could be expected of him. When he lectured his former political friends in the House it was to impress upon them their own folly and inconsistency. He was unable to appreciate — still less respect — the feelings and opinions of those friends who, at the cost of considerable personal distress, found it impossible to agree with him. As the weeks passed and as the schism in the party grew more pronounced, attitudes hardened and the pretence that the differences in the party were differences on particular measures began to give way to the inexorable logic of events.

Whatever the value of Fox's opposition to the war policy of Pitt, he did not allow himself to be moved by any anxiety he may have felt concerning the unity of the party. He supported the principle of the war in 'repelling every hostile attack against this country' and allowed that thus far it was 'just, prudent, and necessary'. Had he emphasized this support, had he concentrated upon eliciting from Pitt the aims upon which the war was being fought and had he directed his fire upon Pitt's incompetent management of the war, then Fox's politics might have been a good deal less unpalatable to the Portland Whigs and they would not have done violence to Fox's own consistency. Yet he blamed Pitt for having refused to negotiate with the French. He did not conceal his distrust for the allies, whose treatment of the Poles was no better than the behaviour of the French:

Anarchy, if it could be introduced into other nations, was in its nature temporary — despotism, we knew, by sad experience, to be lasting.

By co-operating with the allies, Britain might be drawn into a scheme directed at the restoration of the French monarchy, 'for supporting rather the cause of kings, than the cause of the people'. His tirades against the monarchs of Europe developed into declamations against monarchy itself and impressed his listeners with the suspicion that Fox's sympathies lay with the French, a suspicion which seemed all too justifiable by the frequent violence of his language. And such suspicions drove the wedge between Fox and the Portland Whigs ever deeper and ever wider.[1]

Portland continued to embrace the hope that Fox might be won back to respectable opinions upon matters of domestic concern but, as the session wore on, such optimism receded. Although Fox continued to withhold both his name and his countenance from the Friends of the People and the Association for Preserving the Liberty of the Press, he did not disavow their activities and 'appeared the general patron of all such persons and proceedings'.[2] There is nothing to suggest that Fox attempted either to restrain or to direct the activities of these societies. Nor could such attempts have succeeded for by now the reformers in the opposition were well organized and were acting in concert. Fox had remained aloof for too long and had allowed the two societies which had been carved out of the Whig party to canvass their causes out of doors. The fruits of his indecision and weakness of judgement were now being reaped. Fox could not control the reformers in the opposition.

The Association of Friends for Preserving the Liberty of the Press had lately declared war on the loyal Associations which had proliferated throughout the country since November. At a meeting of the Association on 19 January, Erskine declared that the loyal Associations were 'doubtful in law, and unconstitutional in principle . . . a sort of partnership of authority, with the executive power . . . supported by the subscriptions of opulent men, for the avowed object of suppressing and prosecuting writings'. Ten thousand copies of this speech were circulated in the country and at the next meeting of the Association on 9 March a fund was opened for the relief of victims of the prosecutions. This was carrying the defence of liberty a little far. On 20 April, after only £400 had been collected, Erskine told the Association that it was improper to give relief to those successfully prosecuted by the law. Many among those present appeared willing to defer to this judge-

[1] For Burke's comments on this point, see *Observations*, in *Burke's Works*, i. 616–618.
[2] Ibid. 616.

ment and rid themselves of the embarrassing business, but Horne
Tooke contested the decision and forced the meeting to divide.
Although the moderates were in a majority, the two divisions which
were taken (121–80 and 91–63) showed that the Association contained
a fairly large proportion of men who would not be content with half-
measures.[1] While the Liberty of the Press Association was castigating
the loyal Associations — which were looked on by the Portland
Whigs as having delivered the country from impending anarchy — and
while it was attracting the support of men like Tooke, thus justifying
Burke's charge that the reformers would not be able to control the
spirit which they were awakening, the Friends of the People were
running to other extremes. On 21 February Sheridan had boasted to
the Commons that the Association of the Friends of the People 'was
neither dead nor sleeping, but in the full vigour of activity'.[2] Shortly
afterwards the Association published its two reports on the state of the
representation. On 16 March its members authorized Grey to bring
the question of parliamentary reform before the Commons.[3]

Fox was being forced to declare his hand by events which were
running out of his control. For a while, indeed, there remained some
traces of equivocation in his conduct. On 28 March he supported
Sheridan's motion for a committee to enquire into the existence of
seditious practices, in a speech which contained something to placate
both the reformers and the Portland Whigs. He condemned the loyal
Associations 'in the strongest and most emphatic terms, as destructive
both of the peace and character of individuals in all probability
innocent, and totally subversive of every principle of liberty'. At the
same time, he politely acknowledged his dissent from certain friends,
who acted 'on the most honourable principles'. The present disagree-

---

[1] The meetings are reported in *The Morning Chronicle* of 21 Jan., 11 Mar. and
22 Apr. Whitbread admitted to the Commons on 7 May that the Association
contained undesirable members. (*The Parliamentary History*, xxx. 884–5.) Members
of the Association included Erskine, Sheridan, Byng, Sturt, Wharton, Howard,
Courtenay, Grey, Lambton, MacLeod, Maitland, Rawdon, M. A. Taylor, Whitbread, Wm. Smith and Lauderdale.

[2] *The Parliamentary History*, xxx. 466.

[3] *The Morning Chronicle*, 18 Mar. See Veitch, *Genesis of Reform*, 279–80, for the
efforts made by the Friends of the People to restrain the other societies from
activities which might have endangered the success of Grey's motion.

ment 'made no difference whatever in the great line of their political principles; in their disapprobation both of the general system of the present administration, and of the way by which they came into office'. For Windham and the 'Third Party', however, Fox had nothing but harsh and bitter words.[1] But there were to be all too few occasions in the future upon which Fox might hope to satisfy both the reformers and the Portland Whigs. The debates on the Traitorous Correspondence Bill found Fox claiming an exclusive consistency of conduct since 1783 and rejecting Frederick North's conciliatory suggestion that both the Foxites and the 'Third Party' might be justified in their present attitudes because the principles upon which the opposition had rested since 1783 allowed of differing interpretations.[2] As in 1792, however, it was to be the question of parliamentary reform which was to bring the party to a renewed crisis. In the year that had passed since Grey's previous motion, too much had happened to enable Fox to hedge and trim yet again. If he was to continue to maintain an effective political party about him then he must of necessity advance closer to the radicals in the opposition. To do otherwise would destroy any influence over them which he still retained. The attitude which Fox was to adopt on 6 and 7 May 1793, therefore, was to be of crucial importance in the history of the Whig party.

Earlier in the session Fox had said nothing upon the subject of parliamentary reform save to disavow universal suffrage.[3] On 7 May his attitude was dramatically reversed. For the first time, he unhesitatingly indicated his public approval of the Friends of the People. He denied Pitt's arguments that neither the mode nor the time of the application was safe and affirmed that reform was the only instrument of saving the constitution from the creeping paralysis of influence. His objection to universal suffrage was not distrust of the decision of the majority, but the lack of 'any practical mode of collecting such suffrage', without the sinister intervention of widespread influence. Fox's speech, while it did not go the lengths of those of other members of the opposition, indicated that he was unwilling to sacrifice his opinions in

[1] *The Parliamentary History*, xxx. 547–9. It was upon this occasion that heated exchanges between Fox and Burke almost led to a duel, ibid. xxx. 554.
[2] 21 Mar. 1793, *The Parliamentary History*, xxx. 595, 600.
[3] 21 Feb. 1793, ibid. xxx. 462; 2 May 1793, ibid. xxx. 780.

the interests of a fictitious party unity. His decision to support the petition of the Friends of the People made little apparent difference to his own conduct. He neither attended their meetings nor openly espoused their cause. But his speech of 7 May left Portland in an impossible position and thrust him into a closer relationship with the 'Third Party'. Nor could Fox lightly retract the opinions he had so strongly professed. If there is a point of no return in Fox's relations with Portland, that point had surely been reached on 7 May 1793.[1]

Meanwhile, Portland's attitude towards Pitt remained substantially unaltered. Although Loughborough kept the Duke informed of the continental situation for a while, renewed soundings were not forthcoming and the communications lapsed. Portland was flattered with the bestowal upon his son of an acceptable military appointment but this, too, was devoid of significant political consequence. In truth, now, and for long after, the Portland Whigs were unable to overcome their distrust of Pitt and their distaste for his conduct of the war.[2] In parliament none of the Portland Whigs, with the single exception of Portland himself, ever defended Pitt's administration from the assaults of the Foxites. Portland made one of his rare appearances in the Lords to acknowledge his support of the Traitorous Correspondence Bill on 15 April, when he declared that several parts of it were 'highly objectionable'. Yet he reiterated his willingness to uphold the principle of the war 'because he thought it both just and necessary'. It is impossible to understand the painful dilemma in which men like Portland found themselves unless one understands 'that Strange Partiality He feels for the Persons whose principles conduct and character He disapproves'.[3]

The leaders of the 'Third Party' were in close touch with Pitt and Dundas and found them willing to discuss measures. The ministers even tolerated patiently Burke's lengthy instructions upon the conduct

---

[1] For the horrified reaction to Fox's speech in conservative Whig circles see Mrs. Crewe to Portland 19 May 1793, Portland MSS. P.W.F. 3, 174.

[2] Loughborough to Portland 10 and 19 Mar 1793, Portland MSS. P.W.F. 9233, 9234; Amherst to Portland 20 Mar. 1793, ibid. P.W.F. 108.

[3] *The Parliamentary History*, xxx. 731; Loughborough to Burke 23 Mar. 1793, Wentworth Woodhouse MSS., Burke Letters 1; Fitzwilliam to his wife N.R.O. Fitzwilliam MSS., Box 45.

of the war. It is doubtful if such conferences did anything to change Pitt's notions on war policy but he bore them with civility and seems to have impressed Burke's friends with his readiness to listen to their views.[1] Members of the 'Third Party' occasionally spoke out in support of the ministers in the House but their assistance was not always forthcoming. The Traitorous Correspondence Bill aroused even their objections. A conference at Downing Street between the ministers, Burke and Elliot, was required to settle the noxious clauses. Even then only Burke, North and Anstruther spoke during the debates. The other members of the 'Third Party' remained silent in the House. Windham, Elliot, Lord Sheffield, Sir Francis Basset and Thomas Stanley spoke on other occasions, few of them regularly. On certain important motions, ministers would be left to defend their own policy. Relations between themselves and the 'Third Party' were tenuous and unsystematic, resting as they did upon the voluntary and individual willingness of its members to bring themselves forward in defence of the government while leaving themselves open to taunts and insults from the opposition.[2]

The success or failure of the 'Third Party' as an efficient political force depended upon one man. If Portland was to declare his final separation from Fox, and if ministers were to be pushed and prodded into adopting the only policies which could possibly effect the discomfiture of the Jacobins, then Windham was the only politician who might seriously undertake to accomplish these ends. He was possessed of distinguished talents and a disposition so compelling as to endear him to all. The power of his intelligence was disguised by his self-effacing manner as a reserve of strength and firmness which he did not in reality

[1] Elliot to his wife 7 Mar. 1793, Minto, ii. 121–2.
[2] Elliot to his wife 26 Mar. 1793, Minto, ii. 127–8. It is worth noticing that the Portland Whigs and the 'Third Party' sat together on the opposition side of the House. (*The Parliamentary History*, xxx. 389, 598.) Courtenay's sarcastic explanation of this (ibid. xxx. 484), 'the other side was already too much crowded', cannot be accepted because there were only few occasions when the attendance at debates would have made it impossible for the 'Third Party', at least, to have sat on the government side of the House. The custom of opposition seating procedures seems, then, to have exerted a strong influence upon members of the party and allowed the Portland Whigs to indicate their continued attachment to Fox in the most significant manner.

possess. His talents and his nature, allied to unquestioned integrity, gave him a reputation and a standing among his contemporaries which was, perhaps, second only to that of Fox. It was not by accident that Windham was able to rally to him some of the most respectable independents in the House of Commons. Nevertheless, he was peculiarly ill-suited to the role which he was now called upon to play in the political drama of 1793. He was daunted with the prospect of assuming responsibility for matters of state by the doubts and fears which gnawed away at the determination he could summon in his rare moments of enthusiasm and exuberance. Once his energy had been overcome by the exhaustion of his spirits, he would fall away into lethargy, despair and pessimism. Having formed the 'Third Party', he promptly excused himself from leading it. Having committed its members to a distinct support of administration, he escaped to the solitude of Fellbrig, in spite of 'the possibility of having lost an opportunity of distinction'. He consoled his conscience by toying with the preparation of speeches which he never delivered while he ruminated on his inability to act out the part which he himself had chosen.[1] He returned to town in the second week of April when the Traitorous Correspondence Bill was safely in the Lords, but it was a fortnight before he applied himself to the problems in hand. By that time, the gulf which separated the 'Third Party' from the Portland Whigs was beginning to shrink. The hitherto suspended round of social intercourse which normally characterized the conduct of opposition members during sessions was beginning to revive. Elliot and Burke were once more seated at the same dining-table as Portland, Fitzwilliam and Devonshire.[2] From these convivialities Fox and his friends excluded themselves, a significant indication that Portland was freeing himself of the personal influence of his closest friend. At the same time, Windham began to organize informal meetings of his political followers. So close was the texture of Whig society that it was perhaps inevitable that attendances at all such gatherings should be fairly uniform. From

---

[1] *Windham Diary*, 272–4, Windham to J. C. Hippisley 28 Mar., loc. cit. For instances of Windham's inability to lead a party, see his letters to Tom Grenville of 10 Feb. 1793, Ad. MS. 42058, ff. 115–16, and 17 Feb. Ad. MS. 41854, ff. 296–7, Thomas Grenville MSS.

[2] Elliot to his wife 2 May 1793, Minto, ii. 135–9.

the happy renewal of personal contacts there might yet follow some greater measure of agreement in politics. Grey's motion for the reform of parliament came just at that time when these developments were acquiring momentum and the second half of May witnessed no diminution of their gathering force.[1]

The political stalemate of the beginning of the year was beginning — and only beginning — to dissolve. The fundamental doubts, suspicions and uncertainties remained and almost nothing had passed which might yet contribute to their solution. As the session was drawing to its close there seemed little prospect that the Portland Whigs would yet forgive Pitt for their humiliations of the past nine years and, setting these aside, declare a more wholehearted support for his tired administration. And yet Fox was unconsciously driving Portland into a closer relationship with Windham. It was Windham who, at this point, represented the unstable element in the structure of political attachments which had prevailed since February and it was upon Windham that Pitt wisely chose to concentrate his attention in the summer of 1793.

II. THE IMPOSSIBILITY OF PARTY
MAY–DECEMBER 1793

The disintegration of the Whig party was not a sudden event. Like all political parties, it was composed of loosely grouped sections of men who, for a multitude of reasons, had grown accustomed to acting in concert over a number of years. While such co-operation was possible it was natural for its members to emphasize and insist upon those elements of opinion where harmony prevailed. When circumstances thrust new problems and unforeseen priorities into the forefront of political life, the unity of the party became subject to the danger of disruption from differences which were formerly tolerable or irrelevant. Portland and his followers refused to accept that these differences were of sufficient force to nullify the possibility of co-operating with Fox at some future date. Until then, they would, at least, refuse to act with Fox's enemies. Meanwhile, they were a politically paralysed group, taking little or no positive part in affairs, because they were dependent

[1] Elliot to his wife 3 May 1793, ibid. 139–41; *Windham Diary*, 274–7.

for a revival of their fortunes upon circumstances over which they could exert little influence. Although the progress of the allied armies and fleets was to influence the conduct of the Portland Whigs in the next few months, it was developments within the Whig party itself which were to reveal the impossibility of achieving any substantial methods of co-operation and steadily to widen the gulf which separated its members.

It was at this time, too, that Pitt renewed his overtures to certain members of the party. In recent months he had committed himself to the allies by promising to distribute generous subsidies, involving himself in the affairs of the continent to the point at which he might be charged with entertaining the notions of the allies themselves upon what the aims of the war were to be. Nor had the war been conducted as successfully as many had anticipated. The allies were advancing but the notable victory at Neerwinden on 18 March had been but tardily followed up, notwithstanding the optimism which had led the ministers to abandon the West Indian expedition so that troops could be poured into Flanders. If the war was the greatest factor in politics, then the conduct of the war by the government was an issue of paramount importance. The first months of the campaign gave rise to many criticisms of Pitt and Dundas, not only from among the conservative Whigs but also from influential government circles, including the cabinet itself. While the Portland Whigs remained aloof from administration, lending merely tacit and token support for the war, they could not be expected to share responsibility for its conduct. In case of growing criticism of ministers, they might retreat still further away from any sort of distinct support of the conduct of the war and into the arms of Fox. Pitt was enabled to guard against this danger by seeking to enlist the Whigs in his defence against Fox's motion for peace with France on 17 June.

This motion came as no surprise because the Foxite press had been denouncing the war ever since its commencement and, more stridently, since the victory at Neerwinden had secured the Netherlands.[1] In May and June, therefore, Pitt renewed his overtures to certain well-chosen individuals, who can only be regarded as those most likely to have proved amenable to his soundings. During the last few days of May,

[1] E.g. *The Morning Chronicle*, 22 Mar. 1793.

Elliot was offered the post of Governor-General of Madras, a move which doubtless won the approval of Burke.[1] After keeping Carlisle in suspense for several months, Pitt bestowed upon him a Blue Riband, after Loughborough had acted as the intermediary in prolonged and tortuous negotiations.[2] Friendly contacts were maintained between the ministers and Burke and Windham in the early part of June.[3] With the date for the debate on Fox's motion rapidly approaching, after which the ending of the session would allow politicians of all descriptions to leave town, Pitt returned once more to his well-known tactics of trying to detach the conservative Whigs from Fox.

He cannot have been blind to the urgency of the need. Events out of doors were forcing the pace and bringing politicians face to face with problems which they were reluctant to acknowledge. The friends of Fox were once more responsible for making the uneasy compromise of the Portland Whigs difficult to sustain. After the rejection of Grey's reform motion, the Friends of the People had issued an appeal to the people, urging them to continue their agitation and, not least, their petitions to the House. Although the influence of the Association began to decline after May, on account of its disapproval of the proposed convention of reforming societies, this appeal could be interpreted in only one way by the conservative Whigs. The Friends of the People were determined to carry on spreading their poison, without, of course, being disavowed by Charles Fox. Their defiance was mirrored by Erskine in his defence of Frost at the latter's trial in May.

[1] Minto, ii. 146. Elliot refused the offer but returned to town from Minto in June.

[2] Loughborough to Carlisle May 1793, H.M.C. *Carlisle*, 701–2; Pitt to Carlisle 5 June 1793, ibid. 701–2; Carlisle to Pitt 5 June 1793, P.R.O. Pitt Papers, 121; Pitt to the King 6 June 1793, Aspinall, *Later Correspondence of George III*, ii. 47; Lord Grenville to Buckingham 12 June 1793, *Court and Cabinets*, ii. 237–9. *The Diary* of 8 June said that Carlisle was to replace Dundas at the Home Department.

[3] Windham was in touch with both Loughborough and Pitt at this time (*Windham Diary*, 276); Windham to Pitt 8 June 1793, Ad. MS. 37844, ff. 3–4; Pitt to Windham 10 June 1793, ibid. ff. 5–6, Windham Papers. From about this time, moreover, dates Windham's close contacts with the *émigrés*. See Ad. MS. 37855 *passim*, Windham Papers. Burke and the ministers came into contact over the impeachment of Hastings, the leisurely progress of which provoked several debates in parliament in late May and early June. See the debate of 30 May 1793 for Pitt's defence of Burke, *The Parliamentary History*, xxx, 972–3.

Meanwhile the Foxite press embarrassed both the conservative Whigs and the ministers by exaggerating the differences between Pitt and Portland and by printing wild stories about the continued attachment to Fox of several of the most respectable Whigs.[1] Worst of all, for Pitt, at least, was the grim prospect that the conservative Whigs might still return to Fox — and in early June it seemed as if that was on the point of being brought to reality.

At this time Fox was financially embarrassed by debts of over £60,000. On the initiative of Charles Pelham and Dudley North a scheme was set on foot to pay off these debts for him. After no less a sum than £40,000 had been privately promised, a public meeting was held at the 'Crown and Anchor' on 5 June which established a committee to supervise the collection of money and which appointed three trustees to direct its application. Although much was said to the effect that the subscription was to be purely a personal matter, 'without looking to political partialities of any kind', the subscription was, in fact, of some political importance.[2]

The Duke of Portland not only approved of the subscription but he was active in attempting to raise money. Indeed, he assented to the distribution of propaganda relating to the subscription which was disseminated throughout England and Ireland. Further, Portland was by no means the only conservative Whig who was prepared to lend active support to the subscription project. This was in the face of a widespread feeling that the whole proceeding was a 'kind of degradation', which did Fox immense harm in the country.[3] The political implications of the subscription were grasped by Fitzwilliam who observed that 'it will never make a consistency sufficient to call itself

[1] E.g. *The Morning Chronicle*, 11 Apr., 9 May.

[2] Ibid. 6 June. The Committee consisted of: Lord John Russell, Lord G. H. Cavendish, Francis, Crewe, Vyner, Wrightson, Alderman Skinner, Serjeant Adair, Alderman Combe. The three trustees were T. W. Coke, Tom Pelham and Byng. See also Lord to Lady Bessborough 7 June 1793, Earl of Bessborough, *Lady Bessborough and her Family Circle* (1940), 90.

[3] James Perry to Adam 13 June, William Taylor to Adam 11 July 1793, Blair-Adam MSS.; Adam to Portland 27 July 1793, Portland MSS., P.W.F. 47a. The unfavourable opinions of the subscription are illustrated in: Sheffield to Lady Webster 14 June 1793, Ad. MS. 51845, unfoliated, Holland House MSS. The *Public Advertiser* of 8 June called Fox 'an object of public pity'.

the subscription of any body of men'.[1] Moreover, this view can readily be substantiated from a glance at the resolutions which were passed at the 'Crown and Anchor' on 5 June, having been sent to Portland for his approval. These acknowledged the purity of Fox's motives and the disinterestedness of his conduct. These innocuous provisions were offset, however, by those resolutions which adverted to the services of Fox which entitled him to the applause of the country and which merited an 'effective demonstration' of the affection, gratitude and esteem of his friends and constituents. According to Burke, in accepting the assistance of his friends, Fox assured them that he would persist in his present line of conduct. Whether Portland realized the construction which might be placed upon his approval of the subscription or whether this was merely the latest instance of his attempts to prevent the final disruption of the party is difficult to determine. Such evidence as there is suggests that Portland had some reservations concerning the political implications of the subscription but that these were overcome by Adam. Notwithstanding Portland's motives, there can be no doubt but that the national campaign to honour Fox cannot have done other than carry with it political undertones in an age when personalities counted for so much in political life.[2]

The activities of the Portland Whigs in connection with the subscription doubtless convinced Pitt that Fox might still possess personal influence sufficient to prevent them from declaring their separation from him and perhaps to lead them to act in party with him on a future occasion. While the political scene was still fraught with uncertainties — not the least of which was the question of the duration of the war — the Foxite and Portland Whigs might yet have come together again. With 17 June rapidly approaching — the date fixed for debating Fox's motion for peace with France — Pitt may have feared that the Portland Whigs might yet be sympathetic to Fox's views. Not since 18 February had Fox himself instigated a debate on the war and, indeed, so deeply had

[1] Fitzwilliam to Adam 21 July 1793, Blair-Adam MSS.

[2] Serjeant Adair to Portland 4 June 1793, Portland MSS., P.W.F. 19; Adam to Portland 27 July 1793, Portland MSS., P.W.F. 47; the King to Pitt, 7 June 1793, Aspinall, *Later Correspondence of George III*, ii. 47. The King realized the importance of the affair and told Pitt that it 'compleats the career of this Session' of Fox. For Burke's views, see *Observations*, in *Burke's Works*, i. 619.

England committed herself to the support of the allies and so ineptly was the first campaign being conducted, that Fox might well have been expected to find fresh ammunition to level at the ministers. On 14 June Pitt sent for Windham, ostensibly to discuss Fox's motion of the seventeenth, more significantly, to disclose 'some Circumstances arising out of the present State of Politics' which required confidential communication. While rumours of impending cabinet changes swept London, the conservative Whigs were brought once more to consider the future of their party.[1]

Windham and Pitt met on the morning of the debate. Windham had already seen Portland, Devonshire and Mansfield[2] at Burlington House the previous evening and had found that their attitude to Pitt had not softened. Nor were Pitt's present offers likely to conciliate them. For he was not thinking of a party junction at all but was merely trying to detach individuals. To Windham he offered the Secretary-ship-at-War and to Lord Spencer the post of Lord-Lieutenant of Ireland. Before any consideration could be given to this overture, proceedings in parliament occupied the attention of politicians.[3]

The debate of 17 June revealed that there was no ground for com-promise between Fox and the Portland Whigs on the question of war. Although none of the Portland Whigs spoke during the debate,

---

[1] Pitt to Windham 14 June 1793, Ad. MS. 37844, f. 7, Windham Papers printed in *Windham Papers*, i. 137. 14 June: 'The day of my receiving my first note from Pitt.' *Windham Diary*, 277. For the coldness of Fitzwilliam's attitude to Pitt, see Fitzwilliam to Pitt 5 June 1793, P.R.O. Pitt Papers, 135. Rumours of cabinet changes were widely believed, e.g. Lord Jersey to Pitt 16 June 1793, C.U.L. 6958[7], f. 1274. It was expected that either Auckland or Cornwallis would replace West-morland in Ireland. See R. Cunningham to Auckland 26 May 1793, Ad. MS. 34451, ff. 113–14, Auckland Papers; John Lee to Auckland 28 May 1793, ibid. ff. 143–4; *The Public Advertiser*, 18 June 1793.

[2] Previously, 7th Viscount Stormont. A Northite Peer, he was Secretary of State for the Northern Department 1779–82 and President of the Council in the Coali-tion ministry of 1783. Succeeded his uncle as Earl of Mansfield in 1793.

[3] *Windham Diary*, 277; Lord Bessborough to his wife 18 June 1793, Bessborough, *Lady Bessborough and her Family Circle*, 92. Another report says that there was an additional meeting at Windham's 'for the purpose of promoting Connection and Atheism' on the same evening as the dinner at Burlington House. Auckland to Pitt 25 June 1793, P.R.O. Pitt Papers, 110. *The Morning Chronicle* on 15 June was strenuously (and rightly) denying reports that Portland and Pitt were to meet.

Fox's uncompromising speeches upon the issues of war and peace exacerbated the existing party divisions and raised the prospect of fresh disagreements in the future. For Fox was pledging his opinions to accommodate future circumstances and in none of these opinions could the Portland Whigs be expected to concur. In laying down the premise that the only justifiable aims of the war had been accomplished by the successful defence of Holland, he was raising the (quite different) question of what the ultimate purposes of the war were to be and in doing so he threw into the controversies which raged around the war the issue of intervention in French affairs. The debate, and the issues it aroused, went further than the mere discussion of the desirability — or security — of negotiating peace. Fox condemned any attempts on the part of the allies to obtain indemnities, to interfere in French internal matters and, in particular, to dictate to France the form of her government. Windham, on the other hand, supported by Pitt, protested that interference in French affairs might be necessary if there was to be in Paris a government 'as we might with safety treat with'. Even if the war ended in the immediate future, there would be further divisions in the party on the subject of peace and such divisions would follow from just those conflicting constitutional attitudes which had bedevilled the unity of the party since 1792. Those who followed Fox in professing support for the French Revolution and in railing at the conduct of the allies were now advancing one stage further. In refusing to tolerate interference in French affairs, they were condoning republicanism. By pledging their hostility to the reimposition of monarchy upon the French by the allies, they were opening an unbridgeable gulf of opinion between themselves and the Portland Whigs.[1]

The importance of the debate was immediately recognized by the Portland Whigs. According to Burke, who regarded the motion as 'far the worst of Mr. Fox's proceedings':

The efforts of the faction have so prevailed that some of his Grace's nearest friends have actually voted for that motion: some, after showing themselves, went away, others did not appear at all. So it must be where a man is for any

---

[1] *The Parliamentary History*, xxx. 994–1024. There is a list of the minority in *The Morning Chronicle* of 18 June which, including tellers, numbers 49 and not 47 as *The Parliamentary History* states.

time supported from personal considerations, without reference to his public conduct.[1]

After the conclusion of the debate, Burke dined with Windham and doubtless left him in no doubt as to his views upon the overtures which had been received from Pitt. If Windham still entertained any doubts about accepting office, he was relieved of them when Lord Spencer called on him the following day to tell him that he did not wish to accept Pitt's offer. Windham informed Pitt of their decision on 19 June and, although he was still troubled with reservations over the wisdom of his refusal, he was glad to dismiss the aggravating subject from his mind and prepare himself for a brief sojourn in Flanders. Although Pitt said that the interview was 'perfectly satisfactory', a more realistic account was provided by Dundas. He said that 'with mutual profession of entire agreement, and of a disposition to unite, all arrangement is, however, suspended for the present'. Characteristically, Windham had extricated himself from an embarrassing situation by hinting to Pitt that he might take office 'sometime hence' while Spencer had pleaded 'private grounds of family convenience' as the reason for his refusal.[2] Although the negotiations were broken off, the uncertainty which surrounded their conclusion was reflected in the continued spate of rumours, which was not confined to the newspapers. If Pitt had intended to interest Portland in the possibility of coming to some arrangement with the ministry then he had evidently succeeded, for the Duke was bemused, if not dazzled, by the feeling that high offices in the state were at his disposal if he chose to take advantage of his political weight.[3]

---

[1] *Observations*, in *Burke's Works*, i. 622. There seems little real justification for what Burke says about votes. The only Portland Whig who voted with Fox was Tom Pelham who was, in any case, uncertain in politics in 1793. Lord John Townshend, lately returned to parliament, voted with Fox and continued to do so regularly. The rest of the minority included Foxite Whigs, Lansdowne's members, and a handful of independents.

[2] *Windham Diary*, 278. Pitt to Windham 19 June 1793, Ad. MS. 37844, ff. 9–10, Windham Papers. Elliot to his wife 25 June 1793, Minto, ii. 150–1.

[3] Lord Hardwicke to Pitt 21 June 1793, C.U.L. 6958[7], f. 1281. *The Morning Chronicle* of 19 June noticed a report in a ministerial paper that Windham was to be the new Irish Secretary. On 21 June the paper spoke of the imminent retirement of Dundas, of Windham's close friendship with Pitt 'and his immediate appointment to some responsible situation'. For Portland's views, see Portland to Fitzwilliam 22 Sept. 1793, Wentworth Woodhouse MSS., F.31a, unfoliated.

In the days following the conclusion of the negotiation, Portland and his friends were flattered by a pleasing recognition of their public reputations. In early July, Portland was officially installed as Chancellor of the University of Oxford. Honorary LL.D.s were liberally bestowed upon the Duke's friends, including Devonshire, Fitzwilliam, Malmesbury, Mansfield, Elliot, Windham and Frederick North. Portland put forward Burke's name for a similar honour, only to be annoyed when Burke declined acceptance on the grounds that he had not merited the degree when his *Reflections* had been published. Otherwise the ceremonies at Oxford were attended with the greatest cordiality. While the conservative Whigs basked in the social limelight, ministerialists tactfully remained in the background.[1] They were not alone in ostensibly wishing to eliminate considerations of political advantage from Portland's installation. Much to Fox's relief, Portland hinted that his presence at Oxford might prove to be embarrassing. Fox took his point. If he attended the ceremonies, then it was just possible that he might be offered a degree. In that case, he would have to refuse the honour because he differed in politics from the Duke. So Fox and most of his friends stayed away from Oxford.[2] While the political scene was so uncertain as to render any mark of respect for Portland liable to delicate interpretations, it was not surprising that a more overt move should encourage renewed speculation concerning the future of the Portland Whigs. The creation of an earldom for Lord Porchester in the middle of July was just such a move.[3] The situation of Elliot, however, was a far more serious factor in the ambiguous political circumstances of the time.

The offer of the Governor-Generalship of Madras had brought Elliot scuttling back to town from Minto. On 25 June he saw Dundas and told him that he must reject the offer. Dundas then offered the

---

[1] 'Scarce any ministerial people have attended, which is very strange considering their proposing the Duke'. Lord to Lady Bessborough 4 July 1793, Bessborough, op. cit., 94–5. Elliot to his wife 3 July 1793, Minto, ii. 153–4.

[2] Fox to Portland 28 June 1793, Ad. MS. 47561, ff. 140–1, Fox Papers. The only Foxite Whig who appears to have been at Oxford was Lord William Russell. *The Morning Chronicle*, 3 July 1793.

[3] Lady Holland, *Journal*, i. 69; J. Hare to the Duchess of Portland 26 July 1793, Portland MSS. P.W.G. 143.

Irish secretaryship to Elliot as a testimony of the administration's
intention of reforming the government of Ireland. Elliot would not
consider taking such an office while Lord Westmorland remained
Lord Lieutenant. Loughborough vainly strove to bring Elliot into an
arrangement with the government but, by offering him the post of
Vice-President of the Board of Trade, an office which he thought that
Pitt would create for Elliot, he overplayed his hand. Dundas told Sir
Gilbert that Pitt had no intention of creating such an office. Elliot
proceeded to Oxford to attend Portland's installation, after which he
returned to Minto.[1] Yet Elliot's return to London had not been entirely
devoid of consequence, although he was disappointed at the outcome
of the political skirmishings in which he had been involved. He took
with him back to Minto the conviction that ministers were full of good
intentions about Ireland and that they wished to settle its government
with all possible speed.

For a few weeks the situation rested. As Auckland put it: 'The
dispersed and rusticated life of English politicians during the summer
months makes it difficult to collect intelligence.'[2] Windham was in
Flanders from 12 July and it was only after he returned to England on
6 August that the inconclusive state of the relations between the
ministers and the conservative Whigs could be determined more
thoroughly. Windham was in a crucial position. It was through him
that ministerial contacts with the conservative Whigs would proceed.
It was upon his shoulders that the initial responsibility would fall for
bringing the Portland Whigs into a closer relationship with administration. It was to him that waverers in the party would look for some
initiative. Even before his return from the continent, Windham was
under some pressure from Elliot to assist in a scheme which the latter
had concocted. Elliot had written to Dundas from Minto a letter
which strongly insinuated that Spencer would be ready to consider an
offer of the Irish Viceroyalty; if the offer were to be made, then
Windham would be a party to the arrangement. Dundas was interested in the scheme and was impatient for the negotiation to be concluded in view of renewed disturbances in Ireland. Elliot was anxious

[1] Elliot to his wife 25 June 1793, Minto, ii. 150–1 and 151–3. Pitt mentioned to
Windham on 19 June that Elliot might go to Ireland as secretary to Spencer.
[2] Auckland to Lord Henry Spencer 9 Aug. 1793, *Auckland*, iii. 104–5.

lest Malmesbury, the most likely candidate for the Viceroyalty after Spencer, should put himself forward and be found acceptable to the ministers. Windham was justifiably suspicious of a scheme, the success of which would give umbrage to Portland, the failure of which might bedevil future relations between the conservative Whigs and the ministry. Further, Windham himself was still reluctant to involve himself in a closer connection with the government. He refused to involve himself too closely with Elliot's plan and referred it to Portland.

In fact, Windham's opinions were only now beginning to point to the desirability of a union with the ministers. He remained acutely suspicious of Pitt and disliked personal contact with him. Yet he nurtured a bitter and deep-rooted fear of the Foxite Whigs. He believed that Fox's intentions were to render the war unpopular, to destroy the confederacy, to ruin the constitution of Britain and to eliminate all prospect of peace and stable, ordered government returning to Europe. He was convinced that the Foxites were finally separated from the party. As for Fox, Windham refused to entertain the possibility of his being allowed to form part of a cabinet in the foreseeable future. The political differences which separated Fox from the party were not only fundamental; they were permanent. Windham's solution to the problem of party was still unchanged. He continued to advocate the doctrine of a 'Third Party', 'supporting Ministry but not joining them', although he now saw that a union might be necessary 'at some period and in some circumstances'. Windham knew that the question of Ireland might well be the issue upon which a union might most conveniently be negotiated. He visited Spencer at Althorp in late August to collect his latest views. Spencer was not averse to assuming the Viceroyalty but he would not do so unless he was assured of firm support in the cabinet — that is, unless there was a general union and party arrangement. Pitt was too untrustworthy to allow of any alternative to a coalition.[1]

Windham was being sought out as the man most likely to influence both the ministers and the Portland Whigs, from another quarter. For

[1] Elliot to Windham 4 Aug. 1793, Ad. MS. 37852, ff. 212–15, Windham Papers, printed in *Windham Papers*, i. 140–4; Elliot to Windham 13 Aug. 1793, ibid. ff. 216–17; Windham to Portland, draft, 3 Sept. 1793, Ad. MS. 37845, ff. 13–14 Windham Papers, printed in *Windham Papers*, i. 146–50.

Edmund Burke the conduct of the war had reached the height of its folly with the despatch to Flanders of the Duke of York and with the subsequent concentration of attention upon Dunkirk. The allies had enjoyed moderate military success but 'This Republic never can have a Territorial Limit, for it has no Local or Territorial Objects'. After months of indecision, the ministers had at last hit upon a system by which to conduct the war. Yet Dunkirk was totally irrelevant to any plan which might lead to victory, which could only be won by a blow at Paris itself. At the very least, one more campaign would be needed and the co-operation of the allies would be essential if the means of obtaining a secure peace were to be achieved. The republicans must be ruined and destroyed, the abettors of anarchy must be punished, property, aristocracy and monarchy must be re-established upon their ancient foundations.[1] Burke pressed these opinions on Windham during August and his efforts were not without effect. For Windham had been unable to make up his mind about how the ministers should conduct the war but by the end of the month he was coming to share the views of Burke.[2]

The Portland Whigs, however, were not to be so easily convinced. As Fitzwilliam put it, the opinions of Burke and those of the Portland Whigs 'certainly were at a wide distance from each other, and this difference was very systematic'. He felt great resentment at Burke's behaviour in November 1792 and at his approaches to Pitt.

He enlisted overtly into his army: nay, he became the standard bearer [sic] of his empire, and of course the supporter of his future fortune in every situation. . . . I cannot make his sentiments, my own, and until I can do so, they must not be the rule of my conduct, upon so material a point in politics as the support of, or opposition to a Minister.[3]

---

[1] Burke to General Dalton 6 Aug. 1793 (copy) N.R.O. A. iv. 22, Burke Letters; Burke to Windham 18 Aug. 1793, Wentworth Woodhouse MSS., Burke Letters 1, printed in *Correspondence of Edmund Burke*, iv. 132–4. Burke to the Comte de Mercy Aug. 1793 (copy), Wentworth Woodhouse MSS., Burke Letters 1, printed in *Correspondence of Edmund Burke*, iv. 136–50.

[2] Windham to Burke 17 Aug. 1793, Wentworth Woodhouse MSS., Burke Letters 1; Windham to Burke ante 22 Aug. 1793, ibid.

[3] Fitzwilliam to Richard Burke jnr. 27 Aug. 1793, N.R.O. A. iv. 20, Burke Letters.

Fitzwilliam could not see the need for anything like a total suspension of opposition to the ministry. All that could be done was to wait upon events and, in the meantime, instruct M.P.s to vote against important ministerial measures.[1] These were not the only issues upon which men like Fitzwilliam diverged from the views of Burke. Powerful antipathies against Pitt, steadily built up and confirmed for ten years, could not be suddenly dissipated.

I may give occasional support to Mr. Pitt, as I have given occasional support to particular measures of other Ministers, being at the same time, generally and systematically in opposition to them: I do give it to the measure of the present war, to its propriety, to its necessity, to its justice. I have daily occasion to combat both his friends and his foes on the subject, and I do combat this for him; but systematically I am in opposition to him and to his Ministry.[2]

In the mind of Fitzwilliam there was nothing anomalous in his political line. There was no question of choosing between Pitt and Fox. Nobody hated the Friends of the People more than Fitzwilliam. It was a choice between Pitt and Portland. The crux of Burke's position was that the French Revolution was a momentous issue upon which politicians were divided by principle. It was irrelevant to argue that the war with France might soon be over and the party then reunited. The French Revolution was 'a violation of every right divine and human'. The very principle of society itself was at stake and upon this principle there could be no compromise. It was not a particular measure since it underlay opinions on all other issues. Whatever Pitt had done in the past, however ineptly he was conducting the war at the present, he was at least fighting for the survival of civilized society and thus all systematic opposition to him should cease. The personal ties binding the Portland Whigs to Fox must be broken and, following the lead of the 'Third Party', separation must be declared. Although Windham was beginning to accept Burke's opinions more thoroughly, even now he could not admit that a junction with the ministry was desirable His views on this subject were, in fact, almost identical with those of the Portland Whigs but he stressed the doubtful consequences of any such junction rather than the prejudices and principles which coalition would necessarily call in question. He preferred to be in a position

[1] R. Burke jnr. to Fitzwilliam 16 Aug. 1793, N.R.O. A. iv. 19, Burke Letters.
[2] Fitzwilliam to Richard Burke jnr. 27 Aug. 1793, loc. cit.

'maintaining from time to time his own opinion in debate and giving
to Ministry, in causes which he approved, the benefits of a support
which would become of some value from being wholly exempt from
suspicion of any undue motive'.[1] When they realized that Windham
could not serve their purposes, the ministers returned to their former
tactic of exerting pressure on Elliot. Dunkirk provided them with a
convenient opportunity. The Duke of York had departed on 10
August with a force of 37,000 men and the news of the town's
capitulation was eagerly anticipated. Elliot was chosen by the cabinet
to order proceedings at Dunkirk as soon as the town had fallen. In
early September, Elliot accepted this temporary post but almost
simultaneously with his acceptance came the news of the staggering
reverse at Hondschoote. The Dunkirk campaign had failed and the
Duke of York was forced to retreat into Flanders. Elliot's mission
was off and the political situation at home was once more plunged into
confusion.[2]

The debility of Pitt's administration was strikingly revealed by the
Dunkirk fiasco. Although Pitt himself was nonplussed, regarding the
reverse as 'only a temporary check', the ministers concerned in the
affair, Chatham and Richmond, were the focus of strident criticism and
bitter disgust. Even Dundas could not escape the burst of disapproval
which broke like a storm over the heads of the ministers. For a while
some rearrangement of the cabinet was expected and, once more, the
conservative Whigs found themselves in the middle of a political furore
of the first order.[3] The political repercussions of the Duke of York's

[1] R. Burke jnr. to Fitzwilliam 16 Aug. 1793, N.R.O. A. iv. 19, Burke Letters;
Fitzwilliam to R. Burke jnr. 27 Aug. 1793, N.R.O. A. iv. 20, Burke Letters;
Portland to Fitzwilliam 22 Sept. 1793, loc. cit.

[2] Elliot to his wife 10 and 11 Sept. 1793, Minto, ii. 159–60.

[3] Camden was, at this time, looking for an early opportunity of resigning,
Camden to Pitt 1 Sept. 1793, C.U.L. 6958[7], f. 1310. Even before Hondschoote,
Auckland was grumbling to Sheffield of 'a multiplication of blunders and misfortunes', 20 Aug. 1793, Ad. MS. 45728, ff. 160–1, Auckland Papers. Loughborough admitted to Auckland that the failure of the campaign would have unpleasant consequences in England: 'things stand here at great risk', c. 10–13 Sept.
1793, *Auckland*, iii. 114–15. Pitt to Westmorland 15 Sept. 1793, C.U.L. 6958[7],
f. 1320. *The Morning Chronicle*, 13 and 18 Sept. Sheffield to Auckland 22 and 25
Sept., *Auckland*, iii. 117–20.

failure before Dunkirk, however, were twisted and turned into a complicated pattern of confusing possibilities. If it stirred Burke to make a passionate call to the Portland Whigs to serve their country, then, equally, it demonstrated the incapacity of the ministers to conduct a war and thus it alienated the Portland Whigs still further from the ministry. If Pitt was led to renew his attempts to detach the conservative Whigs, then it enabled Fox to hope that upon the conduct of the war the party might again unite its forces and assault the ministry.

The Dunkirk failure found the conservative Whigs even more divided than usual upon the subject of their own political future.[1] Elliot was determined to take office. He had come to reject Windham's thesis that junction should only be achieved collectively after the 'Third Party' had renewed 'the connection with and dependence on the Duke of Portland'. To wait still longer for the Duke to make up his mind would be 'fatal to everything like useful exertion, and fatal probably to our private honours'. The obloquy with which the ministers were overwhelmed after Dunkirk was a source of serious concern for Elliot, and his anxieties about the conduct of the war could not be dismissed lightly.

I see nothing to be done but to support and assist ministers in carrying it on, to obtain additional confidence to their administration by our accession to their counsels, and to make ourselves responsible, as well as them, for this measure, which is as much fully our own as theirs. We are completely responsible for the war now, since we are so for its issue.[2]

The disasters of the war had driven Elliot to reject the 'Third Party' doctrine. He told Windham that 'all things considered, a distinct, separate, and unresponsible corps, even supporting Government, is in effect a formidable opposition'. He was not divided in principle from Windham. Where they differed was whether this was to be the appropriate occasion upon which their principles should be put into practice.[3] With energetic encouragement from Burke, therefore, Elliot accepted the post of Civil Commissioner at Toulon in the middle

---

[1] Elliot to his wife 14 Sept. 1793, Minto, ii. 161–2.
[2] Elliot to his wife 17 Sept. 1793, Minto, ii. 158–9.
[3] Elliot to Windham 18 Sept. 1793, Ad. MS. 37852, ff. 218–19, Windham Papers, printed in *Windham Papers*, i. 157–8.

of September.[1] His acceptance of ministerial office was a portent for the future. The defection from the party of Loughborough had been serious but he had never taken seriously the party differences and the doctrinal dissensions. Elliot, on the other hand, had been one of the party's most respected leaders and during the past year he had acted from conviction in supporting the 'Third Party'. Now that he had chosen to dismiss party considerations as no longer relevant to the political situation, he inevitably brought Windham and Spencer to reconsider their positions.[2]

Although Windham was embracing Burke's opinions on the war with increasing enthusiasm, he was still manifestly reluctant to do anything which might secure their adoption. The soundings of the previous few months had convinced both him and Spencer that Pitt was as untrustworthy as ever. Further, the reverse at Dunkirk made them realize that to defend the war by accepting firmer responsibility for its conduct would involve them in the unpopularity which had lately engulfed the ministers. Both Windham and Spencer, therefore, were unwilling to underline their defence of a war policy which they both considered to be indefensible by taking office. On the other hand, it would have been unthinkable for them to have attacked the conduct of the war. This would only have strengthened the hands of those who were working for the subversion of the constitution. It followed that the 'Third Party' doctrine was still relevant to the political situation. Yet they both realized at last that if the doctrine were to be taken to its ultimate conclusion, it would involve them in an impossible dilemma. If Pitt's conduct of the war became absolutely indefensible and aroused such hostility as to lead to cries for his removal then they, the 'Third Party', must form an administration. If they did not, then Fox undoubtedly would. But an administration opposed by both Pitt and Fox could never stand. How did Windham and Spencer resolve the dilemma? In fact, they never faced it squarely. They simply hoped that the Toulon campaign would end the war and thus solve their problems

---

[1] Burke to Elliot 16 Sept. 1793, Osborn Collection, Copeland Transcript. Burke to Elliot, 18 Sept. 1793, Minto, ii. 165–7; Elliot to his wife 17 Sept. 1793, Minto, ii. 162–3.

[2] *The Morning Chronicle* realized the importance of Elliot's defection and was strenuously denying that he had accepted Pitt's offers as late as 25 Sept. 1793.

for them. Even then there was the gnawing fear that if the Toulon campaign were successful, and if the government of France were reconstituted along the lines laid down by Lord Hood's declaration,[1] then the French would return to the constitution of 1789 and perhaps revolution would start from there once more. All this did not bear thinking about. Not surprisingly, Windham and Spencer were paralysed by indecision and incapable of taking anything like the initiatives which were now necessary to resolve problems which could not be shelved indefinitely.[2]

Their hesitation can partly be explained by the fact that Portland had not yet replied to Windham's letter of 3 September which had hinted at the possible acceptance of the Irish Viceroyalty by Spencer. The reverse at Dunkirk had brought new factors into the political game and Portland was no less aware of them than Windham. The Duke had now realized that the war was becoming unpopular at home and that there was now little prospect of a speedy victory. Nevertheless, he had been an advocate of war with France and he was determined to maintain his support 'until it can be terminated with safety to the principles of good order and the first objects of Civil Society'. Portland did not define what this meant but there can be little doubt that he agreed with Fitzwilliam in viewing 'the miserable system of 89 as the cause of all the miseries and that France must start again from her antient Monarchy'. General principles, however, were no substitute for political sagacity. They did not help him to write the much deferred reply to Windham. Throughout September Portland was torn by indecision. Finally, he turned to Fitzwilliam for advice. This only served to heighten Portland's confusion. Fitzwilliam's detestation of the Friends of the People was ripening into a conviction that Fox and he were totally separated by differences over the war. On the other hand, Windham had shown himself in his true colours the previous November and he was no longer to be trusted. Fitzwilliam was not surprised that Pitt was tempting Windham and by doing so providing yet a further

---

[1] Hood entered Toulon on 9 Aug. 1793. His Proclamation of 23 Aug. 1793 strongly implied that the restoration of the French monarchy was a British war aim.

[2] Windham to Portland 3 Sept. 1793, Ad. MS. 37845, ff. 13–14, Windham Papers, printed in *Windham Papers*, i. 146–50; Spencer to Windham 14 and 18 Sept. 1793, Ad. MS. 37845, ff. 112–15, Windham Papers, printed in *Windham Papers*, i. 151–5.

instance of his insincerity. Portland was rather less bitter towards Windham than Fitzwilliam and he could not accept the view that all thought of negotiation should be suspended. Yet his discussion with Fitzwilliam had forced Portland to define his real objection to Pitt. He despised his practice of nepotism, but more serious was 'his holding his own situation in such a way as to make it inconsistent with the principles we have constantly possessed for us to have anything to do with him'. It was impossible for the Whigs to act *under* Pitt but it might be feasible to negotiate an arrangement by which they could act *with* him. Yet how could Pitt be expected to surrender so much of the power which he had assiduously built up and jealously guarded for the last ten years? On 25 September Portland saw Pitt and tried to discover for himself how far Pitt might be willing to go on the subject of the disposal of offices. Nothing definite was suggested but Portland confessed himself a little less antipathetic to the minister after the interview. Pitt had worked his magic well. The Duke was convinced now that Pitt was thoroughly sympathetic to his insistence upon 'a ministerial arrangement upon those principles and that basis upon which alone I ever could take a part in it myself or advise anyone for whom I had a regard to embark in it'. Portland believed that Pitt was now ready to allow Windham and others to enter the highest offices of state but Portland himself was unwilling to impair his character by joining the government. Portland was not long in realizing that he was playing into Pitt's hands. As soon as the impression which the cordiality of Pitt's manner had made on him had worn away, the Duke felt humiliated and incensed. He had run too close to the edge of the precipice. His own craving for some resolution of the daunting problems which overwhelmed him had jerked him into a false sense of duty which, in turn, would only have destroyed the party and with it Portland's own political influence.[1]

It was one of the supreme ironies in the history of the Whig party that at exactly this point Portland received from Burke a complimentary copy of *Observations on the Conduct of the Minority*. From Burke's point of view, it could not have come at a more unpropitious

---

[1] Portland to Fitzwilliam 22 Sept. 1793, Wentworth Woodhouse MSS., F.31a. Fitzwilliam to Portland 22 Sept. 1793, ibid. draft; Portland to Fitzwilliam 23 Sept. 1793, N.R.O. Box 45; Portland to Fitzwilliam 26 Sept. 1793, ibid.

moment. However forceful and convincing his arguments, they raised, for Portland at least, more problems than they settled. It was all very well for Burke to urge Portland to sever relations with Fox but this might ultimately drive the Duke into a closer connection with Pitt. Burke could blithely tell Portland to forget the past and to soften his attitude towards Pitt because the latter was, at least, striving to defeat Jacobinism in Europe. Yet what was Portland to do when Pitt was ostensibly persisting in his attempts to destroy the Whig party? All of Burke's arguments would have been more convincing had he been able to persuade Portland that Pitt sincerely desired to come to some honourable arrangement with the Portland Whigs. It was one thing to tell Portland what the situation demanded of him but Burke did not have to make the requisite decisions. Nor did he appreciate the subtleties, the delicate manœuvres and the finer points of party diplomacy which overwhelmed Portland in his half-hearted attempts to come to terms with his political difficulties. Nor could Burke understand Portland's personal sense of incapacity. For years he had leaned on others and contented himself with but a nominal leadership of the party. Now he could not escape the odious responsibility of charting a course for the party which would settle the uncertainties of its members. His decisions, whatever their nature, would be productive of political embarrassment and personal distress. His brief skirmish with Pitt had at least taught Portland a lesson he should not have had to learn, but he clung to the moral and renewed his determination to keep his distance from Pitt. Portland thankfully retreated to his former position and closed his mind to the problem of his future relations with the administration. His attitude was poignantly epitomized in a letter which he wrote to Burke, replying to the *Observations*:[1]

... I am not christian enough to turn the other cheek to the man who has given me a blow nor can I lick the hand which has endeavoured to destroy me, I can forgive where I see a real disposition to repentance. I desire no man to disgrace himself, and I am positively certain that you are the last man who would consent to my debasing myself. ... Principles require more proofs than one ... they call for a consistency of conduct as a security as a title for confidence and should I observe the persons who profess to agree with me in one case in

---

[1] 10 Oct. 1793, Portland MSS. 2101 (copy), printed in *Correspondence of Edmund Burke*, iv. 161–6.

principle counteracting and undermining this very principle in another, it would seem to me unreasonable to expect and impossible to give that confidence, which I was once vain enough to hope might have been established, and which had it so pleased Providence, might have prevented the alarming Crisis to which We have been brought. There was an evident want of good Faith then, that Want still remains, however in conformity with the Principles I have professed, in this great cause; and indeed in all its appendages my support, such as it may be will be given completely and unreservedly to those be they who may, who appear to conduct it to the best of their abilities.

Portland fell back upon Burke's own principles, adapting them to suit his present needs, while reverting to his own former declarations about 'the only basis upon which an Administration ought to be formed'. Portland doubtless meant that he would insist upon a party coalition with Pitt for which he intended to impose stringent conditions. Until such a coalition might be achieved, he refused to consider lending Pitt any further support. Portland had proclaimed his renewed determination to pursue the same line with regard to the ministers as he had done for nearly a year, but already the ground beneath his feet was beginning to crumble. Although he might indulge in the most generous eulogies of Fox, acknowledging 'many and striking instances of very superior Talents and Judgement, the most incorruptible integrity, the most perfect disinterestedness', Portland could not much longer conceal from himself the ever-widening gulf which increasingly separated him from Fox.[1]

The lethargy of the months of the recess had brought conservative Whigs of all descriptions to reappraise their political roles and to reconsider their relations with the ministry. Meanwhile, a similar reassessment of the status of the Foxite Whigs had been proceeding, provoked by William Adam's activities as secretary and treasurer of the Whig party. In the summer of 1793 Adam was reviewing the state of the party's finances. He found, in addition to pressing applications for money, debts of over £1,000. He began raising the money in a cautious manner; he suggested to Fitzwilliam that contributions to the annual fund should be increased so that an extra £350 per annum could

---

[1] On 17 Oct. Portland replied to Windham, after a delay of six weeks, reaffirming his support for the war but resting his reluctance to seek closer relations with Pitt on the ministry's inept conduct of the war. Ad. MS. 37845, f. 15, Windham Papers.

be added to the present annual fund of £1,100.[1] Fitzwilliam reacted violently. He refused to pay one farthing on the grounds that the party press poured out republican propaganda. Adam's blithe assumption that the Portland Whigs might stretch their token attachment to the Foxites to the point of subsidizing their propaganda had been destroyed at one blow, a blow, moreover, which demonstrated the unreality of that token attachment. Undeterred, Adam begged Fitzwilliam to allow the annual subscription to continue for one more year, thus paying off the debt.[2] Lord Fitzwilliam's reply revealed the length to which he, second only to the Duke of Portland among the conservative Whigs, held the break in the party to have gone. His opinion, in fact, was directly contrary to that of the Duke of Portland:[3]

... the party was broke up a year and a half ago and the means taken for effectuating that purpose were so sure to do it that it would be pushing charity to an excess, to suppose that men of ability and experience can have taken them, but for that purpose, or (to narrow it as much as possible) with a view to dismiss particular persons — from that time I am free from commitments.

After further negotiations Fitzwilliam and Portland agreed to pay £200 each, their subscription for the present year, 'upon the express conditions of its being applied in discharge of the demands stated ... but I will not, upon any account whatever, contribute a single farthing for the Writers or Printers of Newspapers'.[4]

The discussions leading to this financial settlement were accompanied by other soundings which revealed even more clearly the fundamental rift which existed between the Portland Whigs and the Foxites. Shortly after the reverse at Dunkirk, Adam was able to seize upon the prospect of reuniting the party (perhaps as a means of extricating himself from his financial troubles) which had been voiced, somewhat unenthusiastically, by Fox himself:

Regrets are vain but one cannot help thinking that *if* Burke had died five years ago, *if* Lauderdale had not made his Association for he was the sole cause of it, *if* our friends would have been right headed upon the subject of that associa-

---

[1] Adam to Fitzwilliam 4 July 1793, N.R.O. Box 45.

[2] Fitzwilliam to Adam 21 July 1793, Blair-Adam MSS.; Adam to Fitzwilliam 26 July 1793, N.R.O. Box 45.

[3] Fitzwilliam to Adam 28 Aug. 1793, Blair-Adam MSS.

[4] Portland to Fitzwilliam 23 Sept. 1793, N.R.O. Box 45.

tion, and even after all, *if* last winter they would kept [sic] aloof upon the question of war and contented themselves with talking nonsense about domestic alarms — I really believe any one of these *ifs* would have ruined Pitt and indeed even as it is I think there is a chance of it. . . . Would it be impossible to get our old friends to act with me at least with respect to the conduct of the War, I sometimes think not, and yet they must see that the overturning of Pitt would lead to a Peace they would hardly like.[1]

Adam thereupon protested to Fitzwilliam at the latter's pronouncement that the party was broken up and that unity was now impossible. Adverting to the misconduct of the ministers and (unwisely) to 'the extraordinary terms of peace held out in Lord Hood's Proclamation', Adam expressed the hope to Fitzwilliam that 'any means could be taken to restore harmony'.[2] Fitzwilliam placed the request before Portland while underlining his own convictions:

. . . though it may be my fortune to vote on the same side of the house, I never will *act in party* with men who call in 40,000 weavers to dictate political measures to the Govt . . . whatever may be my private sentiments respecting the criminality of Ministers both before and after in the prosecution of the war, I know not that I shall alter my sentiment upon the subject, and if I did, I must fear the impossibility of Charles's line tallying in the least with mine.[3]

Portland agreed with Fitzwilliam, who passed on to Adam this refusal to consider joining Fox, even upon the sole issue of the conduct of the war. To Adam, the rebuff was 'nothing but the source of lamentation and regret'.[4]

Yet Adam made one last attempt to save the party. He told Fitzwilliam that Fox had not made a final choice in favour of the radicals in the party. He still wished to maintain his connection with the Old Whigs. His support of Grey's reform motion in the previous session was not an indication that he had thrown in his lot with the Friends of the People but merely the preservation of Fox's consistency with the

---

[1] Fox to Adam 18 Sept. 1793, Blair-Adam MSS.

[2] Adam to Fitzwilliam 20 Sept. 1793, N.R.O. Box 45.

[3] Fitzwilliam to Portland 22 Sept. 1793, draft, Wentworth Woodhouse MSS., F.31a.

[4] Portland to Fitzwilliam 23 Sept. 1793, N.R.O. Box 45; Fitzwilliam to Adam 28 Sept. 1793, Blair-Adam MSS.; Adam to Fitzwilliam 3 Oct. 1793, N.R.O. Box 45.

opinions he had formerly voiced in parliament. The disunity in the party ought to be quickly ended.

I own I feel some indignation, too, when I observe some persons avail themselves of that state of things, as a golden Bridge to pass to places, Pensions, contracts honour and titles, without that loss of Character which ought to attend upon such conduct activated by such motives.[1]

Fitzwilliam once more drew Portland's attention to Adam's desperate request that they should at least see Fox to discuss with him the state of the party. Portland was offended by Adam's request though he recognized his good intentions. He would not consent to speak to Fox on Adam's terms:

I must say that it seems true that after *all that had passed*, it is not for *us to seek* an explanation. . . .[2]

Fitzwilliam told Adam that the difference between himself and Portland, on the one hand, and Fox on the other, 'arises from a different view of existing circumstances and the points about which we differ, occupy a very great space in the present political atmosphere'. Discussion with Fox would only exacerbate those differences. Portland and Fitzwilliam would now make no concessions to Fox. Although he might have no formal engagement with the Friends of the People, he 'appears on every occasion, their friend and protector'. Fox and the Portland Whigs were separated by wide differences of opinion about the war. Nothing could be gained by agitating these underlying and uncompromising differences. The only thing which might restore the unity of the party was 'a completely successful termination of the present War'. And Portland himself now admitted that the party was really broken and that everything must be subordinated to a vigorous prosecution of war. It is doubtful if Adam told Fox of these futile overtures with the Portland Whigs. In December Fox was still hoping that the schism in the party might be repaired. Rather curiously, he still expected that the Portland Whigs would support him in the coming session of parliament on one issue at least, the protests which were to be made against the sentences passed upon Muir and Palmer, a cause which Fox embraced reluctantly and into which he had

[1] Adam to Fitzwilliam 31 Oct. 1793, N.R.O. Box 45.
[2] Portland to Fitzwilliam 11 Nov. 1793, N.R.O. Box 45.

been hurried by the precipitation of none other than Lauderdale.[1]

Meanwhile the subscription for discharging Fox's debts had been steadily proceeding. The raising of the money had been entrusted to Adam, who accepted yet another party commission with some annoyance because he had not been informed of the subscription before it had been launched and because he resented the amount of additional work which it involved.[2] Slightly over £40,000 had been immediately subscribed in June but it was not until October that the sum of £55,000 had been raised or promised. Even then a further £10,000 was required to discharge the whole of Fox's debts and to settle upon him a life annuity of over £2,000. Adam was faced with the disagreeable task of asking certain individuals to subscribe a second time and, had the Duke of Bedford not made liberal use of his influence, it is doubtful if the extra £10,000 would have been forthcoming.[3] As soon as the money had been raised, much of it was immediately directed to the liquidation of Fox's debts.[4]

The methods used by Adam to raise the money revealed the link between party and opinion in the country. He either contacted individuals directly to solicit a donation or he made use of the local influence of the friends of Fox as a means of collecting money from their localities. This latter method indicated that the split in the party itself had filtered down to the level of the constituencies. David Hartley wrote to Adam from York where the party had been strongly entrenched declaring that Fox's opinions on the war had 'so far disunited for the present many good Whigs, that it might be dangerous to risque

---

[1] Fitzwilliam to Adam 15 Nov. 1793, Blair-Adam MSS.; Adam to Fitzwilliam 27 Nov. 1793, draft, Blair-Adam MSS. (This letter may not have been sent. It is not in the Fitzwilliam MSS. at Northampton.) Portland to Fitzwilliam 3 Dec. 1793 enclosing a copy of a letter to Adam, N.R.O. Box 45; Fox to Adam 15 Dec. 1793, Blair-Adam MSS.

[2] Adam to Portland 16 July 1793, Portland MSS., P.W.F. 46a. Adam was at this time working on the finances of the Duke of York and the Prince of Wales.

[3] Adam to Bedford 27 Oct. 1793, draft, Blair-Adam MSS.; Bedford to Fitzwilliam (n.d. — *c.* 8 Dec. 1793), 13 Dec. 1793, N.R.O. Box 45. There are many MSS. in the Adam Papers giving details of the subscription. At first £100 was to have been a minimum contribution but many gave less, e.g. Sheridan, Byng, Western and Wilbraham paid only £25.

[4] £25,000 out of the first £55,000 was so directed.

a call of the party, or of any public meetings'.[1] Other prominent men refused to launch the subscription publicly, although they were willing to offer private contributions, because they disagreed with Fox in politics and were unwilling to risk the misrepresentation of their views which might attend upon their acting as local sponsors of the subscription.[2] Others attempted to launch the scheme in their home districts but, almost invariably, they reported to Adam that the cause of Fox was not popular. From Wakefield there were 'no hopes of anything material'. At Manchester a friend of Fox declared that 'the party spirit which rages here with great violence deters many others from joining us'. From Poole came the news that 'the present state of the Public Mind . . . [was] so very unfavourable to the laudable and desirable end proposed'.[3] Many of those who struggled manfully against the prevailing public feeling informed Adam that had the subscription been launched before the war they would have had little difficulty in multiplying manifold the meagre sums which they had managed to collect. Sometimes, however, the reason alleged for the difficulty of inducing the people to subscribe was that of local poverty which resulted from the war.[4] Nevertheless, the attempt to launch the subscription in the country revealed the extent to which the parties at Westminster were now based upon a conscious public opinion which was sometimes not only vocal but violent. The Reeves Associations had done their work well. Most of them, in fact, had already achieved their local objects of rousing the country against the seditious and had ceased their meetings earlier in the year. Inevitably, any scheme for relieving the arch-republican, Fox, of the debts of his debauchery was foredoomed to failure.[5] The issues thrown up by the war were acting as an ideological wedge between politicians and so momentous were the causes at stake that men of all shades of opinion were carrying them to the country. The Foxites largely failed to acquire a broad base of popular approval because their cause could so easily be imprinted

[1] Hartley to Adam 15 June 1793, Blair-Adam MSS.

[2] E.g. Townshend to Adam 21 June 1793, Blair-Adam MSS.

[3] J. Honeywood to Adam 24 Sept., G. Lloyd to Adam 7 July, Mr. Jeffrey to Adam 3 Sept. 1793, ibid.

[4] For the outrages undergone by the Foxites at the hands of the Reeves Associations see Black, *The Association*, 256–9; Mitchell, 'The Association Movement', 67.

[5] Mitchell, op. cit., 75–76.

upon the popular mind as factious, atheistic, republican and unpatriotic once the tentacles of the loyal Associations had extended throughout the land. The Foxites were too late in going to the country and never effectively launched a comparable appeal.

For many reasons, therefore, any prospect of bringing the Whigs to act together again was unlikely to be fulfilled. Fox himself was solicitous for the reunification of the party merely in temporary fits of nostalgia. His views on the continental situation were not advancing one whit closer to those of Portland and Fitzwilliam. He remained bitterly critical of the allies, speaking of their 'scandalous conduct . . . in respect to Poland', and hoping that they might quarrel over the spoils of the second partition. He was delighted when signs began to appear that the war was becoming unpopular in England but his jubilation clouded his judgement and exaggerated the extent of the unpopularity. Fox hoped, as he had hoped during the Oczacov crisis of 1791, that Pitt's inability to conduct foreign affairs might bring his ministry down. He noted with grim approval the growing list of allied failures which had begun with Dunkirk and which had continued throughout October. Yet he was reduced to despair at the continuing anarchy which prevailed within the borders of France. With Sheridan, he made futile representations to the French authorities against the impending execution of Marie Antoinette. All this did not prevent him from indulging in expressions of sympathy for the French people and the cause of the revolution. The events of the autumn tended to strengthen the uncompromising force with which he clung to the opinions he had expressed in public and in private for almost a year. 'I believe the love of political liberty is *not* an error, but, if it is one, I am sure I never shall be converted from it.' He was certainly unwilling to sacrifice those opinions for the sake of achieving a fictitious unity with the Portland Whigs which he undoubtedly recognized as impracticable. With the exception of his confidential confession to Adam and a restrained speech at the Whig Club on 4 November, there is nothing to show that Fox was anything more than indifferent to the possibility of reuniting the party.[1]

[1] For the above, see *inter alia* Fox to Lord Holland of 14 June 1793, Ad. MS. 47571, ff. 28–29, Fox Papers, printed in *Fox's Memorials*, iii. 38–41; 1 Aug. 1793, ibid. ff. 34–35, printed in *Fox's Memorials*, iii. 41–44; 22 Aug. 1793, ibid. ff. 41–43,

Others were less than charitable to the Portland Whigs. One of Adam's reforming friends said that they 'would damn any political party' and described them as 'unfit to be the leaders of a Party and that it was monstrous to think that the mighty genius of Fox should be erased by their weakness'.[1] Contempt for the Portland Whigs and adulation for Fox were coming to characterize the public pronouncements of the Foxite party and among moderate reformers and Foxites in the country the representation of Fox as a towering martyr of liberty was beginning to make itself felt.[2] The Foxites went their way paying scant courtesy to the position of the Duke of Portland. Their political activities, by this time, bore no traces of that solicitude for the unity of the party which might still have been found in 1792.

Since the rejection of Grey's reform motion in May the reform movement in England had been under a cloud. Its energies had been suspended in anticipation of the British Convention which met in October. By their refusal to participate in the proposed Convention, the Friends of the People had lost much of their influence over the other reforming societies.[3] Only when public opinion began to swing against the continuation of the war were Grey and his friends roused from their lethargy. But their behaviour was now more cautious. Grey, in particular, was frightened lest the distresses incurred by the war should drive the people to extreme lengths.[4] It was in Scotland, however, that the tide of reform was running high. The patriotic reaction of 1793 had not stultified the growth of the societies. 'I had no idea they would have stuck so long and so well together,' admitted Robert Dundas in June.[5] With the exception of the Edinburgh Con-

---

and *Fox's Memorials*, iii. 44–48; 17 Sept. 1793, ibid. ff. 58–61 and *Fox's Memorials*, iii. 48–52; 7 Nov. 1793, ibid. ff. 85–86, and *Fox's Memorials*, iii. 56–57; and 21 Nov. 1793, ibid. ff. 87–88; Fox to Adam 18 Sept. 1793, Blair-Adam MSS.; *The Morning Chronicle*, 6 Nov. 1793. Sichel, *Sheridan*, ii. 212.

[1] T. Hill to Adam (n.d. Aug. 1793), Blair-Adam MSS.

[2] *The Morning Chronicle* ran a series of 26 such articles between 2 July and 7 Sept. See also Mr. Lavender to Adam 3 Aug. 1793, Blair-Adam MSS.

[3] Yet they still exerted some influence and they were sometimes approached for help and advice by some societies. See Brunsdon, 'The Friends of the People', 146–7.

[4] T. Bigge to Grey 4 Nov., Grey to Bigge 6 Nov. 1793, Grey MSS.

[5] R. Dundas to Nepean 21 June 1793, quoted in H. W. Meikle, *Scotland and the French Revolution* (Glasgow, 1912), 128.

vention nothing attracted more attention than the harsh sentences
imposed upon Muir and Palmer in August and September, which
outraged the consciences of reformers everywhere and which led to
a clamour for the reform of the judicial system of Scotland.[1]

From the beginning, this *cause célèbre* had been close to the hearts
of the Foxite Whigs. Erskine had offered to defend Muir, the leader of
the Scottish Friends of the People and, although Muir refused, the
Foxites continued to watch the progress of the trials with the greatest
interest. The obnoxious sentences which were passed upon Muir and
Palmer sent men like Romilly and Adam scurrying to their legal text-
books, convinced as both of them were that the two convicted men were
innocent and that the savage punishment was not warranted by the
crimes they were alleged to have committed.[2] During October and
November Palmer wrote to Grey, Fox and Adam beseeching the
interposition of their good offices.[3] Lauderdale had visited Muir in
Scotland and had persuaded Fox, Sheridan and Grey to join with him
in placing before Dundas a memorandum which disputed the legality
of the sentences and which threatened to raise the matter in parliament.
Dundas chose to fall back upon the opinion of the judges whose report
upheld the sentences.[4] As the opening of the new session approached,
therefore, the Foxite Whigs had committed themselves to defend the
two reformers in parliament, a proceeding which could hardly fail
to give umbrage to the Portland Whigs. Fox's attitude to the whole
affair was characteristic of the type of leadership which had proved so
ineffectual in the past. He strongly disliked Lauderdale's unauthorized
initiatives which had drawn others to support Muir and Palmer but he
decided to lend his approval to the application to Dundas. Within a
few days, however, he was growing more enthusiastic about the need
to defend the two men from what he now considered to be a palpable

[1] Veitch, *Genesis of Reform*, 261–3.

[2] Romilly to Adam 11 Sept. 1793, Blair-Adam MSS.; Veitch, op. cit., 256.

[3] Palmer to Grey (n.d. Oct. 1793), 12 Oct. 1793, Grey MSS.; Palmer to Fox
22 Oct. 1793, Ad. MS. 47569, ff. 18–19, Fox Papers; Palmer to Adam 11 Nov.
1793, Blair-Adam MSS.

[4] Henry to Robert Dundas 11 and 16 Nov. 1793, Arniston Letter Book, 78–79;
Robert to Henry Dundas 28 Oct. 1793, *Arniston Memoirs*, ed. G. Ormond (Edinburgh, 1887), 237; Henry to Robert Dundas 11 Dec. 1793, ibid. 240; Veitch, op.
cit., 262–3.

injustice.¹ Once more, Fox's inability to restrain his followers was forcing him to make virtue of his necessities. If Lauderdale, Sheridan and
Grey could jostle their leader into supporting any political moves which
they chose to make, then there could be very little prospect of reuniting
the Whig Party, even if Fox had not already given up the game as lost.

The widening ideological rift between the Foxite and conservative
Whigs had smashed the germinal institutional unity which Adam had
so painfully constructed, destroyed such unity of local organization as
the party had once possessed and had placed the two wings of the Whig
party upon harshly contrasting foundations of public support. It was
impossible to hope for reconciliation now. Yet the near pathological
suspicion of Pitt which gripped Portland and Fitzwilliam rendered any
prospect of their co-operating with ministers unlikely and reduced any
initiatives towards that end to the level of individual machination. As
in former months, such scheming was initiated by Burke and Elliot and
it was directed at Windham. It received its impulse from the reverse at
Dunkirk, the capture of Lyons by the French on 9 October, the
Austrian defeat at Wattignies a week later and the simultaneous
execution of Marie Antoinette. Throughout October Burke and Elliot
were sending desperate pleas to Windham, begging him to come to
town to refute the rumours which had been put about to the effect that
he was increasingly dissatisfied with the conduct of the war. 'If we
criticize, let us criticize to amend, to help, to supply — even possibly
to encourage. But let us strengthen the principles we support.'²
Windham's reluctance to play the role on the European stage which
Burke was pressing upon him was, if anything, reinforced by the
conversations which passed between himself and Spencer during the
latter's visit to Fellbrigg on 6 and 7 October. Having waited in vain
for Portland to reply to his letter of 3 September Windham told Pitt
that he would not enter the government at that time. About a week

¹ Fox to Adam 13, 15 and 17 Dec. 1793, Blair-Adam MSS.

² Burke to Windham Oct. 1793 Ad. MS. 37843, ff. 25–26, Windham Papers,
printed in *Windham Papers*, i. 165–7. Dundas was informed of these attempts to
rouse Windham. See Elliot and Burke to Windham 2 Oct. 1793, Ad. MS. 37852, ff.
220–1, Windham Papers, printed in *Windham Papers*, i. 157–8. 'Mr. Windham is at
his House at Fellbrigg. He takes at present but little part in public affairs, to which
however the public wish and opinion very loudly call him at this crisis.' Burke to
J. C. Hippisley 3 Oct. 1793, Wentworth Woodhouse MSS., Burke Letters 1.

later he received the Duke's letter advising that Pitt's overtures be rejected. It seemed that Windham could continue in his line of unconnected support with the approval of Portland himself and thus all of Burke's persuasive powers were of no avail.[1]

Others were not content to wait patiently for Portland and Windham to bestir themselves. One of Elliot's closest friends, Sylvester Douglas, had been dazzled by the prospect of office for several weeks. As early as August, Elliot had mentioned to Pitt and Dundas the talents and pretentions of his friend and they had expressed their willingness to accommodate him. A most acceptable proposal was not long in coming. The ministers suggested that Douglas should go as Elliot's assistant to Toulon. Malmesbury and Mansfield urged Douglas to accept the offer and the contract seemed to be joined when, at the last minute, Pitt withdrew from his engagement on the grounds that the disposal of such a lucrative office to a member of the Portland party might set a dangerous precedent. It is impossible to discern Pitt's motives in this mysterious affair. If, however, he had intended to whet the appetite for office of yet another conservative Whig then he had succeeded. Douglas quickly swallowed his disappointment. He was soon to be found among the small yet influential group of Whigs who were pressing upon Windham the necessity of his negotiating an arrangement with Pitt.[2]

Meanwhile Burke was pleading the cause of the Royalist rising in La Vendée with Dundas, urging him to send reinforcements to the only theatre of the war which Burke believed might open the line of advance to Paris. Dundas listened patiently but remained unmoved by Burke's arguments. Although he flattered Burke with kind words,

---

[1] *Windham Diary*, 292. Windham to Pitt 11 Oct. 1793, Ad. MS. 37844, ff. 11–12, Windham Papers. For Pitt's regret at Windham's refusal, see Pitt to Windham 13 Oct. 1793, ibid. ff. 13–14, printed in *Windham Papers*, i. 159–61. For Windham's anguish at the execution of the French Queen, see Windham to Burke 1 Nov. 1793, draft, Ad. MS. 37843, ff. 27–28, Windham Papers, printed in *Correspondence of Edmund Burke*, iv. 179–82.

[2] Copies of letters from Douglas to Pitt 11 Oct., Elliot to Pitt 12 Oct., and Pitt to Douglas 14 Oct. 1793 are in C.U.L. 6958[7], ff. 1334, 1335 and 1336. See also Douglas to Windham 14 Oct. 1793, Ad. MS. 37873, ff. 216–23, Windham Papers, Douglas to Windham 22 Oct. 1793, ibid. ff. 224–30.

Burke was aware of the fact that Dundas was merely humouring him.[1]
Hearing of the intended Declaration, which would define the aims of
the war and which was to be published at the end of October, Burke
continued his solicitations, but his advice arrived too late for the
ministers to make use of it. The Declaration was published on 29
October. Its terms went some ways towards satisfying the anxieties
felt by the conservative Whigs upon Pitt's conduct of the war. It
declared that 'interference is become essential to the security and
repose of other powers', and demanded 'that some legitimate and stable
government should be established' in France based upon 'the standard
of an hereditary monarchy'.[2] Even then, Windham thought such terms
too mild and Burke was offended at the references to indemnities. He
felt that insufficient attention was being directed at La Vendée and
this opinion had recently been reinforced by a letter he had received
from the Count D'Artois, asking his intercession with ministers in
favour of the Royalists.[3] For a few days, therefore, Burke renewed his
entreaties to Windham to come to town. On 5 November, however,
Burke realized that nothing could be done to convince the ministers of
their folly in turning a blind eye to the Royalist cause in La Vendée.
'I am not in His Majesty's Service; or at all consulted in his Affairs'.[4]
His letters in November are full of bitter and trenchant criticism of

---

[1] Burke to Dundas 7 Oct. 1793, Osborn Collection, Copeland Transcript,
printed in *Correspondence of Edmund Burke*, iv. 159–61; Dundas to Burke 13 Oct.
1793, N.R.O. A. iv. 10b, Burke Letters (and an additional page of the same letter
in the Wentworth Woodhouse MSS., Burke Letters 1); Burke to Dundas 14 Oct.
1793, draft. N.R.O. A. iv. 10, Burke Letters.

[2] Burke to Dundas 27 Oct. 1793, H.M.C. *Dropmore*, ii. 450–1; Dundas to Burke
29 Oct. 1793, N.R.O. A. iv. 6a, Burke Letters. The Declaration is printed in *The
Parliamentary History*, xxx. 1057–60.

[3] Windham to Burke 7 Nov. 1793, Wentworth Woodhouse MSS., Burke Letters
1, printed in *Correspondence of Edmund Burke*, iv. 189–92; Burke to Windham 8
Nov. 1793, Ad. MS. 37843, ff. 31–33, Windham Papers, printed in *Windham
Papers*, i. 173–6; Count D'Artois to Burke 23 Oct. 1793, *Correspondence of Edmund
Burke*, iv. 166–70.

[4] Burke to Windham 4 Nov. 1793, Ad. MS. 37843, ff. 29–30, Windham Papers;
Burke to Windham 5 Nov. 1793, draft, Wentworth Woodhouse MSS., Burke
Letters 1, printed in *Correspondence of Edmund Burke*, iv. 177–9; Burke to the
Count D'Artois 6 Nov. 1793, copy, Wentworth Woodhouse MSS., Burke Letters 1,
printed in *Correspondence of Edmund Burke*, iv. 183–9.

the war policy of the government although 'The very existence of human affairs, in their ancient and happy order, depends upon the existence of this ministry'.

The operation of our remedies to the French Pestilence is slow. The course has begun late. It is pursued without any true knowledge of its specific Nature. It has been tardily applied — whilst the disorder moves with the pace of a Giant.

Worst of all, the Portland party, by supporting the war 'feebly and unsystematically' was abetting the unceasing attempts of the English Jacobins to undermine the elements of society in England. None of them had awoken to the danger. They had, in fact,

become far more attached than ever to their Jacobin friends, are animated with much greater rage than ever against the ministers, and are become not much less irritable against those of their old friends who act decidedly and honestly in favour of their principles.[1]

While the conservative Whigs were in such a state of disarray, Pitt continued his attempts to detach individuals. Malmesbury was offered an important diplomatic mission to Berlin, rather significantly while he was a guest of the Duke of Portland at Welbeck. Much to Portland's annoyance, Malmesbury accepted.[2] At the same time, Pitt fabricated an 'accidental' meeting with Spencer. He gave an honest account of the aims of the ministers in conducting the war, upon which the conversation seems largely to have turned. He admitted the failures of the previous months yet tried to bring Spencer to realize the very real difficulties under which the Flanders campaign was being conducted. He explained why so much time and effort was being spent in securing the frontier towns. This was merely a prelude to an advance upon Paris and the re-establishment of the monarchy. Spencer told Pitt that Portland still had no wish to enter the ministry. Pitt replied that there were, at present, no vacancies which he could offer, although the prospect of the Portland Whigs coming in collectively (a principle

---

[1] Burke to Elliot 19 Nov. 1793, Osborn Collection, Copeland Transcript; Burke to Windham 25 Nov. 1793, *Correspondence of Edmund Burke*, iv. 201–4 and *Windham Papers*, i. 184–86.

[2] *Malmesbury Diary*, ii. 508; Pitt to Grenville 10 Nov. 1793, H.M.C. *Dropmore*, ii. 464; Portland to Fitzwilliam 11 Nov. 1793, N.R.O. Box 45; Malmesbury to Burke 19 Nov. 1793, Wentworth Woodhouse MSS., Burke Letters 1, printed in *Correspondence of Edmund Burke*, iv. 200–1.

which Pitt seemed prepared to accept) might arise at a future date. For that purpose, communications should be kept open. Nevertheless, Spencer learned that Lord Camden, the President of the Council, was expected to retire in the near future and that he, Spencer, might not be unacceptable in that post and in the cabinet. Pitt's motives, so often bewildering, might be grasped a little more clearly in view of the fact that at this very moment he was discussing with Lord Bayham the possibility of the latter taking the Irish Viceroyalty. Perhaps Pitt wished to convince the Portland Whigs of his good faith and good intentions and, without bringing upon himself the need to dispose of half the cabinet places to them, still continue his attempts to detach them as individuals. For the present, notwithstanding, the situation must perforce remain in the balance.[1]

December, therefore, found both Windham and Spencer, on the one hand, and Portland and Fitzwilliam, on the other, unmoved by Burke's strident demands for some closer co-operation with the ministers.[2] The slight trickle of Whigs who had accepted office had failed to persuade the conservative Whigs to follow them and it had rather bred a feeling of self-congratulation at the purity of their own political motives. Yet there are signs of uneasiness, signs that the conservative Whigs were beginning to realize that they could not persist in their present political line indefinitely. Spencer summed up this vague sentiment when he told Windham, 'The period which is to produce something of rather a more decisive nature in our conduct is now fast approaching'.[3] Yet this something was nothing more than a return to the sterile notions of the 'Third Party'. Spencer, Windham, Pelham, Grenville and the rest were still disinclined to accept office.

---

[1] Pitt to Grenville 10 Nov., loc. cit.; Spencer to Windham 11 Nov. 1793, Ad. MS. 37845, ff. 119–23, Windham Papers, printed in *Windham Papers*, i. 176–82. G. Pellew, *The Life and Correspondence of the Rt. Hon. Henry Addington, First Viscount Sidmouth* (2 vols. 1847), i. 105. There is a long account of Spencer's talk with Pitt in a memorandum by Tom Grenville which he wrote after speaking to Spencer. (Ad. MS. 42058, ff. 128–9, Thomas Grenville MSS.)

[2] Spencer to Tom Grenville 27 Oct. 1793, Ad. MS. 42058, ff. 94–95, Thomas Grenville MSS.; Fitzwilliam to Grenville 7 Nov. 1793, ibid. ff. 120–3.

[3] Spencer to Windham 8 Dec. 1793, Ad. MS. 37845, ff. 124–5, Windham Papers, printed in *Windham Papers*, i. 186–8.

Spencer outlined their position and their intentions in a letter to Tom Grenville:

> I told him [Windham] that I had now strong reason to be sanguine in my Hopes that a body might be collected & kept together sufficiently respectable both as to Number and Character to have weight with Ministers & Parliament, & who might establish themselves in the Confidence of the Publick, by giving the most satisfactory Evidence of the disinterestedness of their motives.[1]

Yet when Windham returned to town on 5 December, he was quickly rounded up by Burke and Anstruther to become part of the small company of conservative Whigs who occasionally dined with Pitt and Lord Grenville.[2] Although Burke's slowly rising influence over Windham was reflected by the success of his efforts to persuade Windham to act as the unofficial mouthpiece of the French Royalists and to canvass their cause with the ministers,[3] Windham still embraced views which would have disgusted Burke. He tended to look favourably upon schemes to indemnify the allies at the expense of France and he was not wholly out of sympathy with the cases of Muir and Palmer which the Foxite Whigs had made their own.[4] It was at this time, nevertheless, that the activities of the British Convention were looming large in the popular mind, against a background of increasing distress and dissatisfaction which the inglorious campaign on the continent had aroused. Lord Mornington crystallized the sentiments of many politicians in November when he noted that 'The general turn of people's minds seems to be to condemn the *conduct* of the war' but he comforted himself with the reflection that 'all will vanish at the first flourish of the trumpets on the first day of the session, unless some great calamity should happen before the meeting'.[5] On 20 December came the news

[1] Spencer to Tom Grenville 10 Dec. 1793, Ad. MS. 42058, ff. 98–99, Thomas Grenville MSS.

[2] Tom Pelham to Lady Holland 7 Dec. 1793, Ad. MS. 51705, Holland House MSS., unfoliated; Tom Pelham to his father 9 Dec. 1793, Ad. MS. 33129, ff. 230–231, Pelham Papers; *The Diaries of Sylvester Douglas*, ed. F. Bickley (1928), 24.

[3] Windham to Pitt 16 Dec. 1793, P.R.O. 190, Pitt Papers. There is a draft of this letter in the Windham Papers (Ad. MS. 37844, ff. 15) and it is printed in *Windham Papers*, i. 190–1; *Diaries of Sylvester Douglas*, 8–9.

[4] *Diaries of Sylvester Douglas*, 17, 21.

[5] Lord Mornington to Addington 8 Nov. 1793, Pellew, op. cit. i. 112.

that Toulon had fallen to the French, destroying at one blow the sanguine hopes which had been focused upon the civil war in France and revealing that France could now be crushed only by long and painful exertions.

5. *The Coalition with the Ministry*

December 1793–July 1794

I. The Repudiation of Party, December 1793–June 1794

It is some indication of the hesitation and the infirmity of purpose which characterized the conservative Whigs at this time that the burst of energy and enthusiasm which moved them after the Toulon reverse only succeeded in edging the party slightly nearer to Pitt. Although consultation over matters of policy became more frequent and more intimate than in the preceding session, it is difficult to detect any more thoroughgoing parliamentary support of the administration on the part of the Portland party. Several of its members in the House of Lords voiced their approval of ministerial policy but in the Commons there remained a dearth of speakers prepared to commit themselves to a public countenance of the government's measures. With the exception of Tom Grenville, the only assistance which Pitt found from among the ranks of the conservative Whigs came from the members of the 'Third Party' and, of these, Windham, Burke and Anstruther formed the most consistent group of speakers. More significant than the change in the relations between the ministry and the conservative Whigs was the internal movement of opinion among the Whigs themselves. On many essential points, Portland found himself adopting 'Third Party' doctrine, and it is almost — but not completely — true to regard the distinction between the Portland Whigs and the 'Third Party' of Windham as having been shaded over to the point of obliteration. Perhaps it is wisest to define the effect of Toulon on the conservative Whigs as the working out and recognition of the trends of the previous months, trends which had demonstrated the palpable impossibility of remaining in any sort of working relationship with the Foxite Whigs. The problem of their future connection with the ministers was shelved by the conservative Whigs, to be worked out at a later period and in a somewhat different climate of opinion. One can see clearly enough that Portland lacked both the courage and the statesmanship necessary for any resolution of this thorny problem but it is hard to see what else he could have done. The ministers, at least, were by no means ready for coalition and in the early weeks of 1794 it was not a practical possibility.

After he had grasped the import of the failure of the British and the Royalists to hold Toulon, the Duke of Portland acted with uncharacteristic resolution. The decisiveness of his conduct was all the more surprising in view of the fact that he was not now acting upon impulse nor was he carried away by a gust of temporary patriotism. He was fully aware of all the confused and contradictory elements in his political role and he seems to have made a manful attempt to come to terms with them. And if his final conclusions were of the nature of a compromise, it was one which allowed of no alternative except that of clinging with obstinate prejudice to his former declarations. He understood that men of his rank and influence were under the obligation of serving their country when the situation called for it. But was the present such an occasion? On the one hand, he believed the existence of the Whig party to be vital to the preservation of the constitution. The constant aim of the present reign had been to destroy that party and with it its unique role of acting as the guardian of the liberties of the people against steadily increasing court and executive influence. During the last eighteen months, attempts had been made to weaken, divide and destroy the party, and there was nothing to suggest that the ministers possessed different intentions now. They were not interested in an honest union with the Whigs and they seemed disinclined to make the concessions — especially in Ireland — which the Whigs would inevitably demand if such a union were to be negotiated. Portland was also able to convince himself that coalition was out of the question by considering its likely effects upon the public mind. In the present circumstances, it was naïve to suppose that Pitt would be willing to change his policy if a handful of Whigs entered his ministry. Those who did so would become his adherents and his creatures. They would participate in a system of government and a series of measures of which they could not possibly approve. The consequent loss of public character and esteem which they would suffer would harm rather than help the ministry. To destroy what remained of the Whig party for such illusory inducements was absurd. Portland was not blind to a further consideration. He realized that public opposition to the war was rising and he saw that it might be harmful for his party to support its present conduct. This was not mere timidity. Portland was a conscientious, well-meaning politician of undoubted integrity. To involve his party in a futile and purposeless coalition with the ministry might only bring down upon the heads of his friends the odium into which the government had been brought through Pitt's ineptitude. Although Portland had supported the war, he had not been consulted about war policy, for which Pitt, and to some extent Windham and Burke, were responsible. The wisdom of Portland's appraisal of political circumstances cannot in substance be faulted. Nor was the Duke prepared to shirk his own responsibilities because of personal considerations. He began to realize in December 1793 that 'support to be effectual must be given completely and indiscriminately, and cannot be dealt out by apportionment or measure'. He had come to the 'determination to support the War with all the effect and energy in my power — that for that purpose it must be clearly understood and manifest that no connection exists between the *friends of the People and me*'.[1]

Windham, Pelham and Grenville found themselves in entire agreement with Portland's views. Windham understood that coalition was necessary if the war was to be prosecuted with the vigour and energy which victory over the French demanded. But he was also aware of the impossibility of achieving a union with the ministry and he would not budge from his formerly expressed determination against taking office as an individual.[2] The only discordant voice to be heard was that of Burke. His rising disgust at 'these ignorant inefficient and incapable Ministers' now knew no bounds. At all costs they must be restrained from their folly by the accession to their counsels of men with a clearer recogni-

[1] For Portland's opinions see Portland to Fitzwilliam 25 Dec., and 31 Dec. 1793, Wentworth Woodhouse MSS., F.31a. Portland to Windham 11 Jan. 1794, Ad. MS. 37845, ff. 17–37, original and two copies, Windham Papers, printed in *Windham Papers*, i. 199–209.

[2] Windham to Mrs. Crewe 26 Dec. 1793, *Windham Papers*, i. 191–4. See also Grenville to Fitzwilliam 31 Dec. 1793, N.R.O. Box 45.

tion of the principles upon which the war should be fought. He cared little about the conditions which must accompany a coalition with the ministers. 'He wishes his best friends to act and not even to act *with* them but *under* them.' He was furious with Windham and Spencer for their refusal to enter the government, and so uncompromising was his advocacy of unconditional coalition that Portland was rather alarmed lest his passion should lead him to adopt unthinking and damaging policies. However violent Burke's denunciations of the supineness of ministers might be, he restrained his persuasions to the writing of letters. He made use of Loughborough to transmit to the ministers a copy of *Remarks on the Policy of the Allies* and took up once more the thankless task of trying to rouse Windham from his lethargy. To Burke's despair, neither of these well-worn contrivances was productive of any result. Nor could it be otherwise while he persistently ignored the practical obstacles to the adoption of his ideas by either the ministers or Windham. Unless he attempted to unravel the complicated problems which inhibited Windham and the Duke of Portland from acting upon his advice, then his influence upon the course of events must of necessity be inconsiderable.[1]

The weeks which followed the news of the reverse at Toulon found the conservative Whigs hurrying to town to attend informal conferences which decided their immediate political conduct.[2] They felt it necessary to render their opinions so explicit as to leave no room for possible misinterpretation. To this end, it was decided that nothing less than a general meeting of the party on the eve of the session would suffice. Until then little could be accomplished. Nevertheless, attempts were made to detach a few of the Foxite Whigs, and Fox was left in no doubt that the Portland Whigs were determined to sever the ties which still bound them to him. Portland, Fitzwilliam and Grenville all saw Fox

---

[1] Portland to Fitzwilliam 31 Dec. 1793, loc. cit.; Burke to Windham 8 Jan. 1794, *Correspondence of Edmund Burke*, iv. 205–6; Loughborough to Dundas 12 Jan. 1794, P.R.O. Pitt Papers, 153.

[2] See the letters of Windham to Tom Grenville of Jan. 1794, Ad. MS. 42058, ff. 145–8; Spencer to Grenville 10 Jan. 1794, ibid. ff. 100–1; Pelham to Grenville 12 and 16 Jan. 1794, ibid. 141–4; *Windham Diary*, 301; Tom Pelham to Lady Holland 13 and 18 Jan. 1794, Ad. MS. 51705, Holland House MSS., unfoliated; J. Anstruther to Windham 7 Jan. 1794, Ad. MS. 37874, ff. 3–4, Windham Papers; Windham to Burke 18 Jan. 1794, Wentworth Woodhouse MSS., Burke Letters 1.

and told him that 'they felt it necessary to take a more decided line than
they had hitherto done, in support of the administration'. Fox interpreted this as their readiness 'to declare formally the separation, or
rather the dissolution of the Whig Party'.¹ Tom Grenville told Fox
that differences between them upon the question of the war and the
spread of democratic principles 'must in their direct course, or at least in
their bearings and consequences, pervade almost all measures of public
discussion'.² Gripped with a sense of determination and a unity of
purpose which they had not hitherto displayed, the conservative Whigs
met at Burlington House on 20 January 'to consider the means of
giving the most effectual support to a vigorous prosecution of the war'.³
Portland's apparently innocent words concealed the fact that the
Portland Whigs were crossing the Rubicon in their relations with Fox.
Burke sensed that the occasion was to be a decisive event in the history
of the party and, despite the interdict under which he felt that he lay in
the mind of Portland, perversely decided to attend.⁴

The meeting was dominated by Portland who made a lengthy and
resolute speech. He declared his own support of the ministry and
exhorted his followers to do the same. For foreign rather than domestic
reasons the ministry must be sustained, whatever setbacks might occur
during the forthcoming campaign. About thirty people were present
at the meeting and there was little dissent from Portland's views.⁵ The
implications were clear. Portland had now pledged his own opinions
to accommodate future circumstances. He had manifestly indicated that

¹ Grenville to Fitzwilliam 31 Dec. 1793, loc. cit.; Windham to Burke 18 Jan.
1794, Wentworth Woodhouse MSS., Burke Letters 1; Fitzwilliam was attempting
to detach the Foxite, Sir William Milner, T. Hill to Adam 15 Jan. 1794, Blair-
Adam MSS. Fox's opinion is contained in his letter to Lord Holland of 9 Mar. 1794.
Ad. MS. 47571, ff. 106–9, Fox Papers, printed in *Fox's Memorials*, iii. 64–68.
² Grenville to Fox 29 Dec. 1793, Ad. MS. 47569, ff. 30–31, Fox Papers, printed
in *Fox's Memorials*, iii. 62–64. In his reply (6 Jan. 1794, Ad. MS. 42058, ff. 135–8,
Thomas Grenville MSS.), Fox reproached Grenville and the conservative Whigs
for breaking up the party. Divided though it was, 'it would have been a body ready
for a better time' and Fox stated that they should have kept up 'a regular and
systematic opposition to a Tory & unconstitutional Ministry'.
³ Portland to Burke 19 Jan. 1794, Wentworth Woodhouse MSS., Burke Letters 1.
⁴ Burke to Portland 20 Jan. 1794, *Correspondence of Edmund Burke*, iv. 221–2.
⁵ Windham to Pitt 20 Jan. 1794 (copy), Ad. MS. 37844, f. 19, Windham Papers.

his former declarations, which had reserved the right to criticize ministerial measures whenever the occasion demanded, no longer applied. He was therefore no longer in 'systematic opposition' to them and the way was thus clear for him to co-operate with the administration whenever he chose to do so. The Portland Whigs were henceforward to be considered as separated in politics from Fox.[1] There was no longer need for a 'Third Party' because Portland's welcome — if overdue — decisions had created 'an independent Party under so very respectable a Head'.[2] Thus far, Portland had adopted the doctrine of Windham's 'Third Party' but, like them, he remained content to defer for the present any final solution of the problematic questions which surrounded the constant and disturbing issue of relations with the ministers.

Ministers had not slackened their attempts to detach individuals from among the ranks of the conservative Whigs. At the end of December Sylvester Douglas was offered the Irish Secretaryship. After hurried consultations with Loughborough (who had instigated the offer) and Mansfield, Douglas decided to accept. Aware of Windham's sentiments respecting the wisdom of succumbing to ministerial allurements, Douglas did not wait for his opinion.[3] Portland, moreover, found the appointment a bitter pill to swallow. He did not openly object but he regarded it as an indication on the part of Pitt that the most glittering political prize of all, the government of Ireland, might yet be placed at the disposal of the Whigs, should they choose to accept it. Yet Portland could never be induced to support the ministerial system of governing Ireland, and without firmer assurances of Pitt's willingness to abandon that system the Duke would prefer to play for time.[4] Much depended on factors which were personal. For Pitt was telling Douglas that Spencer could have the Viceroyalty at an early date and that, because of his former refusal, he, Pitt, was having to

[1] Tom Pelham to his father 20 Jan. 1794, Ad. MS. 33129, ff. 232-3, Pelham Papers.
[2] Frederick North to Windham 28 Jan. 1794, Ad. MS. 37874, f. 6, Windham Papers, printed in *Windham Papers*, i. 209-10.
[3] *Diaries of Sylvester Douglas*, 29-31; Douglas to Windham, wrongly dated 20 Dec. 1793, Ad. MS. 37873, ff. 264-5, Windham Papers.
[4] Portland to Windham 11 Jan. 1794, loc. cit.

consider persons for the post whom he would not otherwise have found acceptable. Further, ministers were full of good intentions towards the Irish Catholics. They desired to admit them 'to a full participation of all the advantages now held exclusively by the Protestants'.[1] Could Pitt be trusted? If so, there seemed some possibility that the Whigs might be drawn into some arrangement with the ministry. But there remained the whole question of Irish offices. The political, family and personal ties which bound together the English and the Irish Whigs were bound to have far-reaching consequences once a member of Portland's party had accepted the Viceroyalty. It was unrealistic to suppose that anything less than some large discretionary power for the disposal of Irish patronage to the Irish Whigs could accompany a Whig régime in Ireland. While this problem had not even been raised, still less settled, any prospect that the government of Ireland could provide a sufficient inducement for Portland to enter the ministry remained illusory.

Pitt, nevertheless, remained in close contact with both Burke and Windham during the early days of the new year. He received from Windham a full account of the Burlington House meeting of 20 January and he accepted some of Windham's suggested changes in the King's speech.[2] It is doubtful if Pitt was interested in obtaining anything more than immediate political support from the Whigs. Both he and Lord Grenville were averse to any thoroughgoing cabinet changes at this time.[3] They could not, however, have been insensible to the dramatic and hostile turn which public opinion had taken against the war. Above all, they could not have been blind to the need for reinforcing the prestige of the government. Pitt's automatic majorities in both Houses would undoubtedly ensure the survival of the ministry but, as Miles put it, 'This is not the moment to depend entirely upon majorities, for, the secret of obtaining them being revealed, their credit is dimin-

[1] *Diaries of Sylvester Douglas,* 34, 36.

[2] Windham says (*Diary,* 301) that Portland's new determination 'relieved me from a state of considerable doubt and anxiety. The effect of this measure was felt, I think, immediately, in the alterations made for the better in the King's speech. . . .' Pitt to Windham 16 Jan. 1794, Ad. MS. 37844, ff. 17–18, Windham Papers; Windham to Pitt 20 Jan. 1794, ibid. ff. 19–20; Pitt to Windham 21 Jan. 1794, ibid. ff. 20–21.

[3] Lord Grenville to Pitt 24 Feb. 1794 (copy), C.U.L. 6958[8], ff. 1405.

ished, and will be of little avail against public opinion'.[1] What was more relevant and, indeed, more pressing, was the necessity for the Portland Whigs to declare an unconditional support for the administration, thus ensuring that it rested upon a wider foundation. Their local and territorial influence, moreover, rendered the support of the Portland Whigs of still greater significance. Because they controlled vast regions of the countryside, their pledged support of administration ensured the loyalty to the constitution of thousands of Englishmen who came directly under their influence. The newly declared role of the Portland Whigs, therefore, helped to stave off the demoralization of the ministry and erected in the country a bastion of loyalty to the constitution. What this role was to mean in political terms, however, only the meeting of parliament could reveal.

The debates on the Address of 21 January 1794 revealed beyond any further doubt that the party was now completely divided. Although the Portland Whigs chose to demonstrate their independence of the ministry by seating themselves on the opposition benches, this merely succeeded in annoying Sheridan to the point where he could not restrain himself from delivering a harsh polemic upon the sordidness of the motives of the Portland Whigs and from ridiculing their political consistency.[2] Portland himself went down to the Lords to announce that he was 'more convinced' than ever of the justice and necessity of the war.[3] Fitzpatrick admitted that 'the Burlington House support of the war was decided'. Fox noted that the Duke of Devonshire had voted for the war although the continuing obstinacy of the House of Cavendish was reflected in the failure of all attempts to persuade its members in the Commons to attend.[4] It was left to Lord Spencer, however, to deliver the fateful verdict upon the state of the party and this he did in unequivocal terms in the House of Lords.

He was extremely sorry to be obliged to sacrifice old friendships, and to abandon political connexions with those with whom he had long been in the

---

[1] Miles to Long 12 Jan. 1794, W. Miles, *Authentic Correspondence with Lebrun* (1796), ii. 134–7.

[2] *The Parliamentary History,* xxx. 1240–2.

[3] Ibid. xxx. 1073.

[4] Fitzpatrick to Lord Holland 22 Jan. 1794, Ad. MS. 51799, unfoliated, Holland House MSS.; Fox to Lord Holland, 9 Mar. 1794, loc. cit.

habit of acting; but such a sacrifice, painful as it was, must be made . . . at so
momentous a crisis every other consideration ought to give way to the welfare
of his country . . . he felt it his duty to make it, and could not help uniting,
with every other well-wisher of his country. . . .[1]

At the same time there persisted the ideological dissensions which had
threatened the unity of the party in the debate of 17 June 1793. Both
Guilford in the Lords and Fox in the Commons rested their amend-
ments to the Address of Thanks upon their opposition to any interference in the internal affairs of France which threatened to dictate the
form of government which that country should adopt. Pitt and
Windham flatly rejected this view while hinting that monarchy was
the only form of government in France which might offer security
to other nations.[2] Not one of the Portland Whigs voted for the amendment to the Address, thus helping to swell the majority to 277 against
a minority figure of 59. This was larger than any minority figure of
the 1793 session and it surprised even Fox.[3]

   Fox's opposition to the war policy of the Pitt administration was
based not only upon his fear that the allies intended to destroy the
republic and restore the monarchy. He also expressed alarm at what
the domestic consequences of allied victory might be. The power of the
crown would know no bounds if the monarchs of Europe triumphed
over the people of Europe. Under the artificially stimulated euphoria
of public service and patriotism which the war fever had spread,
political checks upon the rising influence of the crown were weakening.
The dissemination of false rumours and alarms had enticed away from
the opposition a large number of its adherents. If the war continued —
even worse, if the allies were victorious — then it would be impossible
to restrain the influence of the crown from corroding and undermining
the constitutional liberties of Englishmen. It is difficult to avoid the
conclusion that Fox was really hoping for a French victory over the
allies. Although it is dangerous to apply an excess of logic to Fox's
political creed at any given period, his jubilation at the news of allied
reverses, his indisputable sympathy for the French and his fear of allied
victory allow of no other interpretation. Thus, every military or naval
reverse which drew the conservative Whigs closer to Pitt only separated

---

[1] *The Parliamentary History*, xxx. 1074.   [2] Ibid. xxx. 1245–6, 1283–5.
[3] Fox to Lord Holland 9 Mar. 1794, loc. cit.

Fox still further from Portland. After Toulon, when, as Windham remarked on 21 January, there was no longer any prospect of an end to the war in the foreseeable future, Fox told Fitzpatrick that 'our old friends are worse than ever upon the subject of the war'.[1] Yet he remained sanguine in his view that they would join with him in defending Muir and Palmer, a subject upon which Fox was not prepared to compromise. 'I am sure a stand must be made now, for if what has been done is right there is not a pretence left for calling Scotland a free country, and a very thin one for calling England so.'[2] Fox's sense of conviction was so strong that he brushed aside any consideration for the delicacy of the situation of Portland. He received with surprising equanimity the information that Portland intended to sever the meagre ties which still subsisted between himself and the Foxites.[3] The events of 20 and 21 January left Fox in no doubt as to their meaning. Although he was deeply disturbed by the dissolution of the party (and even contemplated retirement), he realized that to have left the game to Pitt and to the alarmist Whigs would have been dishonourable and dangerous. To Fox 'it seemed some way as if I had the world to begin anew'. He was well aware of the political role which he now considered himself bound in honour to fulfil. With unconcealed weariness he committed himself 'to get together the remains of our party, and begin again, like Sisyphus, to roll up the stone again, which long before it reaches the summit, may probably roll down again'.[4]

This was no temporary, half-hearted pledge. There are signs, for example, that Fox occasionally acted as his own party whip.[5] He realized initially that the Foxites had not learned to act in concert and that his

---

[1] *The Parliamentary History*, xxx. 1245; Fox to Fitzpatrick 1 Jan. 1794, Ad. MS. 47580, ff. 149–53, Fox Papers, printed in *Fox's Memorials*, iii. 263–5.

[2] Ibid.; Fox to Lord Holland *post* 25 Dec. 1793, Ad. MS. 47561, ff. 96–98, printed in *Fox's Memorials*, iii. 57–62.

[3] Tom Pelham to Lady Holland 18 Jan. 1794, Ad. MS. 51705, unfoliated, Holland House MSS.; Tom Pelham to his father 20 Jan. 1794, Ad. MS. 33129, ff. 232–3, Pelham Papers.

[4] Fox to Lord Holland 9 Mar. 1794, loc. cit.

[5] Fox to Grafton 17 Jan. 1794, West Suffolk R. O. Grafton MSS. IIIa, f. 159; Fox to T. W. Coke 7 Feb. 1794, Stirling, *Coke of Norfolk*, i. 411. Adam, of course, continued to act as party whip in the usual course of events. See Whitmore to Adam 20 Mar. 1793, Blair-Adam MSS.

own leadership had not been exerted with sufficient force. On 10 March he confided to the House of Commons that he had wished that the question of the sentences of Muir and Palmer had never come before parliament and he proceeded to disagree with some of the statements already made by his friends.[1] But the magic of his unchallengeable personal qualities and the isolation and even the sense of conviction which gripped the Foxites served to neutralize the bitterness of any animosities which occasionally appeared in their ranks. Nor was there much opportunity for them to indulge in personal recriminations. For the session of 1794 was a busy time for the Foxite Whigs. Their opposition was far more comprehensive than in the previous session. They brought forward more motions of censure upon ministerial measures and proved themselves more than ready to divide the House and make good use of procedural devices. Perhaps even more significant was the unvarying violence of their language and the feeling that they were now irrevocably committed to the course which they had chosen. The opinion that the Portland Whigs were little less than dupes of the minister and dangerous extremists was confined neither to private conversations and letters nor to the pages of the opposition press.[2] Foxite speakers, though not Fox himself, harangued both Houses in occasional bursts of spleen against the inconsistency of those who now chose to co-operate with ministers. Burke, in particular, was usually a favourite target of men like Sheridan, who found it impossible to sit in the House in Burke's presence without insulting or ridiculing him.[3] On only one occasion did Fox make a public appeal for the assistance of the Portland Whigs. On 25 March during the debate occasioned by Adam's motion for a committee to investigate the criminal law of Scotland, he made the following plea:

Good God, Sir, however I may disagree with many of my friends on other

---

[1] *The Parliamentary History*, xxx. 1562. See Francis's trenchant remarks on 1 Apr. ibid. xxxi. 206–7.

[2] 'Our old Whig friends are many of them worse Tories than even those whom they have joined.' Fox to Lord Holland 18 Mar. 1794, Ad. MS. 47571, ff. 110–12. Fox Papers, printed in *Fox's Memorials*, iii. 69–71. *The Morning Chronicle*, 27 Feb, 1794.

[3] For the antipathy between Burke and Sheridan, see their exchanges on 1 and 2 Apr. 1794, *The Parliamentary History*, xxx. 208–11, 377–9.

topics, will they not all agree with me in this? Will they not see all its danger in the same view that I do? Will they not all coincide with me in declaring that no man is safe, no man's liberty secure, if he can be charged generally on the crime of sedition?[1]

Although an occasional demonstration of friendship and sympathy passed through the political barriers which now separated the two groups of men,[2] the old round of social contacts which had done so much to keep the Old Whig party together had almost completely lapsed. Fox could no longer expect anything from the Portland Whigs. He had condemned himself and his party to what seemed an unpropitious and hopeless term in the barren wilderness of opposition. Even Burke, who was always prepared to consider the worst, rejected the notion which flashed through his mind that Fox might still retrieve his fortunes by ingratiating himself once more with Portland and Fitzwilliam.[3] Fox himself had ceased to entertain such expectations. Struggling against hopeless odds, his only political consolation was the belief that the arguments advanced by his followers could not be answered by his adversaries. Yet he himself realized that the most convincing arguments in the world were no substitute for the only real test of political strength, the number of members who would be prepared to follow him into the division lobby.[4] Even Lord Holland noted that the failure of the war was not making the Foxites appreciably more popular, and he observed that it would be 'a great while indeed' before they would be able to augment their numbers and thus be 'of any essential service' to the country.[5]

During the early months of the session the conservative Whigs continued on friendly, though not intimate, terms with the ministers. Portland found the latter willing to confer upon himself, his family and his friends minor though honourable offices of a local or military

[1] *The Parliamentary History*, xxxi. 78; Fox to Lord Holland 9 Mar. 1794, loc. cit., for Fox's opinion that the Portland Whigs would never take office.

[2] E.g. Portland to Adam 6 Feb. and Malmesbury to Adam 15 Apr. 1794, Blair-Adam MSS.

[3] Burke to Richard Burke jnr. 10 Jan. 1794, Wentworth Woodhouse MSS., Burke Letters 1, printed in *Correspondence of Edmund Burke*, iv. 212–14.

[4] Fox to Lord Holland 18 Mar. 1794, loc. cit.

[5] Lord Holland to Fox 27 May 1794, Ad. MS. 47571, ff. 124–7, Fox Papers.

nature.[1] Portland, for his part, was assiduous in furthering schemes for raising corps of cavalry on a local and voluntary basis, and he and his friends played some part in the Volunteer movement which flourished in 1794.[2] Although government initiative had launched the Volunteer Corps in most counties, the fact that such organizations were so frequently based upon the loyal Associations of the previous year is a sufficient indication that the conservative Whigs acted with the government and against the Foxites in placing the country in a posture of armed defence. Once more the party divisions at Westminster were being reflected in the constituencies. The threat of reform and subversion, which continued throughout 1794, was sufficient to render of supreme national importance the political conduct of influential members of both Houses.

The conservative Whigs remained dissatisfied with Pitt's conduct of the war. Portland, indeed, went so far as to send Pitt some advice as to the most efficient and cheapest way of deploying British military resources.[3] Pitt was anxious to draw the conservative Whigs into a closer and more thoroughgoing support of his government's diplomatic policy. In early March he used Loughborough as his intermediary to discover how far they were prepared to support the Prussian subsidy. After Portland had consulted Fitzwilliam, Burke, Windham and Mansfield, their opinion, according to William Elliot, was that 'they could not give any opinion respecting its expediency, as they were unacquainted with the plan of the campaign and other circumstances on which the necessity of it might be founded'.[4] Loughborough, how-

---

[1] See Mr. Morse to Portland 21 Feb. 1794, Portland MSS. P.W.F. 6956, conveying the news that the King had accepted Amherst's recommendation that Lord William Bentinck should be appointed to the rank of major. Portland to Loughborough 26 Feb. and 4 Mar. 1794, 1794, Portland MSS. P.W.F. 9235, 9237, requesting office for a friend. Nepean to Windham either Feb. or Mar. 1794, Ad. MS. 37874, f. 10, Windham Papers, conveying Dundas's offer to Portland of the office of Lord-Lieutenant of Middlesex.

[2] Portland to Amherst 12 Mar. 1794, P.R.O. Pitt Papers, 168. On the Volunteer movement see: J. R. Western, 'The Volunteer Movement as an Anti-Revolutionary Force, 1793–1801' *E.H.R.* (Oct. 1956), lxxi. 605–6; Loughborough to Pitt Mar. 1794, P.R.O. Pitt Papers, 153.

[3] Portland to Windham 3 Mar. 1794, Ad. MS. 37845, f. 35, Windham Papers.

[4] William Elliot to Sir Gilbert Elliot 15 Mar. 1794, Minto, ii. 383n–4n.

ever, reported to Pitt that 'they trusted to the prudence of Govt. to make as good and as secure a bargain as could be got . . . determined to give the fullest support to the measure in all its extent'.[1] The episode reveals far more than Loughborough's misrepresentation to Pitt of the warmth of Portland's feelings towards administration. Although Portland remained cautious in his approval of government policy while he was not in full possession of the facts upon which that policy was based, he was clearly more determined and more resolute than he had previously shown himself to be. He had no hesitation in regarding the opinions of Spencer and Devonshire as identical with his own, although they had not been consulted upon the measure and although Spencer strongly disagreed with the subsidy. He took the opportunity of these contacts with the ministers rather to urge upon them in unequivocal terms his own views of the need for greater exertion than to submit tamely to the system upon which the war was being conducted, of which the Prussian subsidy was but the latest example. Shortly afterwards he was badgering Windham with his suggestion that a committee of Royalists ought to be established and that their cause should be placed upon a more systematic footing.[2] When Pitt brought forward his bill enabling the formation of a corps of French troops in England, he sent a copy to Windham and Portland for their approval.[3] This was a measure to which Portland could lend his enthusiastic support, and he and Burke continued in close contact with ministers while it was before the House.[4] In short, during these months Portland began at last to act the part which he had repeatedly failed to act — that of the leader of his party. Now that he had freed himself of the shackles which had for so long bound him to Fox and which had so frequently left him devoid of initiative and political skill, the Duke was beginning to assert his influence over his party.[5] Forced to rely upon his own political judgement, he was beginning to exercise his modest abilities

[1] Loughborough to Pitt Mar. 1794, P.R.O. 153, Pitt Papers.
[2] Portland to Windham 23 Mar. 1794, Ad. MS. 37845, ff. 37–38, Windham Papers.
[3] Windham to Pitt 23 Mar. 1794, C.U.L. 6958⁸, f. 1420; Pitt to Portland 8 Apr. 1794, Portland MSS. P.W.F. 7071.
[4] Pitt to Burke 11 Apr. 1794, Wentworth Woodhouse MSS., Burke Letters 1; Windham to Portland 13 Apr. 1794, Portland MSS. P.W.F. 9536.
[5] Windham to Portland 13 Apr. 1794, loc. cit.

just at that time when coalition was arising like an ominous spectre on the political horizon.

The administration of Pitt had been the subject of recurring rumour and speculation for several months. Not only had the management of the war given rise to anxiety and criticism but the future of the cabinet itself had provoked widespread discussion. In January there had been unfounded, although significant, reports that Pitt had approached Fox with a view to some arrangement, reports which had arisen in the ministerial press and which had been ridiculed in *The Morning Chronicle*.[1] It was widely believed that the cabinet was torn into two factions — that of Pitt being in a minority — over the conduct of the war.[2] Rumours of impending cabinet changes were frequent and often centred upon Westmorland's continuation at the Castle or upon Richmond and Chatham's future political situations.[3] While these speculations proved to be largely unfounded, few can have doubted the need for strengthening the cabinet. Camden was old and he had frequently expressed his readiness to retreat from politics whenever Pitt found it convenient for him to do so. Chatham and Richmond had been unable to retrieve their reputations after the Dunkirk fiasco and, outside the cabinet, Amherst and Westmorland might be expected to be among the first victims of any cabinet reshuffle.[4] Although the moderate success which attended the early part of the campaign on the continent stifled criticism for a time in early 1794, there can be little doubt that Portland's more vigorous support of the administration was accepted with thankful relief in ministerial circles. Morton Eden declared in January that this support

will do credit to any Ministry, there is no person in the Minority, of whom I entertain so good an opinion, Ld. Spencer is like wise respectable. But it

[1] *The Sunday Reformer*, 19 Jan. 1794; *The Morning Chronicle*, 16 Jan. 1794.

[2] *The Public Advertiser*, 20 Jan. 1794.

[3] *The Public Advertiser*, 16 Jan. 1794, *The Oracle*, 3 Mar. 1794.

[4] In Mar. Pitt was considering whether or not to give Westmorland a cabinet office when he left Ireland, which was likely to be before the next session. See the copies of letters between Hobart and Westmorland of 22 Mar., Westmorland to Hobart of 26 Mar. and Westmorland to Pitt of 30 Mar. in C.U.L. 6958⁸, ff. 1419, 1422 and 1423. See Dundas to Pitt of 29 Apr. 1794, P.R.O. Pitt Papers, 157, for discussion of the possible replacement of the Duke of York by Cornwallis and for criticism of Amherst.

appears to me, we are in a damn scrape and know not how to get out of it.[1]

During the session the support of which Eden approved so warmly perceptibly strengthened. While the Prussian subsidy was being debated in the Lords on 30 April, Portland told the House that

If he had had the honour of being one of his majesty's ministers, he should have been proud to avow his share [of responsibility] . . . and desired to be considered as much a party to this particular measure as any man concerned in it.[2]

Speeches in the House of Lords, however, were no antidote for the spread of a dangerous and insubordinate spirit among the lower ranks of society, which many observers noted with alarm in the early months of 1794. The trials of the leaders of the British Convention had begun in January and had driven the reformers to proclaim the necessity for renewed efforts and unflinching determination in the face of persecution. Mass meetings in many areas of the country reached their culmination in the Chalk Farm Meeting of 14 April. At the same time proposals for another Convention spread throughout the societies. The government decided to strike. On 12 May — the day of Hardy's arrest — Dundas presented to the Commons the King's Message respecting seditious practices. On the following day, the House decided to appoint a Committee of Secrecy to consider measures which the prosecution of the scheme for another Convention might warrant.[3]

During the previous two weeks Windham had been in constant communication with the ministers and had discussed with them the measures which the government should take. These contacts between the administration and the conservative Whigs were to continue unabated for several weeks.[4] The composition of the committees of both Houses is significant. In the Commons, Windham, Burke,

[1] Morton Eden to Auckland 24 Jan. 1794, Ad. MS. 34452, ff. 355–6, Auckland Papers.

[2] *The Parliamentary History*, xxx i. 466–7.

[3] Veitch, *Genesis of Reform*, 299–304; *The Sheffield Register* of 7 Mar. 1794 has a report of a meeting of 5,000 or 6,000 men on 28 Feb. agitating for peace and against the re-establishment of monarchy in France.

[4] *Windham Diary*, 308; Pitt to Windham 5 and 12 May 1794, Ad. MS. 37844, ff. 22–23, 26–27, Windham Papers. See also the letters of Windham to Tom Grenville of 9 May and n.d. May 1794, Ad. MS. 42085, ff. 153–6. Thomas Grenville MSS. Later contacts are described in *Windham Diary*, 310; Portland to Loughborough 7 June 1794, Portland MSS. Copy. P.W.F. 9241.

Anstruther, Tom Grenville, Ossory, Townshend and Ellis sat with
fourteen ministerialists and it would be difficult to find a more alarmist
group of conservative Whig members of parliament. Grey and
Courtenay protested both at the composition of the Committee and at
the manner of its election. Members of such committees were usually
voted by ballot but, according to Courtenay, 'the members were
known before the election'.[1] Fox, for his part, said that the Committee
'was made up of two characters: men who were dupes themselves, or
men who were willing to dupe others'.[2] In neither of the two Houses
were any Foxites included in the Committees. In the Lords, a Committee of nine embraced three of the conservative Whig peers, Portland, Carlisle and Mansfield.[3] It is impossible to avoid the conclusion
that Pitt was striving to gain the greatest possible unanimity from
parliament before proposing the repeal of Habeas Corpus and, in so
doing, he was using the growing custom that the opposition should be
represented in such committees as the Committee of Secrecy in a curious
and interesting manner. Technically, the conservative Whigs were
still in opposition and it was strictly correct for Pitt to omit the Foxite
Whigs from the Committee. In doing so, he was advancing one step
further towards a national coalition with the Portland Whigs without
having to dispose of cabinet offices.

On the subject of disorder and revolution at home, he could expect
complete co-operation from the Whigs and in this he was not to be
disappointed.[4] On 13 June, for example, Lord Mansfield, speaking in
the name of the absent Duke of Portland, declared 'his most perfect
approbation of, and acquiescence in the report made by their committee,
and of the measure now founded upon that report'.[5] When the passionate and persistent hostility of the Foxite Whigs towards the suspension

---

[1] *The Parliamentary History*, xxxi, 474–5, 531, 538–9.   [2] Ibid. xxxi. 555.
[3] Ibid. xxxi. 573.
[4] There was an interesting discussion in 1797 when Sheridan asserted the right
of the opposition to be represented in committees, in that case five out of fifteen.
Ibid. xxxii. 1552–4.
[5] The second half of May and the first half of June were almost wholly taken up
with the committees and the repeal of Habeas Corpus. The Committee of the lower
House was chosen on 15 May. On the basis of the report which it presented the
following day, Pitt moved the repeal, which passed on 18 May in the Commons and
in the Lords, where the Committee had been chosen on the twentieth, on 22 May.

of Habeas Corpus is recalled, it is apparent that there was neither the possibility nor the will to achieve any degree of co-operation whatsoever between the Foxites and the conservative Whigs on this or on any other measures. There was, moreover, little practical purpose in Portland continuing to proclaim his independence of both the ministers and the Foxites. On all the vital measures of the time he was inevitably drawing closer to Pitt and working in continuous harmony with him. Events were leaving him with no room for manœuvre. The heavy British defeat at Turcoing on 18 May had reduced the expectation of achieving even a stabilization of the line of the allies. On 30 May Fox in the Commons and Bedford in the Lords moved to end the war. So outrageous was this prospect that even Fitzwilliam found himself confronting the Lords to deliver an uncharacteristically lengthy oration which stated as a condition of his support of the government the necessity for England to intervene in the internal affairs of France.[1] Yet the euphoric reception accorded to the news of the Glorious First of June, which coincided with displays of unprecedented loyalty to the King on the occasion of his birthday on 4 June, only emphasized the seemingly unpatriotic nature of the conduct of the Foxite Whigs. While co-operation in parliament and the unfortunate progress of the continental campaign were driving Portland into the arms of Pitt, coalition began to seem more acceptable to the conservative Whigs, but it was not to be achieved without the most thoroughgoing searching of Whig consciences. At least, the political scene was now less unpredictable than it had been for several years. Fox had chosen his course and had abandoned Portland. The French had repulsed the allies and only a long and weary war could now save Europe from the contagion of Jacobinism. It seemed, too, that Pitt was now more disposed to think in terms of honest coalition than he had been in 1793. Now that the world around them had ceased to stagger the imagination with its unpredictable fluctuations of fortune, the conservative Whigs might hope once more to find their place in it.

The second report from the Committee of the lower House appeared on 6 June. *The Parliamentary History*, xxxi. 471–97, 497–606, 688–879.

[1] *The Parliamentary History*, xxxi. 673–5.

II. The Party and the Coalition, May–July 1794

The coalition of 1794 was not the first, nor was it to be the last coalition, in the history of the Whig party. It had long been recognized — not least by Burke — that the party might not be of sufficient strength to form a government without the assistance of others. There was nothing in the doctrine of party which disallowed coalition. Now, of course, the Whigs were not mounting an assault on Pitt's ministry and the considerations which suggested the desirability of coalition were not party considerations. Nevertheless, coalition need not be an unconditional surrender to the government. There was no reason why the Whigs should not extort strict terms from Pitt, more particularly in those spheres of politics where they proclaimed the adoption of policies which they took to be of the utmost urgency. The state of the government of Ireland and the conduct of the war were, of course, such questions. Thus there was nothing ignominious in coalition. The Great Wars of the twentieth century have witnessed such coalitions and their justification is that they allowed the mobilization of the country's highest political talents by suspending party animosities at a time when national unity was deemed of paramount importance. Such potent reasoning had its effect upon Portland and the other leading conservative Whigs. But there were other factors and other considerations which clashed with these patriotic ideals. By the spring of 1794, however, they were losing their force. To reject the possibility of coalition simply because Pitt's policy had been tardy, incompetent and misguided may have served Portland's purposes in 1793 but, in the light of the subsequent dangers and disasters, this same argument rather pointed to the urgent need of a coalition, of a reinvigoration of a ministry which had been tried and found wanting. The charge of inconsistency might, indeed, be levelled at the conservative Whigs if they entered the government. On the other hand, if their integrity was indisputable, there was little possibility of such charges affecting the minds of Englishmen at a time of national crisis.[1] The conservative

---

[1] For a good example of the confusing priorities which exercised the minds of the politicians involved, see Spencer to Tom Grenville 27 May 1794, Ad. MS. 42058, ff. 104–7, Thomas Grenville MSS. In discussing the desirability of coalition,

Whigs would be evading their responsibilities if they stubbornly refused
to join the government. The dismissal of the Coalition ministry in
1783 was a further factor which tormented Portland and his friends.
By accepting office, surely they would be countenancing the legitimacy
of that — and subsequent — actions on the part of the King? Perhaps
this was true, but perhaps, too, to join the government when the
country desperately needed new talent was not necessarily an automatic vindication of the King's actions in December 1783. If an
acceptable coalition could be negotiated, the principles of the Whig
party might tend rather to cleanse the administration from within.
The government of Ireland, for example, might be placed upon a new
system in accordance with the doctrines and the party affiliations of
the conservative Whigs. Yet were the party disputes of the past of any
relevance in the present crisis? Was it not nearer the truth to admit that
the former battles between the Whigs and Pitt, opposition and administration, had now become of negligible importance? The only
distinction that mattered was that between Jacobins and the rest. The
events of the winter of 1783–4 were events upon which Whig souls
might brood, but to recall them now as valid reasons for guiding
political conduct was surely to confuse the important issues of 1794.
And yet the bitter memory of 1783 could not be dismissed so easily.
The Whigs had proudly professed the creed of party and of aristocracy.
They had learned from Burke the value of a party administration
resting upon an aristocratic basis. The great families of England were
the rightful rulers of the country, the only power in the land strong
enough to preserve the liberties of its subjects against the influence of
the crown. The fall of the Coalition in December 1783 had witnessed
the victory of the crown, the humiliation of the aristocracy and the

---

Spencer took as his criterion 'the Effect it will produce upon the publick Opinion'.
If they joined the ministry, they might lose credit and perhaps disgust 'some of our
friends who cannot be comprehended in the arrangement'. Yet if they did not join
the ministry, Pitt might fill his cabinet with people who would weaken rather than
strengthen the administration. Spencer came to the conclusion that 'unless a wider
opening in the Cabinet can be offered, we ought to decline pursuing the Negotiation any further, professing at the same time . . . every day more strongly our
determination to persevere in & if possible to add to our Support and Cooperation
with Government'.

renewed challenge to the safety of the British constitution which had continued for a decade. The prejudice of the Whigs against the King and Pitt was grounded upon the notions of the political duties of the aristocracy which Burke had reinterpreted for them earlier in the reign. Something was at stake more important than personal grudges. It was the very spirit which had kept the Whig party of Rockingham and Portland alive throughout years of adversity and gloom.

There were, in addition, several practical difficulties in the way of coalition. There must be a party coalition and Pitt must be willing to dispose generously of cabinet offices if coalition were to be palatable to Portland and his friends. They must naturally be offices which possessed a fair measure of patronage to distribute to the loyal friends of the former opposition. They must be offices which would allow the Whigs to influence ministerial policy. If Burke had done much to destroy the party he had, at least, impressed upon the Whigs the policies which the state of Europe and the government of Ireland required. Such policies were needed urgently. It was now quite out of the question to fall back upon the hope that Fox might be won back to opinions of which the conservative Whigs might approve or that the war might soon be ended. If Portland were to persist in his present political conduct then he might suffer the defection of a continuing trickle of men to administration. Though few had yet accepted office, those who had done so were naturally those with talent and influence. If Windham and Spencer were to leave Portland, then the Duke would lose two of his most able and most sought-after lieutenants and then there might be no reason for Pitt to seek a party coalition. If Pitt wanted to reinforce his government with such ability as the conservative Whigs possessed then it was naturally in Portland's own interest to keep his group together so that he would be in a stronger bargaining position. Portland slowly came to these conclusions as the session wore on. In April he had discussions with Pitt about coalition but nothing significant emerged from these casual soundings.[1] Portland had not yet come to his fateful decision.

It was during May that personal contacts between Pitt and the Portland Whigs assumed something of an intimate character, and at first it was through Windham that this cordiality found its most

---

[1] Devonshire to Portland 9 Apr. 1794, Portland MSS. P.W.F. 2, 706.

significant expression. Out of his close consultations with the ministers concerning the Committee of Secrecy arose some discussion of the possibility of coalition. Windham told Pitt and Dundas that he would have to refer the matter to Portland.[1] It was, however, several weeks before Pitt decided to carry his initiatives to the Duke himself. On 23 May he requested an interview and on the following day the two men met to discuss 'the probability of our forming a ministerial arrangement'.[2]

Pitt laid it down as his wish that the Portland Whigs should take office. He hoped that the rising spirit of Jacobinism 'might make us act together as one Great Family'. He was at present in no position to offer many offices but he assured Portland that every office which fell vacant in the future would be at his disposal. It is not clear if Pitt was attempting to come to some arrangement with the Duke without disposing of half the cabinet places to the conservative Whigs. If he was hoping that Portland would agree to coalition with offices to be arranged gradually as vacancies arose, then he had seriously miscalculated. The Duke reiterated his promise to support the administration if it persisted in its present measures but told Pitt that coalition would need the approval of his associates. Pitt asked him to sound his friends and report their sentiments to him. The Duke thereupon summoned his friends, who were not then in town, to a meeting on 30 May to discuss Pitt's somewhat ambiguous proposals.[3] The beginnings of the negotiations which ultimately seated the Portland Whigs in the cabinet were, however, abruptly interrupted by the illness of the Duchess of Portland and her death on 3 June. The meeting was abandoned. Fitzwilliam took advantage of the interim to avoid coming to town while Windham passed the time in strengthening his informal association with the ministers.[4]

---

[1] 1 May 1794, *Windham Diary*, 308. Pitt to Windham 5 and 12 May 1794, Ad. MS. 37844, ff. 22–23, 26–27, Windham Papers. Windham told Portland of the conversations on 4 May, *Windham Diary*, 308.

[2] Pitt to Portland 23 May 1794, Portland MSS. P.W.F. 7702. It is worth noticing that on 18 May was fought the unsuccessful battle of Turcoing. Portland to Fitzwilliam 25 May 1794, Wentworth Woodhouse MSS. F.31b.

[3] Portland to Fitzwilliam, loc. cit.; Spencer to Portland 28 May 1794, Portland MSS. P.W.F. 8515; Tom Pelham to Portland 30 May 1794, ibid. 7417.

[4] *Windham Diary*, 311–12; Windham to Pitt 12 June 1794, P.R.O. Pitt Papers, 190.

It was not until Friday 13 June that the postponed meeting eventually took place. Those present were Portland, Spencer, Mansfield and Tom Grenville. They agreed unanimously that coalition was a desirable measure. Spencer's former fears that the conservative Whigs would share the odium of ministerial unpopularity seem to have been dispelled by the experience of the previous months, when the Prussian subsidy had not caused the uproar which he had expected.[1] Grenville and Mansfield were strongly in favour of immediate coalition. As for Portland, he was 'more decidedly so than any of them'.

It appears to me to be so clearly for Pitt's interest as well as for that of the Public, that we should be united that I do not doubt the sincerity of His Wishes. . . .

Because Ireland may be saved by it and made a powerful and useful member of the British Empire. Because the true Spirit of Aristocracy and the true Principles of Whiggism may be revived and re-established. Because the Liberty of Europe may be saved. Because at all Events it is the best chance We have of maintaining our own Constitution, and because if We decline taking our share of responsibility in the present moments the danger with which this Country and all the Civilised World are threatened must be unavoidably and greatly increased.[2]

The meeting defined the conditions which should be attached to coalition with the ministry and which should form the subject of the negotiations which the conservative Whigs had now agreed to open. These were:

the Restoration of the French Monarchy and Restitution of Property or at least a Government of which Property forms the Basis

as the aims of the war. An adequate distribution of offices was also demanded. At this time, Portland understood that Pitt would offer a Secretaryship of State, the Presidency of the Council and the government of Ireland. Lord Mansfield was to be accommodated with the

---

[1] Spencer had already been wavering a fortnight earlier. He stated that his opinion was the same as before but 'I may perhaps on being better informed see Reason to change it'. Spencer to Portland 28 May 1794, Portland MSS. P.W.F. 8515.

[2] For this meeting see the lengthy report in Portland to Fitzwilliam 14 June 1794. There is a draft of this letter in the Portland MSS. P.W.F. 3762. The original is in the Wentworth Woodhouse MSS. F.31b.

Great Seal of Scotland and a seat in the cabinet.[1] Pitt had promised that '*He* might consider every other responsible situation which may become vacant, at our disposal'. Inferior offices had not been settled and it was thought that a further meeting might consider their disposal.[2]

The conservative Whigs had overcome many of the difficulties which had ostensibly stood in the way of coalition. Although many details were ambiguous, Pitt's terms were not ungenerous. He had, at least, now realized that nothing less than a party coalition would be considered by Portland, and his recognition of this *sine qua non* of any negotiation was rewarded by a considerable diminution of that acute distrust which had for so long poisoned his relations with the Duke. Yet there was still no definite assurance that Pitt's war aims were quite so explicit as the conservative Whigs wished them to be. Nor was there any enthusiasm at the prospect of coalition on the part of Windham or Fitzwilliam. Windham, it is true, had assented to negotiations, but he had marked his reservations by his silence at the meeting on 13 June. And without Fitzwilliam's approval of the whole project, Portland felt that he would be 'under the necessity of closing the overtures'.[3]

Fitzwilliam had been unable to attend the meeting but he had indicated that he was unwilling even to consider Pitt's proposals. He had, for some time, been ruminating on the desirability of coalition with the ministers but he had been unable to bring himself to admit its necessity.

Upon a general view of the great matters now in agitation, our sentiments and theirs, I believe, tally very sufficiently: but I doubt whether our principles with respect to ways and means do coincide so fully as might be wished.

His hesitation was partly a reflection of his ignorance of the details of Pitt's offers. He urged Portland to obtain the assent of the House of Cavendish to any important decision which was reached and impressed upon him the need for a party coalition.[4] At this stage, therefore,

---

[1] Mansfield was keen to take a seat in the cabinet: 'since my friends wish to have me there, I cannot be kept back by any dread of responsibility'. (Mansfield to Portland 18 June 1794, Portland MSS. P.W.F. 7028.)

[2] Portland to Fitzwilliam 14 June 1794, loc. cit.

[3] Portland to Fitzwilliam 14 June 1794, loc. cit.

[4] Fitzwilliam to Portland 12 June 1794. There is a draft of this letter in the Wentworth Woodhouse MSS. F.31b. The original is in the Portland MSS. P.W.F. 3761.

Fitzwilliam's antipathy to the idea of coalition was based upon a mixture of personal prejudice and ignorance of what was happening in London. At the same time, his thorough disapproval of the government's conduct of the war was double-edged. He despised Pitt's reluctance to embrace the cause of monarchy in France. Only by adopting the cause of the *émigrés* could the ministers hope to end the war. Echoing Burke's views, Fitzwilliam argued that the anarchy in France could only be stilled and order re-established by Frenchmen themselves. By ignoring these considerations, ministers had pursued the wrong principles in the war against Jacobinism and disaster had inevitably resulted. Yet such arguments might lead to the conclusion that coalition should proceed in order that ministers might be persuaded to adopt what Fitzwilliam took to be the policies upon which the prosecution of the war should be based. It is not, therefore, surprising that Fitzwilliam's true objections to coalition soon reasserted themselves when he read Portland's account of the meeting of 13 June and the stipulations with regard to the war which had been agreed on that occasion. Fitzwilliam now agreed that coalition was desirable and necessary. In spite of the strictures which he passed upon the war policy of the government, he recognized that the negotiation should proceed, provided, as usual, that the Duke of Devonshire approved. Yet he had his misgivings. Although he appeared eager to brush aside the difficulties which lay in the path of coalition, he reserved his own position:

... one short word respecting the sentiments of those friends, who have continued staunch since the great separation and still have adhered to you as their leader. ... I trust you think the measure of your acceptance will be favourably received by them, because by them it is important that a favourable construction should be put upon it. ... I hope no objection on their parts will now exist to a junction with the present administration on account of its original formation; bad it was, destructive of true Whiggism: but I trust they will see that present circumstances deeply over-balance that objection, and that they will agree with you in opinion, that the present occasion will prove the revival of its true aristocratic spirit [and] ... the cause of the renewal of power in an Aristocratic Whig party.[1]

---

[1] Fitzwilliam to Portland 15 June 1794. The original is in the Portland MSS P.W.F. 3763. There are drafts of this letter in the Wentworth Woodhouse MSS. F.31b.

It is all the more surprising, in view of Fitzwilliam's recognition of the need for coalition, that he refused to take office himself. He told Portland that

whilst you represent the Whigs and watch over the principles of conduct within, let it be my office to work without.[1]

Fitzwilliam could understand the explanations which might serve to justify coalition but his instincts shrank from lending his wholehearted approbation to the project. He seems to have realized that the most persuasive argument which might be advanced in support of coalition was also that which was the most questionable:

after so long and so unremitted a contention between us as parties perhaps nothing short of a step, as overt, as explicit, as a junction would go the length of persuading the public that contention no longer can continue to subsist between us, that all differences and animosities had now subsided, having given way to what was considered as a great, general and leading public interest.[2]

Fitzwilliam firmly believed in the functions of a Whig party and found it difficult to come to terms with a situation which demanded its surrender to the administration. Assuming the role of keeper of the Whig conscience, Fitzwilliam, the embodiment of aristocratic pride and Whig prejudice, would not involve himself too closely with the coalition. His real feeling was that if the union took place Pitt and the King should be forced to pay the highest possible price for it. The notion of surrender was anathema to him. Marks of the King's favour should be liberally bestowed so as to 'mark beyond dispute, the weight, power and consideration the old whigs are to have in future'. The coalition was not to be the end of the party. It was to be the beginning of merely another phase in its development. This idea was not confined to Fitzwilliam but, in him, it attains its most powerful and most uncompromising expression. Peerages and honours should be given

if the King is now in earnest in having succumbed to the principle of an Aristocratical Administration and feels the wisdom of admitting that useful

---

[1] Ibid.

[2] This and the following are taken from fragmentary drafts of Fitzwilliam's letter to Portland of 15 June, which fragments Fitzwilliam did not include in his final draft of the letter. Wentworth Woodhouse MSS., F.31b.

link between himself and his people as a principle of his government, the better to enable us to give effect to that principle, and to support the Crown by carrying numbers and respectability with us.[1]

Fitzwilliam would not come to town. He was at Milton at this time and then proceeded to Yorkshire. Without his presence, his advice and his complete concurrence in the proposals for the coalition, Portland was unwilling to continue the negotiations. In an attempt to persuade Fitzwilliam to come to town and to take office, the Duke prevailed upon Mansfield, Fitzwilliam's closest friend after Portland himself, to make representations to the Earl.[2]

In spite of the apparent harmony which had prevailed at the meeting of 13 June, Tom Pelham noted that Portland was due to come to town on 17 June 'to settle an arrangement with Pitt, *if it appears practicable, or agreeable to the leaders of our Party*'.[3] On 18 June Portland met Pitt once again. It is some indication of the effect of Fitzwilliam's opinions upon Portland that the whole of the interview was given over to a discussion of the conduct of the war in the light of the Earl's criticisms. Portland was most pleasantly surprised at Pitt's readiness to overcome the obstacles which might have upset the progress of the negotiations. Pitt told him that he was intent upon the restoration of monarchy in France and the recognition of the Regent at 'the first favourable moment for that purpose'.[4] He promised, moreover, that he would strive to involve the French princes and the *émigrés* more closely in the strategy of the war. On the vexed subject of indemnities, Portland said that Pitt wished to direct them to 'the restoration and re-establishment of Order and good Government, an object vastly paramount in his mind to all other considerations'. On the subject of war aims, Portland could hope for little better than these substantial assurances. Although they encouraged him to adhere to his declared policy of coalition, he was beginning to find that his

---

[1] Wentworth Woodhouse MSS., F. 31 b.

[2] Mansfield to Portland 18 June 1794, Portland MSS. P.W.F. '7028; Mansfield to Fitzwilliam 18 June 1794, Wentworth Woodhouse MSS., F.31 i.

[3] Pelham to Lady Holland 15 June 1794. Ad. MS. 51706, f. 145, Holland House MSS. My italics.

[4] Portland to Fitzwilliam 19/20 June 1794, Wentworth Woodhouse MSS., F.31b (drafts in the Portland MSS. P.W.F. 3764).

friends would need some gentle prodding if they were to continue upon the distressing and treacherous road to coalition with the government.

The Duke of Devonshire had refused to press his own opinion — that the conservative Whigs should continue in an unconnected relationship with the administration — and he had decided to leave the problem of coalition to Portland's judgement. During the interview of 18 June, Pitt had increased his bid for the conservative Whigs. He offered the office of Lord Privy Seal to Portland for one of his friends. The Duke promptly offered Devonshire this office but the head of the House of Cavendish wisely refused because his acceptance 'would not be of any use'.[1] Lord Spencer presented additional problems. His former resolution to take office was being shaken by his reflections upon the wisdom of coalition. 'I have entertained very strong doubts on the expediency of our taking such a step,'[2] He now turned down the office he had originally accepted, the Viceroyalty of Ireland. Fitzwilliam's hesitation was exerting its influence upon Spencer and destroying the fragile unanimity which had hitherto existed between the conservative Whigs.[3] Windham was still unhappy about the prospect of coalition while even Lord Mansfield, who had been an ardent advocate of a closer connection with the ministers, was wavering.[4] Only Portland clung to the determination of the meeting of 13 June without reservation or doubt. But without Fitzwilliam's support, he, too, would retract the opinions he had expressed on that occasion.

The future of the party now lay in the hands of Fitzwilliam. Portland informed him of the opinions which Pitt had voiced on 18 June and begged him to reconsider his views. If Fitzwilliam was intent upon 'establishing the standard of aristocracy' within the ministry then he must take office. His influence in Yorkshire was so considerable that, by doing so, he would revive the fortunes of Whiggery in that county. For Portland the principles of the Whig party were neither a set of platitudes nor were they intended merely to be catchwords of partisan conflict at Westminster. Against the raging torrent of

[1] Ibid.; Devonshire to Portland 24 June 1794, Portland MSS. P.W.F. 2, 707.

[2] Spencer to Portland 20 June 1794, ibid., P.W.F. 8516.

[3] Spencer, in fact, was seeking anxiously to discuss political matters with Fitzwilliam. Portland to Fitzwilliam 19/20 June 1794, loc. cit.; Spencer to Tom Grenville 22 June 1794, Ad. MS. 42058, ff. 108–9, Thomas Grenville MSS.

[4] Mansfield to Portland 25 June 1794, Portland MSS. P.W.F. 7029.

Jacobinism they needed to be established in the country to preserve it
from contamination.[1] Fitzwilliam was not unimpressed with Portland's
report. The coincidence of Pitt's views with his own on continental
affairs dispelled his opposition to the principle of coalition. But the
union of sentiments must perforce be sealed by a union of interests.
And now Fitzwilliam declared those opinions relating to the extensive
distribution of honours and offices which he had concealed and omitted
from his letter of 15 June. Unless such marks of respect were forthcoming, the members of the party would be the dupes of the ministers
and they would suffer in public esteem. Even at this stage, he reiterated
his unwillingness to take an official position. He agreed with Portland
that Whiggery must be revived in the country but to do so did not
necessarily mean that he must enter the government. The only
persuasion which Fitzwilliam admitted might influence him to change
his mind was the office of Lord-Lieutenant of Ireland, but that, he
assumed, was out of the question.[2] Portland's dismay knew no bounds.

It is your presence that I want, that I really cannot do without; that I feel
necessary, indispensibly necessary to the quiet and comfort of my mind.[3]

Fitzwilliam was not the man to ignore such a plea from his closest
friend. On 27 June he set out for London.[4]

By the time he had completed his journey, Fitzwilliam was notice-
ably less intransigent. Lord Mansfield saw him and

found him less determined than I could have wished, but strongly inclined to
do what was best upon the whole. I could not remove his doubts, and am
afraid, as I told him, of this overthinking the subject. I brought him to admit
that if *ever* he was to take office this was the time.[5]

Fitzwilliam's return to town coincided, moreover, with the first
reports of Coburg's defeat at Fleurus. Immediately, rumours swept
round London that cabinet changes were imminent. Fitzwilliam could

---

[1] Portland to Fitzwilliam 29/20 June, loc. cit.

[2] Fitzwilliam to Portland 23 June 1794, Portland MSS. P.W.F. 3765.

[3] Portland to Fitzwilliam 25 June 1794. Wentworth Woodhouse MSS., F.31b.

[4] Fitzwilliam to Portland 26 June 1794, Portland MSS. P.W.F. 3766.

[5] Mansfield to Portland 29 June 1794, Portland MSS. P.W.F. 7030. Portland
told Tom Grenville 'I think you will not find him inexorable'. Portland to Grenville 28 June 1794, Ad. MS. 42058, ff. 159–60, Thomas Grenville MSS.

not conceal from himself his realization that his obstinacy might destroy an arrangement which the country now needed more than ever. Although he persisted in telling Portland that he wished to remain outside the government, he admitted to his wife that he saw 'little prospect of escaping office'.[1]

Portland had been keeping Pitt informed about the opinions of Fitzwilliam and they had discussed the state of the negotiation on 1 July. On the following day, Pitt informed Portland of his plan for satisfying Fitzwilliam. He was to receive a definite promise of the Irish Viceroyalty and, until arrangements could be made for withdrawing Lord Westmorland from Ireland, Fitzwilliam could enter the cabinet as Lord President of the Council. When Fitzwilliam became Lord-Lieutenant, Hawkesbury could succeed to the Presidency and Westmorland could, in turn, succeed Hawkesbury as Chancellor of the Duchy of Lancaster.[2] Portland saw the force of these suggestions but he was conscious of some of their attendant difficulties. If Fitzwilliam took the Presidency and later the Irish Viceroyalty, then either Spencer or Mansfield, both of whom had generously stood aside to allow Fitzwilliam to take the former office, would expect its reversion to themselves. In that case, it could not possibly revert to Hawkesbury.[3] Pitt appears to have swallowed with little complaint the obvious need to conciliate the Whigs by allowing them one more cabinet seat. On 3 July he saw the King and received the royal assent to the cabinet changes. It was arranged that Portland should see George III after the levee on the following day.[4] On all sides it was assumed that the arrangements had been completed. Portland's presence at the levee was widely regarded as a certain indication that the Whigs had joined the government.[5] Fitzwilliam had resigned himself to his new station albeit with the greatest reluctance.

---

[1] Fitzwilliam to his wife (n.d.) N.R.O. X. 512/4/1. *The Morning Chronicle* of 27 June assumed that official announcements of the arrangement would appear on 30 June.

[2] Pitt to Portland 2 July 1794, Portland MSS. P.W.F. 7703. Copy in the Pitt Papers 102, in P.R.O.

[3] Portland to Pitt 2 July 1794, Copy, C.U.L. 6958[8], f. 1449.

[4] Pitt to Portland 3 July 1794, Portland MSS. P.W.F. 7704.

[5] Darnley to Portland 3 July 1794, Portland MSS. P.W.F. 1443. *The Morning Chronicle* of 5 July noticed Portland's audience of the King and passed severe strictures upon him.

I do not receive this honor (if it is one) with much exultation; on the contrary with a heavy heart. I did not feel great comfort in finding myself at St. James surrounded by persons, with whom I had been so many years in political hostility, and without those, I can never think of being separated from, publicly or privately, without a pang.[1]

Fitzwilliam was not alone in doubting the wisdom of coalition. Windham had been offered the post of Secretary-at-War and Portland had interpreted his silence (Windham was in Norfolk) as acquiescence. His absence from the party meeting, which took place on the evening of 3 July to settle the arrangements, had prevented him from voicing his reluctance to accept the office. His letter to Portland, expressing his refusal, arrived after the meeting had broken up and only hours before Portland was to attend the levee and speak to the King upon the subject of the offices and arrangements which were to accompany the coalition. The Duke sensed that Windham's change of heart arose from the fear that Dundas in his new office of Secretary for War, would retain control of the war which, as Home Secretary, he had hitherto enjoyed. The Duke thus urged upon Windham that the office which was held out to him could, if he chose to make it so, become 'a real efficient [sic] Cabinet employment'.[2] Tom Grenville travelled through the night and lectured Windham in a desperate effort to dissuade him from destroying the coalition arrangements which had proved so difficult to achieve. He succeeded in breaking Windham's determination to reject office and hurriedly scribbled a note to Portland to this effect. The Duke was thus able to attend the levee and to see the King as Pitt had previously arranged.[3] Nevertheless, the problem which Windham had raised remained unsettled. If Dundas was to take the post of Secretary for War, what would be Windham's functions and powers as Secretary-at-War? In short, were the Whigs

[1] Fitzwilliam to his wife (n.d.), N.R.O. X. 512/6/1.

[2] Windham to Portland 3 July 1794, Portland MS. P.W.F. 9538; Portland to Windham 3 July 1794, Ad. MSS. 37845, ff. 41–2, Windham Papers, printed in *Windham Papers*, i. 216–7; *Windham Diary*, 314.

[3] Portland to Grenville 3 and 4 July 1794, Ad. MS. 42058, ff. 161–4, Thomas Grenville MSS. Tom Grenville to Portland, two letters of 4 July 1794, Portland MSS. P.W.F. 4398, 4399, *Windham Diary* 314.

or were the present ministers to direct and control war policy? If the latter were to be the case, then there seemed to be no purpose in coalition at all. To Fitzwilliam, at least, the crisis had its value.

Dundas does not much like to part with power; but if Pitt wishes the junction, and I have no doubt he does sincerely, he will bring Dundas to his senses. I do not dislike the occurence, for I think it brings the sincerity of Pitt's desire to form the junction to a test.[1]

Having spoken to Windham, who had come to town, on 5 July, Portland had now come to realize the ambiguity of the arrangements respecting his own office, the Home Department. He refused to join the government while the control of Scottish patronage remained undecided and, more particularly, while the Home Department was to be deprived of Indian patronage. But it was the control of the war which was to matter and Portland had no desire to see his office stripped of its former influence in war policy. Portland expostulated with Pitt in the strongest terms. He left him in no doubt that coalition would stand or fall on the issue of control of the war. But Pitt was unwilling to hand over war policy to Portland because 'if all the details of the war . . . were to be settled by communication with a person new both to me and *to others*, I am sure the business could not go on for a week'.[2] He suggested to Grenville, therefore, that Portland should take the Foreign Department while Grenville took the Home Department. By this arrangement, Pitt hoped to soothe the angry Portland who was affronted at the prospect of his cabinet office being diminished in size and influence, by offering him the Foreign Department entire. Grenville immediately agreed to Pitt's request.[3] Thereupon, Pitt went to Dundas and succeeded in wringing from him his assent to the scheme. Pitt was thus able to present his solution of the unexpected difficulty which had arisen in the most diplomatic light to Portland. He told him that it was 'an additional Proof of the eagerness We feel to do whatever is practicable'. At the same time, he insisted that the War Department

---

[1] Fitzwilliam to his wife (n.d.), N.R.O. X.512/5/1.

[2] Pitt to Grenville 5 July 1794, H.M.C. *Dropmore*, ii. 595–6; *Windham Diary*, 314; *The Morning Chronicle*, 7 July 1794.

[3] Pitt to Grenville, loc. cit.; Grenville to Pitt 5 July 1794, H.M.C. *Dropmore*, ii. 596.

should not be placed in new hands.[1] Portland relented, but chose to accept the Home Department with control of the colonies but without the management of the war. A meeting at Burlington House on 6 July provided him with the support of the other conservative Whigs, excepting Windham, whose own problems had been ignored and pushed into the background while Portland was settling the details of his own office.[2] On Monday 7 July Portland and Pitt met at Downing Street to close the agreement. A cordial discussion took place and there seemed every reason to expect that, at last, the Whigs might kiss hands within a few days. News of the junction flashed across London. Windham resigned himself to his new station. Adam wrote to Portland on 7 July, acknowledging 'the rectitude of Your Grace's conduct' but formally severing their political connection. Pitt informed his cabinet colleagues of the conclusion of the coalition negotiations while Portland sent out drafts of the King's prorogation speech to his friends for their perusal. Even the *Morning Chronicle* was forced to admit that coalition was an accomplished fact.[3]

On 9 July, two days before the Whigs were to kiss hands, Dundas came near to wrecking the whole arrangement. He had been brooding at Wimbledon and he had refused to come to town. The loss of patronage, the humiliation of losing half of one of the great government departments and, perhaps, the scanty attention which Pitt had paid to his sentiments brought him to tender his resignation. Further, Dundas was affronted at the inclusion in the cabinet of Windham and the creation of the third Secretaryship. To Dundas it was both undesirable and unnecessary. There were already sufficient cabinet ministers to control war policy and there seemed to him to be no need to add yet one more dissonant voice to the clamour of conflicting opinions. Finally, Dundas was worried about the problem of the general supervision of the war.

    [1] Pitt to Portland 6 July 1794, Portland MSS. P.W.F. 7705 (dated incorrectly 5 July).

    [2] Pitt to Grenville 7 July 1794, H.M.C. *Dropmore*, ii. 597. *Windham Diary*, 314.

    [3] *Windham Diary*, 314–15; Adam to Portland 7 July 1794, drafts in the Blair-Adam MSS.; Pitt to Grenville 7 July 1794, loc. cit.; Pitt to Loughborough 7 July 1794, Campbell, *Lives of the Lord Chancellors*, vi. 350; Pitt to Hawkesbury 7 July 1794, Ad. MS. 38192, f. 9396, Liverpool Papers; Mansfield to Portland 9 July 1794, Portland MSS. P.W.F. 7031; *The Morning Chronicle*, 8 July 1794.

While threatening to resign, he urged Pitt to keep the superintendence of war policy in his own hands and not to allow it to be the subject of cabinet division.[1] Pitt was taken completely by surprise and was overwhelmed with the shock of Dundas's intransigence. If he carried out his threat to resign, he (Pitt) would be 'really completely heartbroken. . . . Had I the smallest idea that it would be the consequence, no consideration would have tempted me to agree to the measure that has led to it'. He therefore begged Dundas to reconsider his position; but even the uncharacteristic posture of Pitt on his knees before him could not sway Dundas.[2] Pitt quickly persuaded the King to write to Dundas and he himself rushed round to Wimbledon to add his personal pleas to the royal expostulations. When Pitt arrived, according to Dundas, he was 'distract and agitated in a manner to make me very uneasy indeed. . . . I begged him to compose himself'.[3] The King's letter, moreover, was a nice essay in royal persuasive diplomacy and by the evening of 9 July Dundas had reluctantly consented to remain in office without demanding any alteration in the arrangements with the Portland Whigs.[4] Coalition could now proceed. The journey along

[1] Dundas to Pitt 9 July 1794, copies in the Arniston MSS., Arniston Letter Book no. 86 and S.R.O. G.D.51. 1/17/24/1, Melville Castle MSS.; Henry to Robert Dundas 13 July 1794, Arniston MSS., Arniston Letter Book no. 91.

It was only after receiving a letter from Loughborough, dated 8 July (ibid. no. 92), suggesting that if the proposed arrangements went through then 'infinite embarrassment and delay' would result and that it might be publicly regarded as a snub against him, that Dundas decided to resign, secure in the knowledge that his views would be supported by at least one member of the cabinet. Or was Dundas's threat to resign a carefully calculated last-minute attempt to preserve his former position?

[2] Pitt to Dundas 9 July 1794, S.R.O. G.D.51. 1/17/24/2, Melville Castle MSS.; copy in the Arniston MSS., Arniston Letter Book no. 87, printed in Stanhope, *Miscellanies*, ii. 253; Dundas to Pitt 9 July 1794, copies in Arniston MSS. loc. cit. no. 88 and Melville Castle MSS. at S.R.O. G.D.51. 1/17/24/3, printed in Stanhope, op. cit. ii, 254.

[3] Pitt to Loughborough 9 July 1794, Campbell, *Lives of the Lord Chancellors*, vi. 349; Henry to Robert Dundas 13 July 1794, loc. cit: the King to Dundas 9 July 1794, Stanhope, op. cit., ii. 255.

[4] Pitt to Loughborough 8.00 p.m. 9 July 1794, Campbell, op. cit., vi. 350; Pitt to the King, Aspinall, *Later Correspondence of George III*, ii. 223; Dundas to the King 9 July 1794, ibid. ii. 222; the King to Pitt 10 July 1794, ibid. ii. 223; Dundas to the King 10 July, ibid. ii. 223.

its stony path had been completed. On 11 July the new cabinet ministers had an audience with the King and, in the presence of a delighted Edmund Burke, they kissed hands and received their seals of office.

6. *Party after the Coalition*

I. THE EFFECTS OF THE COALITION

The terms of the coalition were something of a triumph for the views of Fitzwilliam who had been instrumental in encouraging Portland to demand stringent terms of Pitt. A real party coalition had been achieved. Although there can be no doubt but that Pitt was still supreme in the cabinet, the coalition placed five Portland Whigs in the highest counsels of the state. Portland himself was Home Secretary, Fitzwilliam was the President of the Council, Spencer was Lord Privy Seal, Windham was Secretary-at-War while Mansfield entered the cabinet without Portfolio. The honours which Fitzwilliam had thought necessary were distributed quite generously. Portland obtained a Blue Riband, Lord Titchfield became Lord-Lieutenant of the County of Middlesex, Windham became a Privy Councillor. There were four peerages and one promotion. Welbore Ellis became Lord Mendip, Sir Henry Bridgeman became Baron Bradford, Sir Thomas Dundas became Baron Dundas and C. A. Pelham became Baron Yarborough. The Earl of Upper Ossory, moreover, received an English peerage. Fitzwilliam was promised the Irish Viceroyalty — although specific conditions had not yet been arranged — whenever Westmorland could be accommodated with a station which he considered to be suitable. Burke was not forgotten. Although he did not receive the peerage which had been talked of so frequently in the past three months, he received a generous pension which dispelled the financial anxieties of his last years. George III chafed at giving the Whigs so many honours and favours — a sure indication that the coalition was as fair and as generous to the Portland Whigs as the circumstances of the time permitted.[1]

[1] Stanhope, *Miscellanies*, ii. 251.

Pitt and other members of the cabinet were thankful that the coalition had at last been achieved. Pitt said that 'he placed much dependence on his new colleagues' and Richmond and Hawkesbury acknowledged the fact that the coalition represented an infusion of talent which was none the less welcome for being overdue.[1] Grenville was pleased at what he took to be the annihilation of party distinctions which could not fail to have its effect on the continent.[2] Dundas continued to grumble but resigned himself to his new political station.[3]

Supporters of government received the news of the coalition with mixed feelings. Many of Pitt's friends 'either grumble pretty audibly at the distribution of so great a part of the powers among new comers, or at best, shake their head, and wish that it may answer in the end'.[4] Canning's verdict was, in substance, echoed by many others. Even the most disinterested of politicians, including Wilberforce, approved the individual appointments but thought that Pitt had been too generous.[5] A few rumbles of dissatisfaction were heard at the prospect of Fitzwilliam taking the Irish government, while ambitious men like Auckland and Mornington naturally resented the whole arrangement.[6] Others could not forget the past. Buckingham regretted the cabinet reconstruction 'formed from the ranks of the ancient enemy, so nearly complete, that it wants only the accession of Mr. Fox to render it an efficient administration'.[7]

Portland's friends generally approved of the coalition. The genuine reluctance of the new ministers to take their position was recognized by Sheffield, who thought the junction 'an honest and manly step on

[1] G. Pellew, *Henry Addington* op. cit., i. 121; Hawkesbury to Pitt 17 July, 1794, C.U.L. 6958[8], f. 1461 (copy); Richmond to Pitt 14 July 1794, ibid. f. 1459.

[2] Grenville to Buckingham 9 July 1794, *Court and Cabinets*, ii. 256–7.

[3] E.g. Dundas to Sir Gilbert Elliot 11 July 1794, S.R.O. G.D. 1/17/1/25, Melville Castle MSS.

[4] D. Marshall, *The Rise of Canning* (1938), 75.

[5] Wilberforce to Lord Muncaster 9 July 1794. Wilberforce, *Correspondence*, i. 103–4.

[6] Camden to Addington July 1794, Pellew, op. cit., i. 122–3; Mornington to Addington 27 July 1794, ibid. i. 123; Auckland to Pitt 14 July 1794, draft, Ad. MS. 34452, ff. 461–2, Auckland Papers. See also the important letter of Sir John Mitford to Pitt, summing up the fears and reservations of lesser government men, of 14 Feb. 1795, Stanhope, op. cit. ii. 305–6.

[7] Buckingham to Grenville 8 July 1794, H.M.C. *Dropmore*, ii. 597–8.

the part of the new ministers'.[1] Fitzwilliam was much relieved when he discovered that 'the junction is generally well-received . . . and those who have submitted to situations of responsibility at this period, much applauded'.[2] There were, however, Whigs of the old-fashioned type who considered that Lord Bute and the Tories had triumphed over the Whig aristocracy at last. The pure aristocratic Whiggery of Rockingham lived on in his widow, who condemned the coalition as an attempt 'to blend *Whig* and Tory, to *break all Connections*, and to dispense with *Parties*'.[3]

The Foxites received the coalition with views that were not, in some ways, far removed from those of Lady Rockingham. The tone was set by the *Morning Chronicle*:

Mr. Pitt has completely triumphed in breaking to pieces that great body to whom the people looked up with confidence as to men who would never sacrifice their love of the Constitution to the views of the Court.[4]

In parliament, the Foxites were never tired of jeering at 'the various and discordant characters' who composed the administration. They continued to assert the coalition was not necessary, that the party would have survived its schism when Pitt's deceit and treachery had been understood by the Portland Whigs. Coalition would not have taken place had the Portland Whigs not succumbed to the temptations of court emolument.[5] Although Fox himself participated in the denunciation of the Portland Whigs, going so far as to declare his own solemn separation from Portland at a radical meeting on 9 October,[6] he was, in fact, bitterly hurt by the coalition. He might have concealed his sorrow and his distress in the merry round of conviviality which characterized the private relationships of the Foxite Whigs, but

---

[1] Sheffield to Auckland 30 July 1794, Ad. MS. 34452, f. 469, Auckland Papers, printed in *Auckland*, iii. 223–4.

[2] Fitzwilliam to Portland 26 July 1794, Portland MSS. P.W.F. 3767.

[3] Lady Rockingham to Fitzwilliam 9 Sept. 1794, Wentworth Woodhouse MSS. F.128h.

[4] *The Morning Chronicle* 8 July 1794. On the 15 July, the paper noted that: 'The complete demolition of the ancient Whig Aristocracy, erects the Tories into absolute power.'

[5] E.g.: *The Parliamentary Register*, xxxviii. 448, 452; *The Parliamentary History*, xxxi. 1004–5, 1125, 1241, 1499, 1540.

[6] *The Morning Chronicle*, 11 Oct. 1794.

occasionally he lapsed into lethargy and depression.[1] Nevertheless, his distress carried with it the presumption of his own self-righteousness:

I have nothing to say for my old friends, nor indeed as *politicians* have they any right to any tenderness from me, but I cannot forget how long I have lived in friendship, with them, nor can I avoid feeling the most severe mortification, when I recollect the certainty I used to entertain that they would never disgrace themselves as I think they have done. . . . I think they have all behaved very ill to me, and for most of them, who certainly owe much more to me, than I do them, I feel nothing but contempt.[2]

Opposition was now more fruitless and less hopeful than ever before. Fox's very real personal distress at the coalition was, more often than not, translated into virulent disgust against his former colleagues. He was no longer the Man of the People. He could no longer revel in the prospect of playing the great role in the politics of his country which he had at one time been expected to play. He was now middle-aged, his health was insecure and he had behind him a career of apparent and unbroken failure. His political career had been a series of wild and miscalculated political gambles which had left him beyond the political pale and now, at last, the friends whom he valued most had left him. 'I wish I could be persuaded that it was right to quit public business, for I should like it to a degree that I cannot express.'[3] His ineptness as a party leader and his reluctance to offend his associates by acting against their wishes all too frequently weakened his influence with the Foxites. The vacuum of leadership was willingly filled by either Sheridan or Lauderdale.[4] All that could be hoped for was the overthrow of the ministry by the military failure which Fox usually deluded

---

[1] Wm. Bouverie to Adam (n.d. 1794), Blair-Adam MSS.; Lady Sarah Lennox to Lady Susan O'Brien 9 Sept. 1794, Ad. MS. 51355, unfoliated, Holland House MSS.; Caroline Fox to Lord Holland 18 Sept. 1794, Ad. MS. 51732, unfoliated, Holland House MSS.

[2] Fox to Lord Holland 18 Aug. 1794, Ad. MS. 47571, ff. 143–46, Fox Papers, printed in *Fox's Memorials*, iii. 79–83; Fox to Fitzwilliam 15 Sept. 1796, N.R.O. Box 50: 'every pleasurable idea with regard to politics is quite gone from me; *mais il faut faire son devoir*'.

[3] Fox to Lord Holland 12 Apr. 1795, Ad. MS. 47572, ff. 38–41, Fox Papers, printed in *Fox's Memorials*, iii. 101–6.

[4] Fox to Fitzpatrick 6 Oct. 1796, Ad. MS. 47581, ff. 5–6, Fox Papers; Caroline Fox to Lord Holland 13 Nov. 1794, Ad. MS. 51732, Holland House MSS.

himself into expecting. The Foxites could now only attain power by the humiliation of their country, a humiliation which Fox patiently and gleefully anticipated.¹ Occasionally Fox exerted himself. Following Lauderdale's initiative during the session of 1795, Fox tried to procure a series of petitions from the country protesting against the continuation of the war. But, as Grey saw only too clearly, petitions were not enough to bring Pitt down. Nor would a vote of censure be forthcoming, for the House of Commons would never substitute Fox for Pitt. Grey, in fact, was so troubled by these considerations that he wished to take the issues of war policy and peace to the country as non-party questions.² It was not, then, upon issues arising from the war that Fox might hope to cause Pitt more than momentary embarrassment. A far more promising platform on which to raise the Foxite standard proved to be that of constitutional liberties. The Two Acts of the autumn of 1795 produced a reaction in the Foxites which was little short of electric.

Fox seems to think that upon these Bills it is necessary to have public Meetings wherever they can be had with any probability of success, as he with truth regards this as the most daring attack made on the Constitution since the Revolution.³

The Foxites tried to promote meetings in all parts of the kingdom and their initial enthusiasm led them to canvass vigorously. As Mrs. Crewe put it: 'Charles Fox seems determined we should have a civil war.'⁴ To concert the energies of the parliamentary opposition, an 'association' was formed, modelled upon the constitution of the Whig Club, and its

¹ In 1797 the King said that Fox 'is now become an open enemy of his country'. The King to Pitt 27 Apr. 1797, Aspinall, *Later Correspondence of George III*, ii. 566. Some of Fox's remarks certainly bear out this verdict. In particular, see Fox to Lord Holland 10 Sept. 1795, Ad. MS. 47572, f. 81, Fox Papers.

² Grey to Bigges 20 Aug. 1795, Grey MSS. Fox to (?)Grafton 2 Jan. 1795, Ad. MS. 47569, ff. 52–55, Fox Papers; Tom Pelham to Lady Holland 15 Jan. 1795, Ad. MS. 51706, unfoliated, Holland House MSS.

³ Lauderdale to Grafton 12 Nov. 1795, Grafton MSS. IIIc, f. 734. The people, said Grey, 'must declare open war against the Government'. To Bigges 1 Jan. 1796, Grey MSS.

⁴ Mrs. Crewe to Portland 23 Nov. 1795, Portland MSS. P.W.F. 3177; Grey to Bigges 11 Nov. 1795, Grey MSS.

propaganda was disseminated throughout the country.[1] Lauderdale said with truth that 'The opposition discover more disposition to unite with the public than they have hitherto done.'[2] Early in 1796, however, the bitterness of failure had to be confessed. Lambton summed up the feelings of the weary Foxites. There seemed to be no point in appealing to the people. They were as corrupt as Pitt's majority. Even when resolutions were procured, nothing could be done with them.

Our comfort must be, tho' our undertaking has been unsuccessful, that we have fulfilled a duty satisfactory to our own conscience. . . . I am, like you thoroughly sick of Politics and so indifferent to Parliament that I almost long to have no more to do with it.[3]

A year later, Fox made one of his rare yet significant submissions to the cruel realities of the political position into which he had led his followers, when he wrote to Lauderdale:

If yourself, Guilford, Bedford, and Grey could get the government, and would accept it, you would do much better without me.[4]

While the opposition became consumed with that growing weariness of politics which led to the secession of 1797, the Portland Whigs were establishing themselves in their new political role. The habits of former years could not be shrugged off too quickly. Old political friends had to be rewarded for their fidelity to the party and requests for any official employment from such men usually came to the Portland Whigs, 'as I am yet unaccustomed to solicit Mr. Pitt', remarked Sir Thomas Dundas.[5] Portland himself tried to help his friends but was careful not to offend the cabinet or the King. He usually passed on such requests to the relevant department or to Pitt.[6] Pitt was not ungenerous and seems to have upset some of his own friends by the readiness with

[1] Fox to Grafton 28 Dec. 1795, Ad. MS. 47569, ff. 66–67, ff. Fox Papers; Grey to Bigges 1 Jan. 1796, Grey MSS.

[2] Lauderdale to Grafton 16 Dec. 1795, Grafton MSS. iiic, f. 745.

[3] Lambton to Grey 11 Apr. 1796, Grey MSS.

[4] Fox to Lauderdale 2 June 1797, *Fox's Memorials*, iii. 271–2.

[5] Sir Thomas Dundas to Portland 13 Aug. 1794, Portland MSS. P.W.F. 3507. There were requests for offices and peerages promised during the Regency Crisis and, in some cases, in 1782 and 1783.

[6] But in Jan. 1795, shortly after Spencer became First Lord of the Admiralty, Portland had a list of almost thirty applications for his attention. Portland MSS. P.W.M. 8518. 'List of Applications to be made to Lord Spencer'.

which he was prepared to accommodate Portland.[1] Yet the requests were numerous and Portland found it impossible to avoid disappointing many of his friends. Dundas, moreover, disliked any interference with Scottish patronage and was quick to rebuff the Duke's occasional attempts to satisfy his Scottish friends.[2] The King disliked excessive generosity towards those who had been his personal and political enemies for so many years. Not long after Fitzwilliam had assumed the Irish Viceroyalty, Portland was warning him about 'putting the K — more out of humours than is necessary when we want a *job* or two ourselves'.[3] With the exception of Fitzwilliam's tenure of the Irish government, however, the Whigs seemed to have struck a fairly unexceptionable balance between loyalty to old friends and a full appreciation of their new non-party responsibilities.

Burke had hoped that the coalition government would not be a government of departments, that previous political quarrels could be forgotten and subsumed under a strengthened unity of purpose in tackling the war. Yet the new ministers were advocates of Burke's doctrine that the war could only be won by a blow aimed at the heart of France and they were constantly advocating that this doctrine be put into practice.[4] Although the accession to power of the Portland Whigs did not convert the war into an ideological crusade, it did increase substantially the link between the *émigrés* and the British government and it gradually established in government circles a greater realization of the importance of expeditions to French soil. It confirmed, too, that the restoration of the Bourbons and the restitution of property were necessary preliminaries to any peace treaty. Yet the control of the war was not in the hands of the new ministers. Pitt and Dundas used the peculiar administrative system and the division of responsibilities between several departments to keep that control securely in their own

[1] Sir John Mitford to Pitt 14 Feb. 1795, loc. cit.

[2] E.g. Dundas to Portland 8 Oct., 25 Nov. 1794, Portland MSS. P.W.F. 3486, 3490.

[3] Portland to Fitzwilliam 14 Jan. 1795, Wentworth Woodhouse MSS., F.31e. In the Portland MSS. there is a list of Portland's suggestions to Fitzwilliam concerning the rewards to be given to Irish political friends. P.W.F. 9787 Misc. 25. In the Wentworth Woodhouse MSS. at Sheffield F.I. there is a list of over sixty applications to Fitzwilliam for Irish offices from English friends.

[4] E.g. Fitzwilliam to Portland 8 Sept. 1794, Portland MSS. P.W.F. 3772.

hands. They respected Windham and frequently placed considerable trust in him by the communication of the most confidential matters[1] but his inexperience militated against him. His tireless efforts, however, wrung a few subsidies for the *émigrés* from the ministers and persuaded them to go forward with the ill-fated Quiberon expedition.[2] Windham, in fact, seems to have drawn into his own department the control of all matters relating to the Royalists, but he found his position to be impossible. In the spring of 1796 he resigned this responsibility to other departments. He confessed that he was sick of the frustration which arose from the need to consult other departments whenever he wished to do anything for the Royalists. He was weary, moreover, with the jealousy and the suspicion that he acted 'rather according to my own Ideas, than in conformity to those which the cabinet have finally adopted'.[3] At bottom, Windham realized that the other ministers did not share his concern for the Royalists and that they were uninterested in bestowing upon their affairs the least attention. He and the other Portland Whigs had failed to persuade the ministers to adopt as their consistent policy the cause of the French royalty and the French aristocracy. Nor had the coalition apparently prevented a series of disasters on the continent which continued until Holland had been lost in March 1795. Later in the year, the government decided to explore the possibilities of negotiating peace with the republic. Windham agreed that the nature of the French government should be no obstacle to these soundings[4] but Portland and Mansfield found this a bitter pill to swallow.[5] They acquiesced with reluctance in the cabinet's decision but shifted uncomfortably at the charges of inconsistency which were levelled against them. Objecting to Portland over the professed recognition of the French republic, Laurence reminded the Duke that 'it was on the ground of resisting generally the introduction of the

---

[1] In particular, the vexed question of the recall of the Duke of York. The other Portland Whigs were also intimately involved with this question, e.g. Lord Grenville to Fitzwilliam 13 Sept. 1794, Wentworth Woodhouse MSS., F.31c.

[2] Pitt to Windham 23 Sept. 1794, Ad. MS. 37844, ff. 68–69, Windham Papers; Dundas to Windham 15 Sept. 1794, Ad. MS. 37874, ff. 64–65, Windham Papers.

[3] Windham to Pitt 27 Apr. 1796, Ad. MS. 37844, ff. 122–4, Windham Papers.

[4] Mansfield to Portland 21 Sept. 1795, Portland MSS. P.W.F. 7039.

[5] Portland to Pitt 23 Sept. 1795, P.R.O. Pitt Papers, 168; Mansfield to Portland 26 Oct. 1795, Portland MSS. P.W.F. 6251.

principle here that your Grace and your friends joined the Administration'.[1] A year later, Windham had adopted the most uncompromising of positions on the question of peace.

Do not imagine that in such a state of things I shall be induced to take a new lease of my connection with the Ministry, or do more than drag on in my present situation till I see what turn things take. If I could have been sure that Lord Malmesbury's despicable embassy would succeed and that peace must be the immediate consequence, I should have been out long since.[2]

The Portland Whigs clung fast to the principles which they had adopted before they entered the ministry, and on the question of peace they did not surrender their opinions completely. But they did not succeed in securing their adoption. From this aspect, therefore, the coalition may be judged to have been a failure. Nevertheless, it can at least be said that the coalition infused some much-needed vigour and energy into Pitt's cabinet of old men and incompetents. Windham at last found some outlet for his energies, however dissatisfied he may have been with his station. At the Admiralty, Spencer proved to be an outstanding success. He resisted Dundas's encroachments into his departments and had the force of character to rid the navy of the ageing Lord Hood.[3] Portland made a hesitant and unsteady beginning at the Home Office and leaned heavily on Dundas for a while. It was Dundas, in fact, and not Portland who first suggested the Two Acts in 1795.[4] Portland's very weaknesses, however, have been recognised as something of an advantage. During the harsh period of repression while he was at the Home Office he did not interfere unnecessarily with local magistrates and the Two Acts might have been applied much more severely than they were. Verdicts on the coalition might with justice, however, be left to those whom it affected most closely. That it cannot be dismissed as an unfortunate mistake because of the Fitzwilliam

[1] Laurence to Portland 16 Dec. 1795, Portland MSS. P.W.F. 6251.

[2] Windham to Mrs. Crewe 31 Oct. 1796, *Windham Papers*, ii. 23–25.

[3] There is some evidence to show that Spencer was the driving force behind the dismissal of Richmond. Richmond to Pitt 15 Dec. 1794. H.M.C. *Bathurst*, 706–7; Portland to Fitzwilliam 2 Dec. 1794. Wentworth Woodhouse MSS., F.31d; Portland to Fitzwilliam 4 Dec. 1794, ibid.; *Correspondence of Charles, 1st Marquis Cornwallis*, ed. C. Ross (4 vols., 1859), ii. 281–2.

[4] Dundas to Portland 12 July, 4 Aug., 4 Sept. 1794 and 1 Nov. 1795. Portland MSS. P.W.F. 3479, 3481, 3482, 3495.

affair is attested by the ministers themselves who expressed their satisfaction with the conduct of their new colleagues. Pitt told Lord Westmorland that 'the conduct of all our new friends has been perfectly cordial and satisfactory' and there are many other such testimonials.[3] There seems to have been a real desire on all sides to make the new arrangements work in practice. Much of the credit for this must go to Pitt, who recognized and appreciated the delicacy and the embarrassment of the new situation in which the Portland Whigs found themselves and who, at some risk to his own popularity with his own followers, demonstrated his willingness to do what he could to help his new cabinet colleagues.

II. The Whigs and Ireland

The coalition was to meet its most severe test on the affairs of Ireland. The Whigs had a long-standing interest in the situation of that country, more particularly since the Rockingham–Shelburne administration had granted legislative independence to the Irish in 1782. 'The practice, established in 1782, by which a change of ministry involved a change of viceroy strengthened the connection between political groups in the two countries.'[2] As early as 1784 there is evidence to suggest that the Irish opposition was closely in touch with, and possibly taking orders from, the English opposition.[3] Such connections were hardened in the years that followed. During and after the Regency Crisis of 1788–9 the Irish Whigs demonstrated not only their relationship with their English colleagues but also their willingness and ability to organize themselves on a party basis. Grattan threw in his lot with the English opposition[4] and the Irish Whigs were able to command a short-lived majority in the Irish Commons, which threw off its subservience to the English legislature and invited the Prince of

---

[1] Pitt to Westmorland 19 Oct. 1794, Stanhope *Miscellanies*, i. 8–12. Grenville's similar verdict is in his letter to Tom Grenville 15 Oct. 1794, *Court and Cabinets*, iii. 312–16.

[2] J. C. Beckett, *The Making of Modern Ireland, 1603–1923* (1966), 236.

[3] E. M. Johnston, *Great Britain and Ireland, 1760–1800* (1963). For the family connections which bound the two parties together see ibid. 286.

[4] S. Gwynn, *Henry Grattan and his Times* (1939), 222.

Wales to assume the Regency in Ireland. Only by wholesale dismissal and proscription of the supporters of the Prince's right to the Regency was the Lord-Lieutenant, Buckingham, able to recover his ascendancy, but it was the ruthlessness and severity of these dismissals which served to entrench party into Irish politics. Buckingham observed that the language of Grattan 'is avowedly that of the Cavendish party, and I am told he now avows himself a party man . . . the puppet moved by the wires of Burlington House to the measures of that party'.[1] As early as February 1789 Grattan had organized an informal association which pledged its members (who numbered about fifty Irish M.P.s) to resign if any of them were dismissed.[2] After the failure of their expectations in the spring of 1789, the Whigs organized themselves upon a more systematic basis by forming the Whig Club of Dublin in June. According to one report, two-thirds of the Irish opposition participated in some way or other in this Whig Club.[3] The Irish Whigs 'rested with peculiar security on Mr. Fox and the Rockingham Party, under whose power and with whose aid, Irish freedom was established in 1782'.[4] The Club initially dedicated itself to supporting measures of moderate reform such as Place Bills and the disqualification of revenue officials, but it was not blind to the need for giving birth to similar societies in other parts of Ireland and for this purpose a particularly effective propaganda system was established.[5]

The institutions of party were accompanied by their ideological justification. Grattan proclaimed that their party was beneficial: 'a party united on public principle, by the bond of certain specific measures cannot be carried by individuals and which measures can only succeed by party'.[6] Even Wolf Tone admitted that the Whig Club 'has the merit of giving an elevated tone to our politics by summoning at least private honour to the aid of public system — which has wiped away

---

[1] Buckingham to W. W. Grenville 7 Feb. 1789, H.M.C. *Dropmore*, i. 409–10: 'they have their instructions from their party in England', Buckingham to W. W. Grenville 18–20 Jan. 1789, ibid. 400–1.

[2] Gwynn, op. cit., 232.

[3] Hobart to W. W. Grenville 19 Aug. 1789, H.M.C. *Dropmore*, i. 492. At first the club had 53 members but by Mar. 1790 there were 113. *Memoirs of Henry Grattan*, ed. H. Grattan (5 vols., 1841), iii. 416.

[4] F. Hardy, *The Memoirs of James Caulfield Charlemont* (2 vols., 1812), ii. 202.

[5] Gwynn, op. cit., 243, 245–6; Hardy, op. cit., 205–6.   [6] Gwynn, op. cit., 239.

from our public men the national stigma of insincerity and desertion of principle and party'.[1] The Whig Club was, in fact, a new departure in Irish politics in that it was an attempt to weld together a definite party in parliament with definite aims and upon an ideological basis similar in many ways to that which Burke had propounded in the *Thoughts*.

During the session of 1790 the Irish opposition held together, and even a surprise dissolution did not prevent them winning a landslide victory in the elections in Dublin.[2] Westmorland, the new Lord-Lieutenant had, in fact, been worried. As he told Pitt, 'the associated strength of the Party, aided by many County Members who reluctantly vote in every measure of opposition, for fear of being misrepresented in their Counties' had caused him great concern.[3] In the session of 1791, however, Grattan's moderation and his refusal to take sides in the quarrel between Fox and Burke which was exercising his allies in England were quite unable to prevent the appearance of a schism in the Irish opposition, rather similar to that in England, on the subjects of the French Revolution and reform.[4] At the same time, there is a parallel between the failure of the Friends of the People in England to restrain the reformers and the inability of the Whig Club of Dublin to control the agitation for the repeal of disabilities affecting the Irish Catholics.[5] The Relief Bill of 1792, by which Catholics were freed from disabilities concerning mixed marriages, the practice of the law and the remaining restrictions on Catholic education, was regarded by the aristocratic Irish Whigs as a final and satisfactory measure. Yet the rising tide of agitation out of doors, organized by the Catholic Committee, reached its culmination in the Catholic Convention which met in Dublin on 3 December. The English cabinet decided upon a further measure and the Relief Bill of 1793 admitted Catholics to the same municipal and parliamentary franchise as the Protestants and opened most civil and military posts to them. Yet Catholics were still unable to sit in parliament. The Bill of 1793 was limited in its effect because

[1] Gwynn, op. cit. 253. See also p. 17.
[2] Hardy, op. cit., 224–5; Grattan, op. cit., 460–3.
[3] Westmorland to Pitt 24 Feb. 1790, copy, C.U.L. 6958⁴, f. 765.
[4] Gwynn, op. cit., 249; Johnston, op. cit., 288–9.
[5] W. Lecky, *History of Ireland in the Eighteenth Century* (3 vols., 1913), iii. 16.

there were few boroughs where the Catholics could seriously hope to influence elections.

The progress of the reform agitation and the worsening situation on the continent in 1793–4 began to exercise a divisive effect upon the Whig party in Ireland. The more conservative wing in the party learned to co-operate with the Lord-Lieutenant on questions of domestic security and this led, in the session of 1794, to a gradual defection of members of the opposition.[1] Nevertheless, the news of the coalition of July 1794 aroused the Irish Whigs to expect a change of system now that their English friends had seemingly been handed the government of Ireland. The Ascendancy, therefore, looked upon the future with the deepest forebodings.[2]

The coalition had placed Pitt in an embarrassing position. He did not wish to offend his Irish and English colleagues by handing the government of Ireland over to the Whigs. But, had he not at least promised that Fitzwilliam was to be Lord-Lieutenant as soon as Westmorland could be provided with a suitable post in England, the coalition would not have been concluded.[3] Little was said about the exact terms upon which Fitzwilliam was to go to Ireland but the Portland Whigs seem to have been in little doubt that Irish affairs were to be placed completely in their hands, 'without any other reserve, than what are supposed in every wise and sober servant of the Crown'.[4] Yet such general assump-

---

[1] 'The Government during the summer [of 1793] had made converts of many members who usually had acted in opposition. Lord Shannon and his numerous train, which from the time of the debates on the Regency had been Opposition, now became partisans of the Court from his Lordship being gratified with the situation of First Lord of the Treasury. Mr. O'Neill and his two members also quitted the Opposition, he being gratified with a peerage. Several of the county representatives, by being appointed to high situations in the militia regiments, were become either wholly devoted or much inclined to the Court.' The Journal of Sir Laurence Parsons, quoted in Gwynn, *Grattan and his Times*, 288. See also Grattan, *Memoirs*, iv. 126–7; Hardy, *Memoirs of Charlemont*, ii. 297, 310.

[2] Ibid. ii. 308; O'Beirne to Fitzwilliam 23 Aug. 1794, N.R.O. Box 46: Beresford to Auckland 15 July 1794, Ad. MS. 34452, f. 463, Auckland Papers.

[3] Pellew, *Henry Addington*, i. 122–3.

[4] Burke to Windham 16 Oct. 1794, *Windham Diary* 328–30. 'If the general management and superintendance of Ireland had not been offered . . . that Coalition could never have taken place.' Fitzwilliam to Carlisle 23 Mar. 1795, H.M.C. *Carlisle*, 713–21.

tions were not at this stage defined too closely. Pitt did not choose to confide his own difficulties to the new ministers and he left in dangerous ambiguity the terms of any new Irish arrangement the Whigs might wish to conclude. Unrestrained by contradiction from Pitt, the Whigs proceeded to act as though Ireland was their preserve. With no reference to the cabinet, Fitzwilliam decided to appoint Tom Grenville as his Irish Secretary and advertised his intention of introducing a new system into the Irish government by complaining loudly at the continuing disposal of offices by the outgoing Lord-Lieutenant.[1] Fitzwilliam was not alone in these indiscretions. Portland found Westmorland's distribution of offices equally offensive and he remonstrated with Pitt against it.[2] Nor did Portland refrain from courting Ponsonby and the other Irish Whigs who were in London during the late summer of 1794. Indeed, Portland was trying to restrain them from forcing the new cabinet members to go to extremes in their demands for the reform of the Irish government. Even Burke was worried lest Fitzwilliam should act over-hastily and introduce a Catholic Relief Bill or even propose the union of the two kingdoms.[3] Complaints of indiscretion were not confined to supporters of Pitt. Nor were they levelled solely at Fitzwilliam. Burke saw that the Earl had acted imprudently 'to go so far into detail as has been done until all the circumstances of the Appointment were settled', and he thought that Portland was equally to blame.[4]

Fitzwilliam had been trying to persuade Portland to secure his appointment to the Irish Viceroyalty since August but it was not until October that the Duke, seeing that Fitzwilliam's urgency 'was no longer to be resisted' hinted to Pitt that the appointment 'has escaped the King's memory'.[5] Fitzwilliam was threatening to resign:

in consequence of the certainty which I entertain'd of going to Ireland, I

---

[1] Fitzwilliam to Tom Grenville 11 Aug. 1794, *Court and Cabinets*, ii. 299; Fitzwilliam to Grattan 23 Aug. 1794, Grattan, op. cit., iv. 173–4; Fitzwilliam to Portland 17 Aug. 1794, Portland MSS. P.W.F. 3771.

[2] Portland to Pitt 6 Sept. 1794, P.R.O. Pitt Papers, 329.

[3] Adair to Portland 18 Sept. 1794, Portland MSS. P.W.F. 27; Burke to Fitzwilliam *ante* 26 Sept. 1794, Wentworth Woodhouse MSS., Burke Letters 1.

[4] Burke to Windham 16 Oct. 1794, *Windham Papers*, i. 262–71; Lord Grenville to Tom Grenville, 15 Sept. 1794, *Court and Cabinets*, ii. 301–2; Lord Grenville to Lord Buckingham 27 Sept. 1794, ibid. 305–6.

[5] Portland to Pitt 4 Oct. 1794, P.R.O. Pitt Papers, 329. For Fitzwilliam's

thought it my duty to look forward to the management of the country, and therefore invited the most respectable persons of that kingdom to communicate with me confidentially, and upon the credit of the situation *I held myself out* as being intended for, they have been induc'd to open themselves to me, and to let me into their most private thoughts and opinions of men and things . . . if I have duped them, I have done so, because I was myself duped.

He did not wish to be too closely hedged with conditions. Dismissing the notion 'that I step into Lord Westmorland's old shoes', he asserted that if he went to Ireland, he would not continue with the same men and the same measures.[1] All the new cabinet ministers supported Fitzwilliam and threatened to resign with him if satisfactory conditions for the government of Ireland were not forthcoming. They insisted, moreover, upon the performance of a further promise which had made coalition possible in July, that Mansfield would succeed to the Presidency of the Council. The two wings of the cabinet were held together by Windham, with some assistance from Burke. Although Windham stood by his threat to resign, he acted as the mediator between the two sides and did all he could to influence Fitzwilliam. So close, indeed, was he to Pitt that it was reported that Portland was jealous and suspicious of his intentions.[2]

Fitzwilliam dug his heels in and refused to compromise. 'I shall not go, unless I go with that authority I ought to have, & unless I feel a confidence in the support I shall receive here.'[3] He was consoled by the knowledge that 'if we break, we *all* go together'.[4] His stubbornness rested upon the need to carry through the promises he had already made so rashly. On the other hand:

I shudder at the thought of its breaking off; no one can foresee the consequences that will arise in Ireland: the country was kept in tranquillity last year by the great moderation & management of Grattan & opposition: that sort

connections with Ireland and an assessment of his inexperience of office and his lack of restraint, see Johnston, *Great Britain and Ireland*, 106–7.

[1] Fitzwilliam to Windham 11 Oct. 1794, Ad. MS. 37854, ff. 83–84, Windham Papers.

[2] Windham to Pitt 12 Oct. 1794, P.R.O. Pitt Papers, 330; Pitt to Windham 12 Oct. 1794, Ad. MS. 37844, ff. 76–77, Windham Papers; Windham to Fitzwilliam 12 Oct. 1794, Wentworth Woodhouse MSS. F.311; Bland-Burges to his wife 14 Oct. 1794, *Bland-Burges*, 271–4.

[3] N.R.O. Fitzwilliam MSS. S/12/29.   [4] Ibid. S/12/10.

of management is very difficult to hold for ever. . . . The body of the people
out of doors are but ready to back them, & what line their passions may lead
them to no man can foresee: those in Parlt. will have little power or authority
over them: leaders of a very different description will present themselves.[1]

Fitzwilliam, indeed, was 'much satisfied with all these stoppages on
our part'. If his resolution and his determination to adhere to his principles finally obtained for him the government of Ireland 'it will mark
the character of the transaction, & clear it of all suspicion of an eagerness for Honours, or a willingness to compromise with Ministers'.[2]

The October crisis was a real test of the trust and the confidence
which had been built up between the new and the old cabinet ministers.
It is significant that Portland remained distrustful of Pitt and that
Dundas suggested that the government would be better off without its
new members.[3] With the exception of these two men and Fitzwilliam,
the other cabinet ministers were anxious to prevent a thorough breach
of the coalition and the fact that it held together in the face of a first-
rate political storm is some indication of its former success and cordiality. In some ways the two parties in the dispute, Pitt and Fitzwilliam,
were not separated by insuperable barriers. Pitt was willing to allow
the Earl to go to Ireland, 'provided the line of measures to be pursued is
satisfactorily settled, and all idea of violent change put out of the
question'. Pitt did not foresee any real difficulties as to measures and he
recognized that Fitzwilliam was not demanding a general proscription
of Westmorland's supporters. He flatly rejected the dismissal of
Beresford but did not appear to cavil too closely at the prospect of some
change of personnel.[4] Yet Pitt perhaps realized that more fundamental
issues were in question.

The system of introducing English party into Ireland, the principle of connect-
ing changes of Government here with the removal of persons high in office
there, and particularly the marking of that system in the instance of a person of
Fitzgibbon's situation, weight, and character. . . .

---

[1] Ibid. S/12/18   [2] Ibid. S/12/17

[3] Portland to Windham 19 Oct. 1794, Ad. MS. 37845, f. 61, Windham Papers;
Dundas to Pitt 13 Oct. 1794, Lord Ashbourne, *Life of Pitt* (1898), 183–4.

[4] Fitzwilliam to Burke 21 Oct. 1794, Wentworth Woodhouse MSS., Burke
Letters 1; Pitt to Westmorland 19 Oct. 1794, loc. cit. For Loughborough's
attempts to mediate with Pitt see the letters printed in J. Holland Rose, *Pitt and
Napoleon : Essays and Letters* (1912), 24–26.

were anathema both to himself and to Lord Grenville.[1] These opinions were echoed by Dundas.

The idea of Lord Fitzwilliam going to Ireland was at all times a bad one, because being connected with a faction in Ireland, it was not in human nature for him with the best intentions, to avoid getting into the arms of that faction, and governing upon narrow in place of general principles such as operated, or at least was thought to operate in the Union of Parties.[2]

Before Fitzwilliam departed from England, an agreement upon the points in dispute had been reached[3] but the agreement was so ambiguous that it did not preclude the possibility of misinterpretation.[4] Nevertheless, it should be remembered that few of those who were closely involved in achieving that agreement accepted Fitzwilliam's version of its stipulations. Pitt had stressed constantly that he would not agree to the removal of Beresford or Fitzgibbon but he told Fitzwilliam that they were not to be removed 'immediately' and thus Fitzwilliam was perfectly justified in his contention that Pitt had not forbidden their removal.[5] Others, however, thought that they should not have been removed without cabinet approval.[6] Similar confusion prevailed on the much-discussed subject of a Roman Catholic Bill. Fitzwilliam agreed that he should not bring forward such a bill but 'that the discussion of the propriety may be left open'.[7] To Fitzwilliam this meant that the

[1] Lord Grenville to Tom Grenville 15 Oct. 1794, loc. cit.

[2] Dundas to Loughborough 19 Oct. 1794 (wrongly dated 1792), S.R.O. G.D.51. 1/17/14, Melville Castle MSS.

[3] A meeting of Pitt, Lord Grenville, Portland, Fitzwilliam, Spencer and Windham in Dec. ended in an agreed Memorandum which is printed, *inter alia*, in Ashbourne, *Pitt*, 187–90.

[4] The document is both imprecise and incomplete. I certainly cannot accept the opinion of Johnston (*Great Britain and Ireland*, 112), that 'no Lord-Lieutenant ever set out with more explicit instructions'. Beresford was not even mentioned at the meeting. The Catholic question was 'not discussed at much length, that no decided sentiment was expressed by anyone' except that Fitzwilliam ought '*if possible*, prevent the agitations of the question'. (*Great Britain and Ireland*, iii. My italics.)

[5] Pitt to Fitzwilliam 9 Feb. 1795, Wentworth Woodhouse MSS., F.31f.; Fitzwilliam to Portland 3 Feb. 1795, ibid. F.5, ff. 39–40; Fitzwilliam to Carlisle 6 Mar. 1795, H.M.C. *Carlisle*, 704–11.

[6] Carlisle to Fitzwilliam 19 Apr. 1795, Wentworth Woodhouse MSS., F.31i.

[7] Fitzwilliam Memoranda 15 Nov. 1794, Wentworth Woodhouse MSS., F.29b.

cabinet had left the responsibility of supporting such a bill (if one were to be brought forward) in his own hands.[1] The other cabinet ministers, however, said that cabinet approval was necessary before the Lord-Lieutenant might take any such decision.[2] Fitzwilliam, very justly, was later able to point to the fact that his frequent requests for guidance on this subject had met with no response and that the urgency of the situation left him with no alternative but to lend it his support.[3] On the further question of office changes, Fitzwilliam does seem to have given too liberal an interpretation to the instructions which he carried with him. The rest of the cabinet agreed that, with one or two exceptions, cabinet approval of changes must be forthcoming. Fitzwilliam, however, had already discussed with Grattan and Ponsonby in some detail the changes that he intended to make and he seems to have carried out exactly these promises.[4] Finally, Pitt doubtless felt that by early December there was little possibility that Fitzwilliam, whatever his earlier intentions, had now abandoned the idea of introducing anything like a new system with regard to men or to measures into Ireland.[5] Notwithstanding such clarifications as had been made, the rising anticipation in Ireland that Fitzwilliam's appointment would introduce the long-awaited new dispensation into Irish affairs was not quelled.[6] Moreover, the various interpretations which could be, and were, placed upon this so-called clarification make it difficult to resist the conclusion that Pitt was guilty of indefensible negligence in omitting to draw up a definite agreement with Fitzwilliam which could not have been misconstrued. He can hardly have been ignorant of the opinions which Fitzwilliam and his friends had been propounding for so many years nor can he have been unaware of the expectations in Ireland that threatened to lead to a new system of government. If he could not

---

[1] Pitt's notes from letter(s) of Fitzwilliam end. 8 Mar. 1795, P.R.O. 325, Pitt Papers. Fitzwilliam said in 1799: 'I made most distinct declarations, that, in case of its being so brought forward, it should receive my full support.' (*The Parliamentary History*, xxxiv. 672.)

[2] Lord Grenville to Portland 21 Mar. 1795, H.M.C. Dropmore, iii, 35–38.

[3] Fitzwilliam to Carlisle 23 Mar. 1795, loc. cit.

[4] Grenville to Portland, loc. cit.; Fitzwilliam Memoranda, loc. cit.

[5] Pitt to Loughborough (n.d. — probably 7 Dec. 1794). Campbell, *Lives of the Lord Chancellors*, vi. 348.

[6] O'Beirne to Fitzwilliam 15 Dec. 1794, N.R.O. Box 46.

wriggle free from his commitment to allow Fitzwilliam to go to Ireland, then he cannot be excused for his failure to place the Earl's Viceroyalty on the most explicit conditions.

The early days of the Fitzwilliam régime in Ireland were marked by an almost fastidious desire on the part of Fitzwilliam himself to do nothing without first obtaining the consent of the cabinet.[1] He found the Catholic Bill already in agitation, but he attempted to prevent it from coming before the Irish parliament.[2] It was not until 15 January, however, that he told Portland that he had dismissed Beresford a week earlier and appointed Ponsonby to the post of Secretary of State. At the same time, he had given up all hopes of arresting the Catholic Bill and he therefore asked Portland for guidance. Rather curiously, he said that if he heard nothing from him on this subject, he would support the Bill.[3] Complaints of a new system were beginning to reach England by this time but Pitt was so overwhelmed with other '*pressing* things' that it was with some reluctance that he began to direct part of his attention to the activities of the new Lord-Lieutenant.[4] When he opened the Irish parliament on 22 January, however, Fitzwilliam's speech from the throne did not mention the Catholic Bill. Yet he had come to the conclusion that the Bill could not be stopped and his letters to Portland in the following days contain many hints of the desirability and even the necessity that the Castle should support the measure.[5] Portland appeared to be more concerned about Fitzwilliam's office changes, which had caused ominous rumblings of displeasure in London, but still he provided no clear instructions.[6] Fitzwilliam became anxious at

[1] Fitzwilliam to Portland 7 Jan. 1795 (copy), Wentworth Woodhouse MSS., F.4. For Fitzwilliam's Vice-Royalty, see T. H. B. Mahoney, *Edmund Burke and Ireland*, ch. ix.

[2] Fitzwilliam to Portland 8 Jan. 1795, ibid. F.5, ff. 5–7.

[3] Fitzwilliam to Portland 15 Jan. 1795, ibid. F.5, ff. 11–16, printed in H.M.C. *Dropmore*, iii. 9.

[4] Pitt to Windham 16 and 17 Jan. 1795, Ad. MS. 37844, ff. 86, 88, Windham Papers.

[5] Fitzwilliam to Portland 23 Jan., 29 Jan. 1795, Wentworth Woodhouse MSS., F. 5, ff. 23–27, 30–33; Fitzwilliam to Carlisle 6 Mar. 1795, H.M.C. *Carlisle*, 704–11.

[6] Portland to Fitzwilliam 2 Feb. 1795, Wentworth Woodhouse MSS., F. 31c; the King to Pitt 29 Jan. 1795, Aspinall, *Later Correspondence of George III*, ii. 298–9. Holland Rose, *Pitt and Napoleon*, 31–32, remarks that inclement weather

the cabinet's silence on his office arrangements and on the Catholic
Bill. This silence can be explained quite easily. There was no guidance
from London because no decisions had been taken there. The first
cabinet to concern itself with Irish affairs did not meet until 7 February. Fitzwilliam's office changes were disapproved of, but he was not
instructed to reverse them. He was told to provide the cabinet with
more information about the Catholic Bill and this at a time when urgent
decisions were needed.[1] These directives, such as they were, came too
late to be of use. On 10 February Fitzwilliam formally asked for advice
on the Catholic Bill.[2] He had persuaded Grattan to wait until the King
and the cabinet had agreed to the measure before bringing it forward.
Two days later, however, Grattan sought and received leave from the
Irish lower House to introduce his bill, but its terms were held back
pending news from London. The response of the cabinet was equivocal.
They demanded more information of the motives and facts which
might have justified the measure but they did not demand its outright
rejection. Although Windham said that the cabinet meeting of 18
February came to no conclusion on the Bill, it is likely that either then
or shortly afterwards it was decided to demand its suspension, and
Portland wrote to this effect to Fitzwilliam on 20 February.[3] On the
following day the cabinet met again and decided that Fitzwilliam must
be recalled from Ireland. The Bill was stopped and Fitzwilliam's
successor, Lord Camden, was directed 'to reinstate all those who have
been removed by his predecessor, and to support the old English
interest as well as the Protestant Religion'.[4]

---

prevented the mails from leaving England between 10 and 23 Jan. and suggests that
this nullifies charges of cabinet neglect and incompetence. Yet this does not explain
why the first cabinet to deal with Ireland did not meet until 7 Feb. See also
Mahoney, *Edmund Burke and Ireland*, 396.

[1] Fitzwilliam to Portland 3 and 5 Feb. 1795, Wentworth Woodhouse MSS., F.5,
ff. 39–40, 41–42; Portland to Fitzwilliam 8 Feb. 1795, ibid. F.31; Pitt to Fitzwilliam
9 Feb. 1795, ibid.

[2] Fitzwilliam to Portland, 10 Feb. 1795, Wentworth Woodhouse MSS., F.5,
ff. 48–54.

[3] Fitzwilliam to Portland 10 Feb. 1795, loc. cit.; Portland to Fitzwilliam 16 and
18 Feb. 1795, ibid. F.31e; *Windham Diary*, 334; Portland to the King 19 Feb.
1795, Aspinall, *Later Correspondence of George III*, ii. 304–5; Portland to Fitzwilliam 20 Feb. 1795 (copy), Wentworth Woodhouse MSS., F.31f.

[4] The King to Pitt 10 Mar. 1795, Stanhope, *Miscellanies*, ii. app. xxvi–vii.

There is no simple explanation which might serve to clarify the many and complex problems involved in the tragedy of Fitzwilliam. It is not clear why it was thought necessary to recall him. Grattan's Bill had, it is true, been introduced into the Irish Commons but there had been no proceedings on it and both Fitzwilliam and Grattan would have been agreeable to delay, although Grattan would not have tolerated the loss of the Bill.[1] Pitt, of course, must have been relieved to have the opportunity of ridding himself of an Irish government which seemed bent on offending his closest and most steadfast friends in Ireland. However, it was not Pitt but Portland who suggested recall, and when he did so Pitt could have done no other than agree. Portland's justification for recalling Fitzwilliam is, at best, cloudy. So far as his motives can be fathomed, he appears to have thought that Fitzwilliam had been carried away by his popularity with the Irish and that he had fallen unreservedly into the hands of Grattan and Ponsonby. He felt, moreover, that Fitzwilliam was arousing and leading the Irish to dangerous extremes which threatened the preservation of English government in Ireland.[2] The attitude of the King may have been a further consideration with the Duke, although even the King's objections to the Catholic Bill[3] need not have led to a demand for Fitzwilliam's recall. Finally, Portland was aware that some of the Irish Whigs themselves disapproved of the Bill and he may have been loath to antagonize them by maintaining in their midst a Lord-Lieutenant of whom they increasingly disapproved.[4] Whether his motives justified his taking the initiative in demanding the recall of Fitzwilliam may well be doubted. But there can be no doubt that Portland was gravely at fault in leaving Fitzwilliam's requests for advice and guidance unanswered until it was too late to restrain him from the actions which

[1] Grattan to Burke 19 Feb. 1795, Wentworth Woodhouse MSS., Burke Letters 1.

[2] Portland to Fitzwilliam 21 Feb. 1795, ibid. F.31f.

[3] The King's attitude to the Bill was outlined in a memorandum of 6 Feb. 1795, Stanhope *Miscellanies*, ii. App. xxii–v. The King greeted the news of the Bill with the 'greatest astonishment' and attributed 'the total change of the principles of government' in Ireland to 'the peevish inclination of humiliating the old friends of English Government in Ireland, or from the desire of paying implicit obedience to the heated imagination of Mr. Burke'.

[4] Portland to Fitzwilliam 16 Feb. 1795, loc. cit.; Hardy, *Memoirs of Charlemont*, ii. 347.

avowedly led to his recall. Portland actually confessed to Fitzwilliam: 'most heavily do I feel the blame which you may impute to me for not having warned you sooner'.[1] But the other cabinet ministers, especially Pitt, must share the blame for not having provided Fitzwilliam with clear directives both before his departure and after. Loughborough admitted that policy had not been sufficiently clarified before Fitzwilliam left for Ireland, and it seems impossible to dispute this verdict.[2] It is amazing that a cabinet was not summoned earlier than 7 February to discuss Irish affairs in view of the storm which Fitzwilliam's measures had created perhaps two weeks before. Yet Fitzwilliam's conduct cannot escape criticism. He had done much to arouse an unnecessary feeling of expectation among the Irish Whigs and reformers and his party proclivities had led him to adopt measures which even he suspected would be disliked by Pitt and the other cabinet ministers. If his instructions had been ambiguous, it remains true that few people interpreted them in the way that Fitzwilliam did. The tragedy of the Fitzwilliam affair is very largely the story of Portland's incompetence and Fitzwilliam's failings as a statesman, for Fitzwilliam did not realize that a coalition in England must mean a cessation of party in Ireland, and Portland did not possess the political courage to tell him before it was too late.

The Portland Whigs in the government supported Pitt against Fitzwilliam and there was hardly a breath of resignation in the air.[3] They begged Fitzwilliam to remain in the cabinet but Fitzwilliam's anger knew no bounds. He had never wished to take office but, for the sake of his friends, he had agreed to do so and now those same friends were responsible for his humiliation and for the reversal of his policy — the policy which he had learned from them.[4] It was against Portland, however, that Fitzwilliam's anger was directed. He pitied the patheti-

---

[1] Portland to Fitzwilliam 21 Feb. 1795, loc. cit.

[2] Loughborough to Grattan 28 Feb. 1795, Grattan, *Memoirs*, iv. 197–9; *Portrait of a Whig Peer . . . 2nd Viscount Palmerston*, ed. B. Connell (1957), 370.

[3] For a rather unconvincing discussion of this point see Mahoney, *Edmund Burke and Ireland*, 270. It is doubtful if the Portland Whigs in the cabinet had changed their minds on concessions for the Irish and most unlikely that fictitious notions of 'cabinet solidarity' counted for very much.

[4] Fitzwilliam to Burke 4 and 9 Apr. 1795, Wentworth Woodhouse MSS., F.31g.

cally bewildered Duke but he was unable to forgive him for his desertion, and Fitzwilliam decided to hold no future intercourse with him.[1] The heat of Fitzwilliam's fury might have been cooled had he not been so convinced that he had been right. He had no doubt whatsoever that his Whig principles, if translated into practice, would have saved Ireland from the fate into which he was convinced that country was falling. He had not been trying to annihilate the English supremacy in Ireland. By weakening the Ascendancy he was not weakening the English government. He was strengthening the position of the Lord-Lieutenant. By supporting the Catholic Bill he had been striving 'to make monarchy and aristocracy palatable and amicable in the sight of the many'.[2] If these were Whig principles then his friends had deserted both him and them. When the recall of Fitzwilliam came before the House of Lords, Fitzwilliam's passionate hostility to his friends knew no bounds. Portland, Spencer and Mansfield inside the cabinet and Carlisle and Carnarvon outside the cabinet spoke against him.[3] Fitzwilliam found himself supported by Foxites in both Houses who renewed the cry that Pitt's consistent objective had been to destroy and to humiliate the Whig party and its members. Fitzwilliam himself subscribed without reservation to this view, yet he cut a strange and lonely figure during the next few years, denouncing the political basis upon which Pitt's ministry rested while refusing to oppose its measures.

The effects of the recall of Fitzwilliam upon the subsequent history of Ireland were extensive and critical. If the Protestant Ascendancy had been maintained, the price which had to be paid was the alienation of the Catholics. No longer could they trust the Ascendancy. No longer could they hope for the reforms which they had demanded and which the Viceroyalty of Fitzwilliam had for a time promised to provide. Although Grattan made one last effort to accomplish a moderate reform by introducing a Catholic Bill on 5 May 1795, his motion was lost by 155–84. While we may doubt, with Lecky, 'Whether the introduction of a few Catholic gentry into the Legislature' would have

[1] Fitzwilliam to Tom Grenville 2, 3 Apr. 1795, ibid. F.31i (copy). The original is in Ad. MS. 41855, ff. 62–65, Thomas Grenville MSS.

[2] Fitzwilliam to Burke 9 Apr. 1795, loc. cit.

[3] 8 May 1795, *The Parliamentary History*, xxxi. 1502–21. The Commons debated the issue on 19 May.

quietened the country,[1] there can be little doubt that the recall of Fitzwilliam led to more widespread disorder and provided the United Irishmen with the stimulus which brought them the loyalty of large sections of the Catholic community.[2] The Fitzwilliam affair, moreover, served to clarify, and to close, the mind of George III on the question of Catholic Emancipation.[3] And the effects of the King's decision on this subject were to resound until and beyond the end of his reign.

III. EPILOGUE

There was one who was, perhaps, even more grieved than Fitzwilliam at the outcome of the ill-fated Viceroyalty. 'My heart is almost broken,' mourned Edmund Burke.[4] He felt himself more responsible for the coalition of July 1794, which had brought such disasters upon Fitzwilliam, than was perhaps warranted by events. Suspicion of his own guilt in the murky business was matched by a strange inability to understand what was happening. 'I am lost and confounded . . . I have nothing but to take refuge in oblivion, until I take refuge in the grave.'[5] He was pitifully incapable of understanding what had happened, pathetically unable to offer any realistic advice or consolation to any of the parties concerned in the unhappy dispute. He thought the only solution now was for Fitzwilliam to be reappointed to his post, to return to Ireland and to compose the rifts which had appeared in that nation.[6] For a time, he did not even see the obvious objections to this fantastic proposal but eventually he came down to earth. 'In truth I

---

[1] Lecky, *Ireland*, iii. 323.

[2] Ibid. 313–14. One should not overlook that by (unjustifiably) publishing his two letters to Carlisle, Fitzwilliam himself may have served to aggravate popular disorder.

[3] The advice tendered by Loughborough and the Archbishop of Canterbury confirmed the King in the views he had set out in his paper of 6 Feb. Loughborough to the King 10 Mar. 1795; the King to the Archbishop of Canterbury (?) 16 Mar. 1795; the Archbishop of Canterbury to the King 19 Mar. 1795, Aspinall, *Later Correspondence of George III*, ii. 317–20, 321, 322.

[4] Burke to Fitzwilliam ante 2 Mar. 1795, Wentworth Woodhouse MSS., Burke Letters 1.

[5] Burke to Grattan 2/3 Mar. 1795. MS. in the National Library of Ireland, Copeland Transcript.

[6] Burke to the Duke of Devonshire 11 Mar. 1795, Chatsworth MSS.

hardly know where I am.'[1] He deplored the return to power of the Junto in Ireland yet he was aware of the contradictions of his own position. He admitted that Pitt, one of the ministers responsible for the treachery which had been perpetrated upon the noble Fitzwilliam, was 'necessary to the Existence of the antient order in Europe'.[2] Burke would have approved of Fitzwilliam's apt observation: 'Things and persons no longer go together, agreement on the subject, is not agreement with the Person.'[3] The experience of these months had taught Burke some lessons. He had come to distrust entirely all experiments in coalition government. Party men could not maintain their rectitude against the wiles of their enemies. Pitying Portland's spinelessness in the government during 1796, Burke attributed his weakness to the fact that he had lost his connections. Party and connection could be maintained in a coalition government only so long as the party men chose to keep faith one with another. In 1795 they had not done so. Fitzwilliam had been deserted by his so-called party colleagues. Thus the coalition of July 1794 had been a disastrous mistake.[4] Party, as a union of honest and disinterested men, had been destroyed. All that was left now was the necessity for good men to unite against the menace of Jacobinism. There was now no possible distinction between politicians other than that between the good and the bad, the loyal and the traitorous. The government must unite with the propertied classes and it could not but prevail 'being possessed of all the Revenues and all the forces of the State'.[5] The Foxites would then be helpless. In any case, they were not really a party at all. They were too much divided amongst themselves and they were despised by the public. They were too few in numbers and they could not possibly form an administration should they ever be called upon to do so.[6] Burke deplored the clear-cut division of political opinion in the state which had now come to be focused on Pitt and Fox:

[1] Burke to Grattan 20 Mar. 1795 (copy), Wentworth Woodhouse MSS., Burke Letters 1.

[2] Burke to Fitzwilliam 14 Mar. 1795, ibid.; Burke to Hussey 28 Nov. 1795, ibid., printed in *Correspondence of Edmund Burke*, iv. 326–8.

[3] Fitzwilliam to Burke 30 Aug. 1796, Wentworth Woodhouse MSS., Burke Letters 1.

[4] Burke to Fitzwilliam 13 Dec. 1796, ibid.

[5] Burke to Fitzwilliam 20 Dec. 1796, ibid.

[6] Burke's letter to William Elliot 26 May 1795, *Burke's Works*, ii. 245.

and that there appears a sort of necessity, of adopting the one or the other of them, without regard to any public principle whatsoever. This extinguishes party, as party; and even the Nation as a Nation. Everything is forced into the shape of a mere faction, and a contest for nothing short . . . [of] the sovereign authority, for one or the other of the chieftains: I was in serious hopes that the party which was at last rallied under its proper standards . . . might, either in Ministry, or out of Ministry, as the public necessities required, become some sort of Asylum for principles moral and political, and might control that disposition to factious servitude, which could see nothing, in the constitution or the country, but the power of one or two individuals: . . . not one stone upon the other, is left in that party — nor do I see the least possible chance for its reconstruction either from the same materials or from any other.[1]

While events had brought Burke to reject the idea of party and to declaim against what posterity can recognize as instances of the development of his former ideas in practice, the mantle of party had fallen to Fox and it was he who was to wear it, none too comfortably it is true, in the future. Coalitions flourish and oppositions wither in the heat and storm of war, and Fox thought it necessary to lay some emphasis upon the principle of party at a time when even his nephew was beginning to reach the conclusion that the Portland–Pitt coalition was the death-knell of party.[2] But for Fox himself 'party is by far the best system, if not the only one, for supporting the cause of liberty in this country'. The coalition had all but destroyed party, but Fox was determined to preserve 'what little remains of this system, or to revive it if it is supposed to be quite extinct'. The constitution needed party at all times. Coalitions might shatter party from time to time because 'men are always liable to act both corruptly and absurdly'.[3] Party might even flourish in republics. It was not bound to one form of government any more than its uses might be limited to those of one period.[4] Fox largely reiterated Burke's well-worn view that one of the greatest justifications for party lay in the fact that no other political instrument

---

[1] Burke to Fitzwilliam 2 Sept. 1796, Wentworth Woodhouse MSS., Burke Letters 1.

[2] Lord Holland to Fox 13 Sept. 1794, Ad. MS. 47571, ff. 159–60, Fox Papers.

[3] Fox to Lord Holland 5 Oct. 1794, ibid. ff. 165–70, printed in *Fox's Memorials*, iii. 86–93.

[4] Fox to Lord Holland 15 Dec. 1794, ibid. ff. 189–92, printed in *Fox's Memorials*, iii. 93–96.

could resist the ever-increasing influence of the crown. Britain was a great country with a great empire and thus she had great patronage 'which must always be liable to be abused for the purpose of improper influence'.[1] Victory over the French would add substantially to the empire, thus producing more patronage than ever before, which would be at the disposal of the crown. On the other hand, while the war was going badly, the liberties of Englishmen were being seriously curtailed. On both counts, then, there was a role for party to play in England.[2] The aristocracy must join together to defend the constitution because they were men of independent fortune and thus less liable to the seduction of court emoluments, and because 'the Public should see that there are some Persons of Rank and Property who attend to the general interest of the country'.[3] Fox, and even some of his successors, failed to divest Whiggism of its aristocratic exclusiveness by making an effective appeal to the middle classes in the country. By continuing to assert the sanctity of the principle that power must be distributed in proportion to property, the Foxites remained outside the mainstream of reforming opinion in the years to come. Fox also followed Burke's doctrine of the value of party for the individual. Strength and judgement were to be found by acting in party and the power of self-interest to motivate personal and political decisions would be restrained. Party, in fact, was the 'only substitute that has been found, or can be found, for public virtue and comprehensive understanding'.[4] With all its strengths and weaknesses, the idea of party was inherited by Fox and the Foxites and carried by them into the new world of the nineteenth century. As political conditions changed, the idea of party underwent corresponding developments. Grey, for example, is to be found in 1820 expounding one of the uses of party as that of providing an alternative government and this idea was not unfamiliar several years earlier.[5] Although the old notions persisted and 'Broad-bottom' was still to be found in political discussion in the middle of the nineteenth century, party lost

[1] Ibid.; Fox to Lord Holland 5 Oct. 1794, loc. cit.
[2] Fox to Lord Holland 15 Nov. 1795, ibid. Ad. MS. 47572, ff. 96–97, printed in *Fox's Memorials*, iii. 123–6.
[3] Fox to Grafton 21 Dec. 1794. Grafton MSS. iiia. f. 160.
[4] Fox to Lord Holland 5 Oct. 1794, loc. cit.
[5] Foord, *His Majesty's Opposition*, 447–8.

its overtones of disreputability and its stigma gradually dropped away.

After the coalition of 1794 the Foxites were almost alone in the barren land of opposition. The events of 1792–4 had given party a new impulse and a new ideological content. Fox was left with a party which was less reactionary than the Old Whig party had been and, despite the vicissitudes and the failures of the following years, it did not cease to advocate reform. A few of those who had followed Portland in 1793 and 1794 drifted back to Fox in the 1790s and in 1797 the Prince of Wales returned to his old political allegiance.[1] The party of Fox continued to grow in size. The coalition with Grenville in 1804, however, was of negligible importance, for Grenville brought with him perhaps a dozen members of parliament, and his group was never absorbed into the larger mass of Foxites which numbered considerably more than 100 after 1807 and something approaching 200 after 1818.[2] The Foxites remained true to their principles in these long and fruitless years of almost unbroken opposition. Their hostility to the inclusion of court men in the cabinet contributed to the failure of the negotiations of 1812. A recent writer has declared that 'out of a stern regard for Foxite principles the leaders forfeited several opportunities to enter the Ministry' between 1807 and 1830.[2] During these years, party and opposition became respectable political instruments. Indeed, by 1806 Chathamite principles had been rejected even by the followers of Pitt.[4]

Inside the Whig party, the institutions which had already been established continued in operation. Adam's party fund was at work early in the nineteenth century and he continued to manage elections for the Whigs. The devices both organizational and procedural which had been utilised earlier were strengthened and served to lend stability to a party which suffered chronic weaknesses from lethargy, indolent leadership and internal feuds. Nevertheless the materials of party had been fashioned. It remained to build upon the work which Adam and others had begun and which convenience and necessity had confirmed and consolidated. While patronage and influence declined as preponderant influences in politics, the conflict of public life came to focus more clearly upon the government and opposition parties.

---

[1] Lord Holland, *Memoirs*, i. 76–79.   [2] Foord, *His Majesty's Opposition*, 453.
[3] Ibid. 451–2.   [4] Ibid. 430–9.

Conclusion

The party schism which we have discussed in these pages poses several problems which need to be clarified if we are to obtain a better understanding not only of the internal groupings within the opposition but also of the nature of party itself in the later eighteenth century. The lines along which the party divided in those months of crisis in the winter of 1792–3 and which hardened in 1794 present one such problem. Historians have tended to over-simplify the groupings within the Whig party and the opinion that the Foxites represented a group dedicated to parliamentary reform is one such example. In fact, although most of the parliamentary reformers within the Old Whig party, though not all, joined Fox, about one half of the Foxite party did not support the various proposals for the reform of parliament which were mooted from time to time. This fact alone should dispose of the argument that the Whig opposition from 1784–9 was already divided into reformers and non-reformers and that the events of 1789–92 merely broke the party along pre-existing lines of division. Nor, by this time, does it make sense to talk of the Northites as a distinctive political group within the opposition. Although very few of them joined Fox, they were by no means agreed as to whether to support Portland or Windham's 'Third Party' in 1793. Although it is true that certain individual Northites were prominent in the attempts which were made to come to some closer connection with the ministry between 1792 and 1794, it is doubtful if they represented anyone but themselves, and certainly they cannot be said to have led an organized group. Any generalizations, therefore, about the conduct of the Northites or about their political loyalties in the early 1790s need to be examined very closely indeed. Further, any attempt to impose some kind of 'structural' interpretation upon the disruption of the Whig party requires drastic qualification. There are too many cases where family and patronage and such factors fail to explain the conduct of the members of the opposition. In some instances, members go clean contrary to the political loyalties of their group. And, in any case, about one third of the members in opposition did not owe their seats to a patron or were not drawn into the party by family connection. There is doubtless some truth in all these explanations and, taken together with factors which are too commonly overlooked, they might help to provide some kind of complex explanation of the break-up of the Whig party. Belief in a principle for its own sake, prejudice, fear, ignorance and hesitation — such human qualities and weaknesses accompany the more tangible elements in all historical explanation and doubtless played their part in dividing and finally breaking the Old Whig party.

The fact that the break-up of the party was so protracted is itself an interesting commentary upon facile attempts to explain the Portland schism within the bounds of any one theory of politics or human nature. Between 1792 and 1794 the wide variety of conflicting opinions within the Whig party was complicated by the rapidity with which external events drove members of the opposition to adopt attitudes and to take actions which frequently defy all attempts at categorization. Politicians had now to adapt themselves and their behaviour to circumstances which were unprecedented and to problems which admitted of no obvious or simple solution. The ideas and the loyalties of the past had to be re-examined — perhaps even discarded — before the Whigs could decide their future political roles. The idea of party itself came into question and the Foxites were the first to reject the tacit agreement surrounding the doctrinal basis of the Whig party which had prevailed for over two decades. Yet in doing so they did not reject party as such. They asserted that it was they and not the conservative Whigs who were behaving consistently with the past history of the party. The validity of this claim may well be doubted but it remains true that they sought justification for their actions in a party ideology which was later to undergo development and elaboration in their hands. Nevertheless, the conservative Whigs claimed an exclusive consistency of conduct yet they found themselves in the dilemma of having to join a ministry which had for so long been the very object of their denunciations. How could they reconcile their party proclivities with a coalition with Pitt? They sincerely regarded coalition as being nothing short of their public duty and, further, as being of direct service to the state in that their accession to power would improve the direction of national affairs. They could only resolve the dilemma by having recourse to the argument that 'party' did not presuppose an organized body of men necessarily in opposition to the ministry. 'Party' as a body of men united in fundamental principle could operate from within the government itself. It might serve to cleanse, to invigorate and to render more popular the government itself. There had been nothing in the Burkeian doctrine of party to forbid coalitions and so the Portland Whigs might with some justification claim that their behaviour was neither so inconsistent nor so self-interested as the Foxites were maintaining. The very ambiguity of party doctrine, in fact, could allow of both interpretations. Yet the fact that party doctrine was so ambiguous does not render it spurious. That all sections of the opposition were so eager to claim that their conduct was justified by reference to the past history of the party indicates that it was a most potent element in contemporary political argument. The appeal to party, in fact, could be a most effective means of keeping a political group together. Yet it was to be the Foxite opposition which acted as the vehicle for future party development. Because it was so ambiguous, the idea of party was capable of infinite elaboration and refinement. The break-up of the Old Whig party demonstrates the persistence of the older notion of 'connection' while the newer and more modern concept of the ideological unity and institutional coherence of a political party was struggling to establish its role in the political system. In this latter process, a certain measure of development had been achieved by the end of the eighteenth century, but it is to the Foxite Whigs of the nineteenth century that we must look for the completion of this decisive step in constitutional history.

APPENDIXES

APPENDIXES

Appendix I

An Estimate of the Size and Membership of the
Whig Party, 1780–92

The following estimate can only be regarded as approximate because
the fluctuating membership of eighteenth-century parties is notorious.
Lack of information about a member's party activities and the absence
of an objective criterion of party membership render all such estimates
extremely hazardous. Nevertheless, the Whig party of these years
maintained a relatively stable membership. Neither should the difficulty
of this undertaking nor the tentative nature of the conclusions reached
be allowed to gainsay the fact that contemporary estimates cohere
fairly closely to those reached in this appendix. Materials which have
proved useful in compiling the following lists include: the many lists
of members in the Adam Papers, which range from a State of the House
in 1784 to subscription lists in the 1790s; the list of *Peers and Commoners*
to be won over, in the Portland MSS. (9883 Misc. 51); subscription
and patronage lists in the Wentworth Woodhouse MSS. at Sheffield
(F.1 and F.115); the *Third Party Circular* in the Essex Record
Office (Braybrooke MSS. D/DBy c 9/44); the appendices printed in
J. Norris, *Shelburne and Reform* (1963) and R. Mitchison, *Sir John
Sinclair* (1962), and the biographies in the *History of Parliament*. Other
sources such as parliamentary speeches and division lists and the lists
of members occasionally given in contemporary newspapers have
proved helpful. It has been found convenient to begin the estimate
with a reiteration of Christie's conclusions (*The End of North's
Ministry*) and to trace the size and membership of the party in chrono-
logical fashion from 1780.

(a) The Rockingham Whigs, 1780–4

After the election of 1780 the size of this party was estimated at 77 by Christie (*The End of North's Ministry*, 212, nn. 1 and 2). Of these, the following did not sit in 1784 on the eve of the general election:

Lord Althorp, H. S. Bridgeman, Lord R. Cavendish, Sir L. Dundas, A. Keppel, W. Keppel, T. Lucas, Sir G. Savile and J. S. Stewart.

To the remaining 68 the following members can be added:

G. Damer returned to England in 1782 from the West Indies. Eight members were returned at by-elections: Lord G. A. Cavendish, J. Cotes, Sir H. Fetherstonehaugh, G. Fitzwilliam, F. F. Foljambe, J. Hare, D. Hartley, J. Lee.

Five former Northites can be described as acting with the Fox party by 1784: J. Courtenay, J. Craufurd, J. Nesbitt, J. Nicholls, T. Pelham. On the eve of the election of 1784, therefore, the size of the Whig party can be roughly estimated at 82 members.

This calculation is in harmony with those of contemporaries. In 1783 Gibbon, as is well known, estimated the number at 90. In July 1782, Selwyn estimated the number at 80 (H.M.C. Carlisle, 633). See also Christie (*The End of North's Ministry*, 374) for an estimate of 89 in March 1783.

(b) The Rockingham Whigs and the Election of 1784

Of the 82 members of the party, 29 failed to reappear after the election. Of these, 19 had represented over 500 electors.

County members: Sir T. C. Bunbury, G. Byng, Sir R. Clayton, T. W. Coke, R. H. Coxe, F. F. Foljambe, T. Grenville, W. H. Hartley and Lord Verney.

Members for constituencies with over 1,000 electors: F. E. Anderson, Lord J. Cavendish, B. Grey, D. Hartley, Sir R. Hotham, H. Pigot and W. Braddyll.

Members for constituencies with 500 to 1,000 electors: W. Baker, R. Gregory and R. Walpole.

Members for constituencies with less than 500 members: G. Fitzwilliam, P. Honeywood, T. Lucas, H. Minchin, Sir J. Ramsden, B. Thompson, W. Tollemache, Lord J. Townshend and T. Walpole.

Member who sat for Scottish burghs: J. Craufurd.

To the 53 members who retained their seats must be added a further 6 members who had not sat before the election and who supported the opposition:

J. Bridgeman, O. Bridgeman, P. Francis, the Earl of Inchiquin, J. G. Phillips and W. Windham.

After the election of 1784 the Rockingham party numbered 59 members — a net loss of 23 at the general election.

(c) The Party of Lord North, 1780–4

After the fall of his ministry North could command the support of over 100 Members of Parliament. In July 1782 Selwyn estimated the number as high as 120. Yet North's party was declining rapidly. In March 1783 Robinson calculated North's strength at 106, 56 of which he considered to be 'doubtfuls' (Christie, *The End of North's Ministry*, 374). Since many of North's followers sat in government boroughs or in seats whose patrons supported Pitt and the King in 1784, it is not at all surprising that the election of 1784 was a disaster for North's party.

North's personal following: estimated at about 40 in 1780 (Christie, *The End of North's Ministry*, 200–3). Only 20 sat after 1784: W. Adam, J. Campbell, F. Charteris, P. C. Crespigny, Sir W. Cunnynghame, W. Dickinson, Sir J. Eden, H. Fane, C. Greville, T. S. Jolliffe, W. Jolliffe, W. Keene, Lord Melbourne, A. Moysey, G. A. North, Lord North, Lord Palmerston, H. Penton, Sir R. Sutton, Lord Westcote.

Patrons who remained loyal to North: estimated as providing about 80–90 members in 1780 (*The End of North's Ministry*, 209). Only 12 of these members both remained loyal to North and the Coalition and survived the election of 1784: L. Brown, T. Caswell, E. Clive, W. Clive, Lord Lisburne, Sir J. Morshead, J. Purling, W. Rawlinson, Francis, Robert and William Seymour-Conway and H Strachey.

Independents and others who supported North after 1784 numbered 13: J. Anstruther, Sir F. Basset, T. Davenport, P. Delme, W. Ellis, Sir J. Erskine, W. Ewer, Sir J. Frederick, J. Kenrick, T. Onslow, J. Ord, H. Pelham and Lord C. Spencer.

To the above 45 members can be added a further 6 who entered parliament in 1784 and who supported North:

D. Howell, T. Hunt, Lord Malden, Sir P. Parker, G. Seymour-Conway and H. Seymour-Conway.

The party of Lord North, therefore, numbered 51 members after the election of 1784.

(d) *Other Members who had sat before* 1784 *and adhered to the Coalition*

There were 12 such members: W. P. A. A'Court, G. Anson, G. K. Elphinstone, C. Howard, R. P. Knight, R. Ladbroke, E. Morant, T. Powys, C. Pierrepoint, C. Taylor, T. Whitmore and Sir C. Warwick-Bampfylde.

(e) *New Members in* 1784

There were 10 such members: Sir D. Carnegie, W. Colhoun, J. Dawkins, St.A. St. John, Capt. MacBride, F. H. MacKenzie, T. B. Parkyns, R. L. Savile, C. Sturt and W. Wrightson.

Total

Rockingham Whigs after 1784	59
Lord North's party after 1784	51
Other members who sat before 1784 . . .	12
New members in 1784	10
	132 members

(f) *New Party Members* 1784–90

Between the two general elections the following 34 members entered parliament and supported the opposition:

On petition: H. Minchin.

Changes of Allegiance: Lord Feilding, W. Hussey, Sir J. MacPherson and N. Newnham.

At by-elections: T. Anson, C. Ashley, R. Beckford, G. Byng jnr., Sir

R. Clayton, J. Craufurd, J. C. Curwen, L. Damer, Viscount Downe, Sir G. Elliot, G. Forrester, W. Fullarton, C. Grey, W. H. Lambton, Lord John Russell, Lord William Russell, J. S. Stewart, M. A. Taylor, G. Tierney, Lord John Townshend, R. Vyner and J. Walwyn.

Northite members entering parliament at by-elections 1784–90: Sir G. Cooper, Sir F. Gregg, T. C. Jervoise, J. W. Payne, R. Stephenson, Sir G. Webster and R. Wilbraham.

(g) *Members who left Parliament or defected from the Opposition,* 1784–90

Those who left parliament were: G. Anson, C. Barrow, *L. Brown*, J. Bridgeman, *T. Caswell*, *F. Charteris*, Sir P. J. Clerke, *T. Davenport*, *P. Delme*, *W. Ewer*, C. Howard, *T. Hunt*, *T. S. Jolliffe*, Lord Maitland and E. Morant.

Members italicized were followers of Lord North.

Those who defected were: G. Dempster, *H. Fane*, H. Minchin, J. Nicholls, *T. Onslow*, *Sir R. Sutton*, Lord Westcote.

Members italicized were followers of Lord North.

While gaining 34 members between the general elections of 1784 and 1790, the opposition lost 22. Adding this net increase of 12 members to the total of 132 members of the opposition in 1784 it can be concluded that the opposition numbered 144 on the eve of the election of 1790.

1. This estimate is roughly in line with those of contemporaries. The North MSS. at Waldershare contain a calculation of 125, which is incomplete in that it omits the names of members beginning with A, B and C, (quoted in *History of Parliament*, i. 534) for the year 1788, and for the same year the Third Party Circular estimated the opposition at 155.

2. The absorption of all the Northites save the personal following of North into the mainstream of the opposition is shown by the same two estimates which assess North's party at 17. Yet, according to the calculations made above, there were still 46 members who can be described as Northites on the eve of the election of 1790.

(h) The General Election of 1790

The following 43 members of the opposition were not returned:
W. P. A. A'Court, C. Ashley, R. Beckford, Sir D. Carnegie, Sir
G. Cooper, J. Craufurd, P. C. Crespigny, Sir W. Cunnynghame,
W. Dickinson, G. K. Elphinstone, Sir J. Eden, W. Ellis, G. Forester,
Sir J. Frederick, W. Fullarton, C. Greville, T. C. Jervoise, J.
Kenrick, T. Lister, Capt. MacBride, F. H. MacKenzie, Viscount
Malden, F. Montagu, A. Moysey, N. Newnham, J. Nesbitt, J. Ord,
Sir P. Parker, Lord Palmerston, J. Purling, A. Rawlinson, W.
Rawlinson, S. Salt, R. L. Savile, G. Seymour-Conway, R. Seymour-
Conway, W. C. Sloper, R. Stephenson, G. Tierney, Lord J.
Townshend, Sir G. W. Vanneck, Sir C. Warwick-Bampfylde and
W. Wrightson.

The following 40 members of the opposition entered parliament in
1790: Sir J. Aubrey, W. Baker, R. Bingham, E. Bouverie, W.
Braddyll, J. Buller, J. R. Burch, Sir T. C. Bunbury, J. B. Church,
Sir H. Clinton, T. W. Coke, T. C. Crespigny, L. Dundas, T.
Erskine, C. Forester, T. Grenville, Lord G. H. Grey, J. Harcourt,
W. H. Hartley, H. Howard, W. Lee-Antonie, S. Long, Sir T.
Maitland, R. Milbanke, Sir W. Milner, P. W. Powlett, M.
Robinson, Lord Sheffield, Sir J. Sinclair, H. Speed, B. Thompson,
T. Thompson, Lord Titchfield, C. Townshend, Sir J. Vanneck,
Lord Verney, C. C. Western, J. Wharton, S. Whitbread jnr. and
P. C. Wyndham.

The list includes 8 members who suffered spectacular defeats in 1784:
W. Baker, W. Braddyl, Sir T. C. Bunbury, T. W. Coke, T.
Grenville, W. H. Hartley, B. Thompson and Lord Verney.

No comprehensive lists of the State of the House immediately
following the election of 1790 have been found. Estimates made by
government and opposition supporters are invariably flattering to the
respective sides and, obviously, little reliance can be placed upon such
guesswork. In fact, the election did not change the balance of forces in
the House. The above estimate allows a conclusion of a net loss to the
opposition of 3, from 144 to 141.

(i) *The Opposition from* 1790 *to December* 1792

The following 5 supporters of the opposition left parliament: J. Burgoyne, T. C. Jervoise, Lord North, Lord Verney and W. Weddell.

During the same period N. MacLeod switched his allegiance from Pitt to the opposition.

The following 9 members came in at by-elections and supported the opposition: C. Ashley, R. Beckford, W. Ellis, J. C. Jervoise, F. North, J. Rawdon, W. C. Shawe, J. H. St. Leger and General Tarleton.

During these two years, therefore, the opposition lost 5 and gained 10 members. In December 1792, therefore, there were about 146 members in opposition.

(j) *Patronage*

Of these 146 members, about one-third did not owe their seats to a patron or were not drawn into opposition through family connection.

Over one-half of the members of the party had entered parliament since the Fox–North Coalition of early 1783.

Appendix 2

'The Third Party', 1793

Name	Windham's List	Sheffield's List	Whig Club Secession
J. Anstruther	×		×
C. Ashley	×	×	
Sir F. Basset		×	
Ld. Beauchamp	×		
*C. Boone		×	
W. Braddyll	×	×	×
E. Burke	×	×	×
Sir R. Clayton			×
*D. P. Coke	×	×	
*Sir G. Cornewall		×	
J. Dawkins	×	×	×
Vct. Downe	×	×	×
Sir G. Elliot	×	×	×
Sir J. Erskine			×
*W. Evelyn			×
Ld. G. H. Grey		×	
W. H. Hartley		×	
Ld. Inchiquin			×
R. P. Knight	×		
R. Ladbroke			×
*Sir J. Leicester			×
*Ld. Middleton	×	×	×
F. North	×	×	
Ld. Ossory	×	×	

C. Pierrepoint	×	×	
T. Powys	×		
*C. Rainsford	×	×	
*Sir M. W. Ridley	×		
Ld. Sheffield		×	×
Sir J. Sinclair		×	
*H. Skeene	×		×
*H. Sloane	×	×	
T. Stanley	×		
J. H. St. Leger			×
*J. Tempest	×		
C. Townshend	×	×	
*T. Tyrwhitt			×
W. Windham	×	×	×

38	23	22	18
	23 +	7 +	8 = 38

* = 12 M.P.s not in the Whig party, most of whom were independents.

38 − 12 = 26 Whig party members in the 'Third Party'.

Appendix 3

The Portland Whigs

R. Beckford
Ld. E. Bentinck
R. Benyon
R. Bingham
O. Bridgeman
Sir H. Bridgeman
Sir T. C. Bunbury
J. Bullock
Ld. G. A. Cavendish
J. Campbell
Sir H. Clinton
E. Clive
W. Clive
J. Cotes
G. Damer
L. Damer
Ld. Duncannon

C. Dundas
W. Ellis
A. Foley
C. Forester
Sir T. Gascoigne
Sir F. Gregg
T. Grenville
Wm. Jolliffe
W. Keene
J. Lee
Ld. Lisburne
Sir J. MacPherson
Ld. Melbourne
E. Monckton
Sir J. Morshead
G. A. North
T. B. Parkyns

C. A. Pelham
H. Pelham
T. Pelham
J. W. Payne
J. Scudamore
F. Seymour-Conway
H. Seymour-Conway
W. Seymour-Conway
Ld. C. Spencer
J. S. Stewart
H. Strachey
Ld. Titchfield
B. Thompson
Sir J. Vanneck
J. Walwyn
H. Walpole
J. Webb

= 51 M.P.s

Appendix 4

The Foxite Whigs

*W. Adam
*T. Anson
 W. L. Antonie
*Sir J. Aubrey
†W. Baker
 E. Bouverie
*J. Buller
 J. R. Burch
 G. Byng
*Ld. G. A. H.
   Cavendish
 W. Colhoun
†J. B. Church
*E. Coke
*T. W. Coke
*T. C. Crespigny
†J. Courtenay
*J. Crewe
†J. C. Curwen
*Sir C. Davers
†T. Erskine
 Sir H. Fetherstone
 R. Fitzpatrick

*H. Fletcher
*E. Foley
 C. J. Fox
†P. Francis
†C. Grey
*J. Hare
 J. Harrison
*J. Harcourt
*D. Howell
*H. Howard
*Wm. Hussey
*J. C. Jervoise
 St. A. St. John
†W. H. Lambton
†D. Long
*†Sm. Long
*Ld. Ludlow
†N. MacLeod
*†Sir T. Maitland
†R. Milbank
*Sir W. Milner
*J. G. Phillips

*†P. W. Powlett
 W. Plumer
*J. Rawdon
 M. Robinson
†Ld. J. Russell
*Ld. W. Russell
 W. C. Shawe
†R. B. Sheridan
*H. Speed
 Ld. R. Spencer
 C. Sturt
 C. Taylor
†M. A. Taylor
*Gen. Tarleton
†T. Thompson
*R. Vyner
 C. C. Western
†J. Wharton
†S. Whitbread jnr.
*R. Wilbraham
*Sir E. Winnington
*P. C. Wyndham

=66 M.P.s

* = did not vote for reform in May 1793
† = Friends of People

Others who supported Fox in opposition include: W. Smith, J. Martin and R. S. Milnes (who were members of the Friends of the People) and N. B. Halhed, Sir W. Lemon, H. Bankes, T. Kemp, J. Langston, H. Peirse, E. Lechmere, Sir R. Mostyn, Sir G. W. Shuckburgh, H. H. Coxe, R. W. Wynne, H. Thornton and R. Thornton.

This estimate does not exhaust the total number of M.P.s who voted with Fox on particular divisions. It seems safer to extract from the old Whig party those members who acted with Fox quite regularly, to draw attention to others who joined him, and leave to future historians the task of calculating the strength of Fox's party after 1794. Most of the above 66 can be recognized as Foxites fairly early in the session of 1793.

Bibliography

I. Original Sources

British Museum

Auckland Papers, especially Ad. MS. 34448, 34451–2, 45728.
Fox Papers, especially Ad. MS. 47560–1, 47565, 47568–72, 47580–1.
Hardwicke Papers, especially Ad. MS. 35392.
Hertford Papers, especially Egerton MS. 3260.
Holland House Papers, especially Ad. MS. 51355, 51467, 51705–6, 51732, 51799, 51845.
Liverpool Papers, especially Ad. MS. 38192.
Pelham Papers, especially Ad. MS. 33129.
Windham Papers, especially Ad. MS. 37843–5, 37848–9, 37852, 37873 –4.
Thomas Grenville MSS., especially Ad. MS. 41851–2, 41854–5, 42058.

Public Record Office

Pitt Papers, especially 110, 121, 135, 152–3, 157, 168, 190, 325, 329.

Sheffield Public Library

Wentworth Woodhouse MSS., especially Burke (BK) 1, 8, 10, 37; F. 1, 4, 5, 5, 29b, 31a–i, 32e, 34g, 63b, 115a–e, 128h.
Rockingham MSS., especially R. 164.

Scottish Record Office

Melville Castle MSS. G.D. 51.

The Prior's Kitchen, Durham. Grey MSS.
The University Library, Nottingham. Portland MSS.
Northamptonshire County Record Office. The Burke Letters, Fitzwilliam MSS., main series and in three other series: Boxes 44–46, 50; X 512 and S/12.
Cambridge University Library. Pitt MSS. 6958, 4–9, copies.

Hertfordshire County Record Office. Baker MSS. Acc. 452.
Bury St. Edmunds and West Suffolk Record Office. Grafton MSS.
Blair-Adam MSS., Blair-Adam, Kinross.
Arniston Letter Book, Arniston MSS., Arniston Castle, Scotland.

II. Printed Sources

Historical Manuscripts Commission

Bathurst MSS.; Carlisle MSS.; Donoughmore MSS.; Dropmore MSS.;
Rutland MSS.; Various Collections V.

The Parliamentary History.
The Parliamentary Register.
The Annual Register
Works of the Right Hon. Edmund Burke (2 vols., 1834).

III. Newspapers

The Morning Chronicle; *The Public Advertiser*; *The Morning Post*; *The Morning Herald*; *The Diary.*
Other newspapers have been used in part: *The Oracle*; *The Gazetteer*; *The Sunday Reformer*; *The Sheffield Register.*

IV. Pamphlets

A Defence of the Rockingham Whigs, (1783).
A Fair Exposition of the Principles of the Whig Club, (Dublin, 1790).
An Examination into the Principles, Conduct, and Designs of the Minister, J. Stockdale (1783).
Considerations on the approaching Dissolution of Parliament, W. Combe (1790).
Letter from a Country Gentleman to a Member of Parliament, W. Combe (1789).
Letter to the Electors of Westminster 1793, Charles James Fox.
View of the Political State of Scotland 1788, L. Hill.
Thoughts on a Letter addressed to Thomas Connoley, by a Whig, (1790).
The Whig Club: or a Sketch of Modern Patriotism, C. Pigott (1794).

V. Correspondence, Memoirs and Diaries

Place of publication London unless otherwise stated.
Countess of Airlie, *In Whig Society* (1921).

Arniston Memoirs, ed. G. Ormond (Edinburgh, 1887).

Journals and Correspondence of William, Lord Auckland, ed. Bishop of Bath and Wells (4 vols., 1861–2).

Lady Bessborough and her Family Circle, ed. Earl of Bessborough and A. Aspinall (1940).

Bland-Burges : Letters and Life, ed. J. Hutton (1885).

The Correspondence of Edmund Burke, ed. Lord Fitzwilliam and Sir R. Bourke (4 vols., 1844).

Lord John Campbell, *Lives of the Lord Chancellors and Keepers of the Great Seal of England* (10 vols., 1845–69).

The Memoirs of James Caulfield Charlemont, ed. F. Hardy (2 vols., 1812).

Correspondence of Charles, 1st Marquis Cornwallis, ed. C. Ross (4 vols., 1859).

The Diaries and Letters of Madame D'Arblay, ed. A. Dobson (5 vols., 1904–1905).

Georgiana, extracts from the correspondence of Georgiana, Duchess of Devonshire, ed. Earl of Bessborough (1955).

Diaries of Sylvester Douglas, First Lord Glenbervie, ed. F. Bickley (1928).

Memorials and Correspondence of Charles James Fox, ed. Lord John Russell (4 vols., 1853–7).

Memoirs of Sir Philip Francis, ed. J. Parkes and H. Merrivale (2 vols., 1867).

Memoirs of the Court and Cabinets of George III, ed. Duke of Buckingham and Chandos (4 vols., 1853–5).

The Later Correspondence of George III, ed. A. Aspinall, vols. i and ii (Cambridge University Press, 1962, 1963).

The Correspondence of George, Prince of Wales, ed. A. Aspinall, vols. i and ii (Cambridge University Press, 1964).

Memoirs of H. Grattan, ed. H. Grattan (5 vols., 1841).

Journal of Lady Elizabeth Holland (2 vols., 1908).

Lord Holland, *Memoirs of the Whig Party during My Time* (2 vols., 1852–4).

The Political Memoranda of Francis, Duke of Leeds, ed. O. Browning (1884).

The Diaries and Correspondence of James Harris, First Earl of Malmesbury (4 vols., 1884).

W. Miles, *Authentic Correspondence with LeBrun* (1796).

The Life and Letters of Sir Gilbert Elliot, First Earl of Minto, ed. Countess of Minto (3 vols., 1874).

A. G. Olson, *The Radical Duke* (Oxford, 1961).

Portrait of a Whig Peer . . . 2nd Viscount Palmerston, ed. B. Connell (1957).

Letters and Life of George Selwyn, ed. E. S. Roscoe and H. Clergue (1899).

G. Pellew, *The Life and Correspondence of the Rt. Hon. Henry Addington, First Viscount Sidmouth* (2 vols., 1847).

Lord Stanhope's *Miscellanies* (2 vols., 1861, 1864).

The Correspondence of William Wilberforce, ed. by his sons (2 vols., 1840).

The Diary of William Windham, ed. Mrs. Frances Baring (1866).

The Windham Papers, ed. Lord Rosebery (2 vols., 1913).

Sir N. Wraxall, *Historical Memoirs of My Own Time*, ed. R. Askam (1904).

————*Posthumous Memoirs* (3 vols., 1836).

VI. SECONDARY SOURCES

Lord Ashbourne, *Life of Pitt* (1898).

A. Aspinall, *Politics and the Press* (1949).

D. G. Barnes, *George III and William Pitt* (Stanford, 1939).

J. C. Beckett, *The Making of Modern Ireland 1603–1923* (1966).

E. C. Black, *The Association* (Harvard University Press, 1963).

J. Brooke, *The Chatham Administration* (1956).

P. A. Brown, *The French Revolution in English History* (1918).

O. Browning, *The Flight to Varennes and other Historical Essays* (1892).

I. R. Christie, *The End of North's Ministry 1780–82* (1958).

————*Wilkes, Wyvill and Reform* (1962).

C. B. Cone, *Burke and the Nature of Politics: The Age of the French Revolution* (University of Kentucky Press 1964).

J. W. Derry, *The Regency Crisis and the Whigs 1788–9* (Cambridge University Press, 1963).

A. S. Foord, *His Majesty's Opposition 1714–1830* (Oxford, 1964).

S. Gwynn, *Henry Grattan and His Times* (1939).

J. Holland Rose, *William Pitt and the National Revival* (1911).

————*William Pitt and the Great War* (1911).

————*Pitt and Napoleon: Essays and Letters* (1912).

E. M. Johnston, *Great Britain and Ireland, 1760–1800* (1963).

W. Laprade, *England and the French Revolution* (Johns Hopkins Studies, ser. xxvii, nos. 8–12, Johns Hopkins Press, Baltimore, 1909).

W. Lecky, *History of Ireland in the Eighteenth Century* (3 vols., 1913).

Sir G. C. Lewis, *Administrations of Great Britain* (1864).

C. M'Cormick, *Memoirs of Edmund Burke* (1798).

T. MacKnight, *The Life and Times of Edmund Burke* (3 vols., 1860).

Sir P. Magnus, *Edmund Burke* (1939).

T. H. B. Mahoney, *Edmund Burke and Ireland* (Harvard University Press, 1960).

D. Marshall, *The Rise of Canning* (1938).

H. W. Meikle, *Scotland and the French Revolution* (Glasgow, 1912).

Sir L. Namier and J. Brooke, *The House of Commons, 1745–1790* (*History of Parliament*, 3 vols.), H.M.S.O., 1964.

E. and A. Porritt, *The Unreformed House of Commons* (Cambridge University Press, 1909).

J. Prior, *Memoir of Edmund Burke* (2 vols., 1826).

J. Redlich, *Procedure of the House of Commons* (3 vols., 1908).

W. S. Sichel, *Sheridan* (2 vols., 1909).

Earl Stanhope, *Life of the Right Honourable William Pitt* (1861).

A. M. Stirling, *Coke of Norfolk and his Friends* (2 vols., 1912).

————*The Hothams* (2 vols., 1918).

W. C. Sydney, *England and the English in the Eighteenth Century* (2 vols., 1891).

C. C. Trench, *The Royal Malady* (1964).

G. S. Veitch, *The Genesis of Parliamentary Reform* (1913).

J. Watkins, *Memoirs of Sheridan* (2 vols., 1817).

W. H. Wilkins, *Mrs. Fitzherbert and George IV* (2 vols., 1905).

VII. THESES

P. J. Brunsdon, 'The Association of the Friends of the People' (M.A., Manchester, 1961).

P. Fraser, 'The Conduct of Public Business in the House of Commons 1812–1827' (Ph.D., London, 1957).

J. T. Murley, 'The Origin and Outbreak of the Anglo-French War of 1793', (D. Phil., Oxford, 1962).

VIII. ARTICLES

H. Butterfield, 'Charles James Fox and the Whig Opposition, 1792', *Historical Journal* (1949), ix, 3.

I. R. Christie, 'George III and the Debt on Lord North's Election Account.' *E.H.R.* lxxviii (October 1963).

C. C. Davies, 'The Nootka Crisis.' *E.H.R.* lxx (1958).

J. Ehrman, 'The Younger Pitt and the Oczacov Affair.' *History Today* (July 1959).

A. S. Foord, 'The Waning of the Influence of the Crown.' *E.H.R.* lxxii (October 1947).

D. E. Ginter, 'The Financing of the Whig Party Organization, 1783–1793.' *American Historical Review*, lxxi. 2 (January 1966).

D. E. Ginter, 'The Loyalist Association Movement of 1792–1793 and British Public Opinion.' *Historical Journal,* ix. 2 (1966).

D. Large, 'The Decline of the Party of the Crown and the Rise of Parties in the House of Lords, 1783–1837.' *E.H.R.* lxxviii (October 1963).

H. W. Meikle, 'The King's Birthday Riots in Edinburgh, May 1792. *Scottish Historical Review,* vii.

A. Mitchell, 'The Association Movement of 1792–1793.' *Historical Journal* iv. 2 (1961).

J. M. Norris, 'The Policy of the British Cabinet in the Nootka Sound Crisis., *E.H.R.,* lxx (1955).

J. Steven Watson, 'Parliamentary Procedure as a Key to an Understanding of Eighteenth Century Party Politics.' *The Burke Newsletter* (summer 1962).

———'Arthur Onslow and Party Politics' in *Essays in British History presented to Sir Keith Feiling,* ed. Hugh Trevor-Roper (1963).

J. R. Western, 'The Volunteer Movement as an Anti-Revolutionary Force.' *E.H.R.,* lxxi (October 1956).

Index

Wakefield, 163
Walpole, Horatio (1752–1822), 25
Walpole, Thomas (1727–1803), 244
Walwyn, James (1744–1800), 247,
252
Warwick-Bampfylde, Charles War-
wick (1753–1823), 246, 248
Watson Wentworth, Charles, 2nd
Marquis of Rockingham (1730–
1782): party of, 1, 10, 20, 22–3,
26–8, 52, 68, 129, 132, 211, 219,
244–6; Mary, Marchioness of
Rockingham, 211
Webb, John (?1730–95), 252
Webster, Sir Godfrey (1748–1800),
247
Weddell, William (1736–92), 249
West Indies, 140
Westcote, Lord (1724–1808), 245,
247
Western, C. C., 248, 253
Westminster Election (1784), 3, 15;
(1788), 14–16, 82
Westmorland, John Fane, 10th Earl
of (1759–1841), 78, 144 n. 1,
188, 203, 209, 218, 220–5
Wharton, John, 248, 253
Whig Club, the, 13–14, 56,
112, 119–21, 127–8, 131, 164,
213
Whig Club of Dublin, the, 14, 218–
20
Whig Party, the, xiii–xv, 1–5, 7–33,
39, 44–5, 54, 72, 78–81, 84–6,
89–90, 94–102, 106–7, 109–10,
113–16, 119–21, 122–5, 128–9,
130–1, 134–5, 139–40, 144–5,
148–9, 150–2, 153–6, 158–64,
167, 171–2, 174–8, 181–5, 191,
192–4, 196–7, 201–2, 237–8,
243–9
Whitbread, Samuel (1720–96), 59,
248, 253
Whitmore, Thomas (?1742–95),
246
Wilberforce, William (1759–1833),
210
Wilbraham, Roger (1743–1829),
247, 253
Willis, Dr. F. (1718–1807), 35
Windham, William (1750–1810),
8, 41, 49 n. 4, 56, 85, 108–10,
116, 119, 124–9, 131, 135, 137–
139, 141, 144–8, 149–51, 153–
155, 167–9, 171–2, 174, 176–7,
179–80, 183, 186–7, 189, 194–5,
197, 201, 204–6, 216–17, 223,
228, 237, 245, 251
Winnington, Sir Edward (1749–
1805), 253
Wraxall, Nathaniel (1751–1831), 3,
15
Wrightson, William (1752–1827),
142 n. 2, 246, 248
Wyndham, Percy Charles (1757–
1833), 248, 253
Wynne, Robert Watkin (c. 1754–
1806), 254

York, 162
York, Frederick, Duke of (1763–
1827), 21, 36–7, 150, 152